Contents

3 Editorial:
Gospels Across Worlds

7 *Mary Ann Beavis*
The Parable of the Talents (Matthew 25:14-30): Imagining a Slave's Perspective

22 *Louise Gosbell*
The woman with the 'flow of blood' (Mark 5:25-34) and disability in the ancient world

44 *Francis J. Moloney*
A Study of Mark 16:6-8
Hope in the Midst of Failure

55 *James R. Harrison*
The Historical Jesus as 'Social Critic': An Investigation of Luke 6:27-36

77 *Chris Spark*
Digging, Going Deep, Laying a Foundation: Luke 6:48, Ancient Building and Cultural Communication

86 *Peter G. Bolt*
What Actually Happened on Resurrection Morning? A Clear and Simple Account

101 *David Evans*
A Jerusalemite Source for the List of Nations in Acts 2?

Book Reviews

115 Wim J.C. Weren, *Studies in Matthew's Gospel: Literary Design, Intertextuality and Social Setting*

117 Jonathan T. Pennington. *The Sermon on the Mount and Human Flourishing: A Theological Commentary*

119 Bradley T. Johnson. *The Form and Function of Mark 1:1-15: A Multi-Disciplinary Approach to the Markan Prologue*

121 Armin D. Baum, Detlef Häusser, Emmanuel L. Rehfeld (eds.), Der jüdische. *Messias Jesus und sein jüdischer Apostel Paulus*

124 Rhonda Burnette-Bletsch (ed.). *The Bible in Motion: A Handbook of the Bible and Its Reception in Film Part I + II*

128 Samuel Byrskog, Tom Holmén, Matti Kankaanniemi (eds.), *The Identity of Jesus: Nordic Voices*

131 Stephen S. Liggins, *Many Convincing Proofs: Persuasive Phenomena Associated with Gospel Proclamation in Acts.*

135 Brian J. Wright, *Communal Reading in the Time of Jesus: A Window into Early Christian Reading Practices*

Gospels Across Worlds

The Four Gospels and Acts arose from the first-century world as part of the first-century movement that sprang up in the wake of Jesus the Nazorean, a first-century Galilean. It is remarkable that these first-century works have been read and studied well beyond their original geographical and cultural origins and long after their original time-zone. Their ability to speak into different cultures and periods is continuing testimony to the impact of the remarkable man who is at the centre of their view.

As the SCD Centre for Gospels (and Acts) Research enters its second year, with a growing number of members, it is one more small part of the world where Gospels discussions continue, as they have for centuries. But at the same time, today's discussions have their own distinctive flavour, as new generations of readers continue to taste and see the delights of these books bringing the life, death, and resurrection of Jesus front and centre, for any who care to take them up and read.

But different readers bring their own point of view to this reading experience. How they feel the impact of the Gospels depends upon the many factors in their own make-up that work together to create them into the individual that they are, amidst the cultural and relational network in which they make sense of their world.

Jesus was a master of riddles. Using a variety of parables, metaphors, and other one-liners to engage his original hearers, this brilliant teacher sought to tease their minds into active thought (as Dodd put it). The oral nature of his parabolic teaching may have lost something by being written down, but perhaps not a great deal, since the parables still intrigue and engage and tease, despite being embedded in the forward movement of Gospel narratives. But here, as elsewhere, the readers' repertoire either gets in the way of the Gospels' rhetorical purpose or enhances it. Who, for example, best gets some of Jesus' economically oriented parables? Modern capitalist readers so familiar with using money to make more money hearing of the slave burying his *talent* in the ground are quick to side with his master and condemn him as 'unfaithful'. But what about readers who chafe under oppressive regimes themselves and realise that this slave might have taken the only course open to him, in order to passively resist getting involved in a system that was inherently corrupt and exploitative? Or, as Mary Ann Beavis explores in relation to Jesus' parable of the Talents, what about someone who sees the world as a slave, rather than a slave-owner? How do the riddles of Jesus work on them?

How the world of medicine has changed across the centuries! Jesus and the Gospel writers lived even before the revolutionary changes brought about by Galen in the 2nd century, let alone the sophisticated medical understandings of our contemporary world. Still with plenty of illnesses to afflict them, if they were to find any cure or relief, then their world offered only Hippocratic medicine, magic, or desperate prayer. What was it like to be ill in such a world? Or as Louise Gosbell explores in relation to the woman with the flow of blood, what was it like to be disabled? If you were, how would you hear Jesus' encounter with this woman?

As the Gospels' message about Jesus has been read and accepted, the resultant believing communities have continued to preserve the Gospels so that they might be further read and believed. Focusing upon the intriguing final paragraphs of Mark's Gospel, with all their attendant interpretive issues, Frank Moloney reads with this believing community in view. What does this enigmatic account of Jesus' tomb bring to the ambiguous and fragile lives of believing communities living in the kind of broken world in which human beings have always lived and moved and had their being?

Jesus knew the first-century world of politics, and its social system in which reciprocity was deeply embedded. A favour given was expected to curry a favour in return. Whether in the deeply Hellenized Palestine of his own day, or in the wider Graeco-Roman world in which the Gospel of Luke later circulated, how would Jesus' radical view of how the world ought to be, clash with the world of reciprocity as it actually was? Carefully exposing the differences, Jim Harrison wonders whether Jesus' world could accommodate the social critique of reciprocity which arose from his view of the 'profligate generosity of the Father'? What would they make of that, and what changes would occur, should they be persuaded?

Real flesh-and-blood people are located in a certain place at a certain time. The way we all see the world is affected by the environment we know. By that known world we familiarise ourselves to the unfamiliar. Chris Spark asks questions about what kind of building techniques coloured the minds of those hearing the parable of the builder. Did Jesus' original hearers attempt to domesticate his words by picturing the building techniques they knew from Galilee? And when Luke's Gospel took that parable out to the wider world, did it undergo transformation to accommodate hearers familiar with a different kind of house?

My own essay seeks to pick through the various details of the Gospels' resurrection narratives. How does an historian approach the report of the discovery of an empty tomb, originally delivered in such fear, perplexity and doubt? Two competing epistemologies yield two opposite sets of results. Read from the world of rationalistic scepticism, the Gospel accounts are filled with discrepancies that cannot—or is it *must not?*—be read towards coherence. On the other hand, read from a more robust empiricism, as remarkable as the core historical claim might be, the accounts can be read as dovetailing around a harmonious sequence of events. Dealing with difference in sources is a normal part of historical procedure, even for the history lying behind the Gospels. The clear and simple account is as remarkable today as it would have been just three days after Jesus died.

But the world of the first century seems to be so far away from our present times. Once Lessing opened his wide ugly ditch, it seems to have never been adequately closed, emerging over and again in a variety of new forms! Intriguingly, some kind of historical gap already seems to have opened by the Pentecost following Jesus' death. For amongst others, Acts describes members of the crowd present that day in terms of people-groups long gone. David Evans explores this list of names against other such lists, and helps twenty-first century eyes open into the first century to explain what may have been going on. It seems a better understanding of the ancient world brings a better understanding of what its texts reported about its people. And if this is so for the Jesus' movement, perhaps even with Jesus himself—as Karl Barth put it—the gap has already been crossed from the other side.

Different worlds of time and space, culture and philosophical point of view. Worlds that seem fixed, but are somehow touched and transformed by the world of the Gospels text. By focusing over and again on the man crucified in first century Judea as Messiah, these texts continue to engage readers of all kinds, transporting this great variety from many and different worlds into the world of Jesus Christ to puzzle, annoy, intrigue, critique, and even transform. If so, continuing in Gospels and Acts research seems to be an imperative.

Peter G. Bolt
Executive Editor

The Parable of the Talents (Matthew 25:14-30)
Imagining a Slave's Perspective

MARY ANN BEAVIS

Scholars often take it for granted that slaves made up part of the membership of the earliest churches, as did slaveholders.[1] Slaves are addressed directly in 1 Cor. 7:21-24, Eph. 6:5-8, Col. 3:22-23, 1 Tim. 6:1-2, and 1 Pet. 2:18-25; their presence is presupposed in Tit. 2:9-10, Gal. 3:28, 1 Cor. 12:13 and Col. 3:11. The late second-century critic of Christianity, Celsus, famously observed that the church of his time was made up of 'only foolish and low individuals, and persons devoid of perception, and slaves, and women, and children, of whom the teachers of the divine word wish to make converts' (*Contra Celsum* 3.49; cf. 3.50, 52, 53, 54).[2]

Who were these slaves, and why were they attracted to the teachers of the Word, as Celsus put it? If the accounts of household conversions in Acts (16:13-15; cf. 10:44-48; 12:12-17; 16:27-34; 18:8) bear any historical weight, then some slaves would likely have been baptised along with free family members, with or without the slaves' understanding or consent.[3] Jennifer Glancy remarks, 'Slaveholders chose baptism not only for themselves but also for others who belonged to them, including, presumably, enslaved adult members of the household'.[4] The pious freedman Hermas, raised by a slave dealer and sold to a woman named Rhoda whom he came to 'love as a sister' (Herm. *Sim.* 1.1) may have belonged to this category. Another category of slave converts would have been people who voluntarily sought baptism and incorporation into the *ecclesia*, such as the Ethiopian eunuch (Acts 8:26-40), although in the New Testament, unequivocal evidence of such persons is scarce. If the traditional identification of Onesimus (Phlm. 8-21) as a slave convert of Paul holds, then he would be a rare example, although it is possible that as a member of Philemon's household, he had already been baptised, and Paul's instruction to Philemon to receive him 'no longer as a slave but more than a slave, a beloved brother' (Phlm. 16) was a reminder of Onesimus' spiritual equality in the *ecclesia*, rather than a veiled request for manumission. Extracanonical literature renders other examples of devoted Christian slaves: Rhoda, the (presumably) Christian slave of Mary of Jerusalem (Acts 12:12-17);[5] the aforementioned Christian prophet Hermas; Perpetua's slave Felicitas (*Martyrdom of Perpetua and Felicity*); Sabina (*Martyrdom of Pionius* 9.3-4); the two unnamed slave women (*duabus ancillis*) mentioned by Pliny the Younger

---

1 E.g., Glancy, *Slavery in Early Christianity*; Osiek, 'Early Christian Families', 198-213; Albert Harrill, *Manumission of Slaves*.
2 'Celsus' View of Christianity', <www.bluffton.edu/courses/humanities/1/celsus.htm> [accessed 11 April 2018].
3 See Glancy, *Slavery*, 46-49.
4 Glancy, *Slavery*, 49. On the question of child baptisms, see Glancy, *Slavery*, 48.
5 Glancy, 'Christian Slavery', 4.

(*Letter* 10.96-97); Callistus, the runaway slave who became bishop of Rome in 217 C.E. (Hippolytus, *Refutation of All Heresies* 6.43.11), Patrick of Ireland.[6]

Although the topic of early Christianity and slavery has generated a substantial body of scholarship, most of the focus has been on Christian slaveholders and their treatment of the enslaved persons in their households. The question of why the enslaved would seek to join the *ecclesia* (apart from being compelled to as part of Christian households) has received very little attention, with the exception of Harrill's work on the manumission of early Christian slaves.[7] Clearly, the practice of corporate manumission 'as a conscious tool of mission to gain converts' in some ancient church communities would have appealed to slave members.[8] However, most Christian slaves, whether their conversion was voluntary or involuntary, never received manumission, whether by their Christian slaveholders, or at the expense of their churches.

In addition to the question of why slaves were attracted by the ecclesia, the question of how they experienced early Christian preaching and teaching that overwhelmingly reflected the perspectives and assumptions of slaveholders has seldom been raised. Glancy notes that Patrick's comments on the evils of slavery is a rare example of a once-enslaved Christian's condemnation of ecclesial hypocrisy, although Patrick does not condemn slavery per se: 'They [the Christians of Gaul] send suitable holy men to the Franks and other peoples, with so many thousand solidi to ransom baptized captives; whereas you [the British king Coroticus] kill them [Irish captives] or sell them to a foreign people which does not know God; you commit the members of Christ as though to a brothel'.[9] Elsewhere, Glancy asks the broader question of what was 'the position of [...] enslaved bodies within the Christian body? Given the circumstances of a household baptism, could slaves' experiences as members of the community obliterate the disadvantages of their slave status, even within the cult?'.[10] On a similar theme, with specific reference to the tension between the hierarchical household codes (Eph. 6:5-9; Col. 3:22-24; Tit. 2:9-10) and the egalitarian baptismal formula (1 Cor. 12:13; Gal. 3:28; Col. 3:11), Carolyn Osiek asks:

> What impact might this formula have had on everyday life? It seems to declare that this equal access to salvation in Christ overcomes social differences. Did its interpreters sharply distinguish between the realm of eternal salvation and the realm of mortal life? When slaves were baptized, did they expect this new commitment to bring change to their lives? When they came to the assembly and heard these texts read, perhaps there was some kind of equalizing shape to the worship, so that everyone was treated with some sort of evenness with regard to quality of food and drink—though Paul's complaint that some who come to the Lord's Supper in Corinth eat ahead of others, some get drunk and others go hungry does not sound promising (1 Corinthians 11:21-22). Even if at the common meal at the assembly, there was some measure of commonality, someone had to serve. There is no record of a Saturnalia-like upsetting of social roles here, and when they went home, back to life as usual, did it make

---

6 See St. Patrick's Confessio, www.confessio.ie/more/article_kelly# [accessed 11 April 2018].
7 Harrill, *Manumission of Slaves*.
8 Harrill, *Manumission of Slaves*, 181. On corporation manumissions, see 178-82. The ancient sources he cites as examples are Herm. *Sim.* 1.8; Herm. *Mand.* 8.10; *Const. App.* 4.9.2; 2.62.4; Justin, *1 Apol.* 67.6; to this list can be added Patrick, *Ep.* 10, 14. Harrill further observes that the manumission of slaves from the common chest continued to be a missionary strategy until the time of Augustine (181). He argues that the often-cited example of Ignatius' *Ad Polycarp* 4.3, which admonishes slaves not to expect to be manumitted at the expense of the church, is not a blanket condemnation of the practice, but a warning against greed (158-67).
9 Patrick, *Ep.* 10, 14, quoted in Glancy, *Slavery in Early Christianity*, 80.
10 Glancy, *Slavery in Early Christianity*, 49.

any difference? Again, we are reminded that the Household Codes enjoin masters to be fair, but slaves to serve all the more willingly. Did some have expectations of something more?[11]

Citing the *Letter to Polycarp* 4.3, she notes Ignatius' teaching 'that slaves should not be mistreated or treated with contempt, but neither should they expect to be manumitted at community expense; apparently the question had arisen and was perhaps enacted as policy in some churches [...]. Clearly, there is no vision here of a world without slavery'.[12] More optimistically, Larry W. Hurtado describes the 'extended exhortation and encouragement' to Christian slaves (1 Pet. 2:18-25) in which the beatings they received from their masters are likened to the sufferings of Christ ('likely as Christian slaves of pagan masters') as 'a striking step in a world in which slaves typically counted for little in dignity. [...] This sort of compassionate rhetoric addressed to slaves was unusual, if not unique, in the Roman world'.[13]

These disparate examples of scholarly attention to questions of the subjectivity of early Christian slaves are scarce in the literature, although several recent studies do focus on the involvement of slaves in the *ecclesia* as opposed to 'early Christian slavery',[14] seeking evidence of the religious roles of early Christian slaves, and of 'hidden transcripts' of endurance and resistance in the sources. Did the slave members of the *ecclesia* appreciate the admonitions of early Christian preachers (likely slaveholders themselves) to endurance and willing service, or did they chafe at the hypocrisy of what Frederick Douglass centuries later, and in a very different cultural and political context, called 'slaveholding religion'—a religion that he contrasted starkly with 'the Christianity of Christ': 'The man who wields the blood-clotted cowskin during the week fills the pulpit on Sunday, and claims to be a minister of the meek and lowly Jesus'?[15] Would enslaved members of the *ecclesia* be edified or insulted by the admonition to be 'submissive to their masters and to give satisfaction in every respect; they are not to answer back, not to pilfer, but to show complete and perfect fidelity, so that in every way they may be an ornament to the doctrine of God our Saviour' (Tit. 2:9-10)?[16] What kind of 'disrespect' offered by baptised slaves to 'believing masters' does 1 Tim. 6:1-2 address—were they demanding equality, or at least better treatment, 'on the ground that they are members of the church'? Likely, the responses of baptized slaves were many and varied: pious acceptance, spiritual solace, seething resentment, demands for full equality, requests for manumission, resigned indifference. My aim in this article is to offer an imagined 'slave's-

---

11 Osiek, 'Early Christian Families', 206.
12 Osiek, 'Early Christian Families', 206.
13 Hurtado, *Destroyer of the Gods*, 177. See also Moxnes, 'Beaten Body of Christ', who suggests that this passage represents the creation of an 'inner body' as a symbol of healing through the comparison of slaves' suffering to the beaten body of Christ. Whether or not the actual slaves addressed in the epistle, as opposed to the abstraction of 'the suffering person' who is made into a 'full person' through a 'different knowledge' (140), found healing, or even comfort, in identification with the sufferings of Christ is questionable. This line of argumentation comes perilously close to a theology that 'glorifies suffering and perpetuates victimization by convincing persons who are oppressed to suffer violence willingly' (Reid, *Taking Up the Cross*, 14).
14 E.g., Shaner, 'Religious Practices of the Enslaved'; Elliott, *Roman Family Empires*, 85-96, 231-68.
15 Douglass, *Life of Frederick Douglass*, < www.gutenberg.org/files/23/23-h/23-h.htm> [accessed 11 April 2018]. The question as to the value of cross-cultural comparisons between ancient and North American slavery is debatable. I agree with Keith Bradley that although there are salient differences (i.e. American racialism and abolitionism were unknown in antiquity; I would add that the Christian overlay of much North American slave discourse also distinguishes it from ancient slavery), comparison can be helpful (Bradley, 'Roman Slavery', 482; 'Engaging with Slavery', 542). Similarly, North American slave narratives (or freedom narratives; see Powery and Sadler, *Genesis of Liberation*) may be formulaic and highly edited, but nonetheless historically valuable (see Starling, *The Slave Narrative*, 221-248). With these limitations in mind, comparative material will be used for illustrative purposes in this article.
16 All quotations from the bible, unless otherwise specified, are from the NRSV, Anglicized Edition.

eye view' of a Matthean parable featuring slave characters as it might have been understood by a baptised slave in antiquity.[17]

The Parable of the Talents (Matthew 25:14-30)

Feminist scholars have long been engaged in the study of women and other marginalized persons whose presence in early Christianity has often been overlooked, due to the male bias of the sources and the androcentric presuppositions of traditional scholarship. As Katherine A. Shaner notes: 'Feminist historians of early Christianity have shown that the questions that scholars bring to those materials often hide women from our view, an insight that applies to scholarship about slaves'.[18] Similarly, African American interpreters have drawn attention to the slaveholder bias inherent in many biblical texts. Mitzi Smith observes:

> The biblical text sometimes lends itself to support oppressive structures and disregard for human freedom and dignity in societies. A Gospel narrative, inclusive of slave parables replete with stereotypes, did not have to be perverted to support the inhumane system of slavery and its routine physical, spiritual, and psychological cruelties against African slaves. Matthew's Gospel, for example, abounds with slave parables in which exemplary stereotypical slave behavior serves as a model for persons desiring membership in the kingdom of heavens.[19]

The obliviousness, and even resistance, of traditional scholarship to the presence of slaves in the parables is illustrated by the translation of *doulos* as 'servant' in many modern translations (e.g., ASV, ESV, GNT, KJ21, HAV, NCV, NIV, TLB), despite the unambiguousness of the terminology: *doulos* means 'slave'.[20] Glancy notes the reluctance of some prominent scholars to recognize that the 'servants' in the parables are, in fact, enslaved persons, e.g., Joachim Jeremias, who held that the *doulos* of Matt. 18:23-35 was a 'satrap'; Duncan J. Derrett, who insisted that the *doulos* was a 'minister'; according to W.R. Herzog, he was an 'important retainer'.[21] Others have attempted to situate the master-slave relationships depicted in the parables within the framework of patron-client relationships, and thus as 'voluntary'.[22] Glancy further observes that, '[a] recent trend in parable scholarship that claims to situate the parables in the context of first-century realities nonetheless overlooks or minimizes the relevance of the institution of slavery'.[23] Although Glancy offered this critique nearly twenty years ago, these examples illustrate the reluctance of prominent New Testament scholars to engage with the first-century reality of slavery, despite the routine brutality exhibited toward the parabolic *douloi* by their *kyrioi*. With reference to the Matthean parables, Glancy notes: 'In the Greco-Roman world, the most pervasive image associated with slavery was that of a body being beaten; in turn, ancient readers would associate representations of beaten bodies with slaves. Thus, as Matthew turns repeatedly to the figure of the slave at

---

17 Cf. Munro, *Jesus, Born of a Slave*, 351.
18 Shaner, 'Religious Practices', 2.
19 Smith, *African American Interpretation*, 77.
20 See Glancy, 'Slaves and Slavery', 88.
21 Glancy, 'Slaves and Slavery', 85, citing Jeremias, *Parables of Jesus*, 210; Derrett, *Law in the New Testament*, 33, n. 1; Herzog, *Parables as Subversive Speech*, 136. On the discomfort of traditional NT scholarship with slavery, see also Beavis, 'Ancient Slavery', 39-43.
22 Glancy, 'Slaves and Slavery', 69, citing especially Bernard Brandon Scott, *Hear Then the Parable: A Commentary on the Parables of Jesus* (Minneapolis: Fortress, 1989), 205.
23 Glancy, 'Slaves and Slavery', 69 n. 11.

disciplinary moments, he reinforces a stereotype ubiquitous in antiquity'.[24]

The following discussion of the parable of the three slaves in Matt. 25:14-30[25] will proceed from the likely assumption that there were enslaved persons among the congregants of the earliest churches who gathered to hear the Gospel, or parts of it, read aloud, and presuppose that the form of the parable they heard would have been similar to the text as it stands.[26] In its earliest iterations, the parable may or may not have been presented as part of a longer eschatological discourse, as it is in Matthew 24-25. Some of the slaves in the audience would have been baptized along with other members of the household; some would have sought out membership in the *ecclesia*, like other slaves who joined cultic associations (*collegia*), with their masters' consent.[27] Some might have simply accompanied their slaveholders as part of their household duties. A few of these slaves might have had managerial duties like those in the parable, but most would likely have 'labored at more onerous tasks, ranging from mining to attending to their owners' bodily needs'[28]—mostly likely, the latter. Some might be owned by other *collegia* or municipalities.[29] Enslaved hearers of the parable would not necessarily have been surprised, or even encouraged, by the presence of slave characters in the story, since the theme of faithful and unfaithful slaves, as constructed by slaveholders, was commonplace in ancient literature.[30] What might these enslaved hearers of the parable have made of it in terms of their own experiences and aspirations?

As noted above, the situation envisioned by the parable, where the slaveholder entrusts three of his slaves with sums of money ('talents') 'to each according to his ability' (*hekastō kata tēn idian dynamin*; Matt. 25:14) has struck some modern interpreters as so implausible as to suggest that the three *douloi* were not actually slaves but free servants, agents or clients of their kyrios,[31] but both slaves and masters in the *ecclesia* would have seen it as nothing out of the ordinary for managerial slaves to be responsible for the administration of their wealthy master's estates and finances.[32] A *talentum* was worth approximately 6000 drachmas, or approximately 16 years' wages for a male day labourer, twice that for female labour,[33] so the sums are substantial: 'A talent was one of the largest values of money in the Hellenistic world. A silver coinage, it weighted between fifty-seven and seventy-four pounds. One talent was equal to six thousand denarii. It was, then, a large sum of money'.[34] From the viewpoint of the ordinary slaves and other poor hearers of the parable, the sums would have been astronomical, but not unthinkable for élite slaves to administer.

A slave might interpret the assignment of these huge sums of money to the slaves as a test set by the slaveholder. As Winsome Munro observed, 'at every level of the tradition, it is evident that the slave-type experience of trying to satisfy the all-powerful master, and to this end to read his apparently capricious mind and disposition aright is the clue to the parable's message'.[35] In fact,

---

24 Glancy, 'Slaves and Slavery', 84.
25 A variant of this parable is found in Luke 19:12-27.
26 That is, the question of whether an 'original form' of the parable was told by Jesus will not be discussed here. For discussion of this issue, see Glancy, 'Jesus and Slavery'.
27 Harrill, *Manumission of Slaves*, 147-52.
28 Glancy, 'Slaves and Slavery', 72.
29 Harrill, *Manumission of Slaves*, 152-55.
30 Glancy, 'Slaves and Slavery', 78-79.
31 Glancy, 'Slaves and Slavery', 88.
32 Glancy, 'Slaves and Slavery', 88.
33 EDB, 'Talent'; Schottroff, *Lydia's Impatient Sisters*, 92-95.
34 Scott, *Hear Then the Parable*, 224.
35 Munro, *Jesus, Born of a Slave*, 337. Munro's contention that the parable's apparent sympathy for the third slave is evidence that Jesus himself was, or had been, a slave has not gained much acceptance in subsequent scholarship. For critique of Munro's hypothesis, see Glancy, *Slavery in Early Christianity*, 100, 123, 127-29.

there is evidence that slaveholders sometimes deliberately withheld their true intentions from slaves as a strategy to keep them in line. For example, Tertullian recommended that his fellow slaveholders should offer slaves certain privileges and some independence so as to test them: 'Do not wise property owners offer and permit some things to their slaves on purpose in order to test them and to see whether and how they make use of things thus permitted, whether they will do so with moderation and honesty? However, is not that slave deserving more praise who abstains totally, thus manifesting a reverential fear of the kindness of his master?' (*Cult. fem.* 2.10.5-6).[36] Slave-hearers of the parable might suspect a trap—what does the master really expect? Does he want the slaves simply to guard the money, to invest it—or is he setting them up to squander it in defiance of what Tertullian calls the 'reverential fear' they owe him? From the wording of the parable, this is difficult to discern, since the master gives the three slaves no explicit instructions about how he wants them to handle the money; he simply gives them the talents and departs for an unspecified 'long time' (Matt. 25:19). Slave hearers might be especially apprehensive for the third slave, considered to be less capable by the slaveholder (25:15). Would he rise to the challenge, or fail the test?

As Osiek notes, the sum entrusted to each slave is a *peculium*,[37] in this case, a sum of money given the slaves to manage. Richard Gamauf, citing the second-century jurist Florentinus, notes that *peculia* could come to slaves by different means: 'In the first place, the assets forming a *peculium* could have been acquired by the slave on his own initiative, either through saving or by earning rewards from third parties. Only then does Florentinus mention assets provided by the master'.[38] A slave hearer might surmise that the first two slaves were known by the slaveholder to have previously amassed a *peculium* through their own efforts: 'At the humble beginnings of a *peculium* there might be a slave saving food to sell it. Such savings grew through austerity and the willingness to do services for others in addition to the duties towards his master'.[39] Although the slaveholder legally owned the *peculium*, it was treated as if it was owned by the slave on the master's sufferance.[40] A slave hearer might surmise that the third, less 'able' slave had not managed to amass much of his own *peculium*, and therefore be uneasy about how he would respond to the test. Possibly, more ambitious slave listeners would identify with the first two slaves, who presumably already had a reputation for managing their own and their master's property shrewdly.

The key to the slaveholder's unspoken expectations is foreshadowed in v. 16: 'The one who had received the five talents went off at once and traded ["worked"] with them, and made five more talents'. The general verb *ērgasato* here implies trading or investing.[41] The second slave doubles his *peculium* in the same way (v. 17). The less experienced slave 'went off and dug a hole in the ground and hid his master's money' (v. 18). Several interpreters have pointed out that it is actually the third slave, who only receives one talent, who acts consistently with Jewish jurisprudence:

> This activity shows him prudent and trustworthy. In commenting on the Mishnah, 'If he guarded it [money] in the manner of guardians [and it was lost] he is not liable', the Gemara quotes Rabbi Samuel: 'Money can only be guarded [by placing it] in the earth'. In the ancient world, underground was the only safe place, and the finding of buried treasure was not unusual. Josephus remarks how people buried treasure against the ill fortunes of war. By

36 Arbesman, Daly and Quain, trans., *Tertullian: Disciplinary Works*, 144.
37 Osiek, 'Early Christian Families', 205.
38 Gamauf, 'Slaves Doing Business', 334.
39 Gamauf, 'Slaves Doing Business', 335.
40 Gamauf, 'Slaves Doing Business' 334-35.
41 Viviano, 'Matthew', 668.

burying the silver the third servant ensures a verdict of responsible behavior, at the time of accounting.[42]

Similarly, Richard Rohrbaugh writes:

> And what about the third slave, the one so bitterly rebuked by the returning master and vilified in virtually all Western interpretation for failing to invest the money? In Matthew, he buries the deposit for safekeeping. The rabbis argued that this was precisely the right thing to do so the deposit [...] could be returned intact (b. Baba Mezi'a 42b; m. Baba Batra 4:8). In fact they ruled that burying the deposit meant the trustee was not liable if a loss occurred. Though the Lukan slave ties the money in a cloth—thus taking what the Mishnah specifies as the riskier course—he nonetheless preserves the pound as any honorable man would. He does not participate in the scheme to double the master's money, but honorably refrains from taking anything that belongs to the share of another.[43]

Although the Jewish sources cited here are centuries later than the Gospel (with the exception of Josephus), if indeed the historical Jesus uttered some form of this parable, possibly the audience was expected to sympathize with the prudence of third slave. In the Matthean parable, however, it is clear from his reaction that the slaveholder's expectation is that the slave would double the *peculium* (vv. 26-27). Further, a slave acting with honour would indeed be unexpected, since in the context of an honour-shame culture, slaves were without honour. As Orlando Patterson notes, 'What was universal in the master-slave relationship was the strong sense of honor the experience of mastership generated, and conversely, the dishonoring of the slave condition'.[44] Correspondingly, slavery is loss of honour: 'the so-called servile personality is merely the outward expression of this loss of honor'.[45] Moreover, ancient stereotypes about slaves held them to be 'unscruplous, lazy, and criminous'.[46] However, as Glancy notes, since slave authorship is rare in ancient literature, we have little evidence of how slaves regarded themselves as persons, or to what extent they accepted or resisted their exclusion from the 'game of honour'.[47] To the extent that a Jewish slave-hearer had internalized or resisted 'the conception of degradation held by their masters',[48] they might have admired the third slave's unsuccessful attempt to assert his honour, or winced at his failed effort.

The third slave's failure to discern the slaveholder's expectations recalls what Tertullian describes as the 'reverential fear' that slaves should feel in pursuit of their masters' sometimes inscrutable intentions: should he take the conservative course dictated by Jewish law (if he was aware of it); should he abstain from seeking his own benefit (Tertullian's peference); or should he follow the bolder course exemplified by the other slaves? Whether or not slave hearers of the parable would describe the fear expressed by the third slave (v. 25) as 'reverential', they would have recognized fear as a motivating factor in the responses of all three slaves:

> Although the faithful slaves do not identify fear as a motivation, surely they are aware that vulnerability to abuse is inherent in the situation of the slave. In the words of Richard Saller, 'the lot of bad slaves was to be beaten and that of good slaves was to internalize the

---

42 Scott, *Hear Then the Parable*, 227.
43 Rohrbaugh, 'Biblical Views', 23.
44 Patterson, *Social Death*, 11.
45 Patterson, *Social Death*, 11.
46 Bradley, *Slavery and Society*, 65.
47 Glancy, *Slavery in Early Christianity*, 28.
48 Patterson, *Social Death*, 97.

constant threat of a beating'. By concluding with examples of wicked slaves enduring corporal punishment, the parables allude to what is probably the strongest incentive slaves had for loyalty to their owners, that is, the disciplinary retribution.[49]

As Mitzi Smith says, 'Slaves are always expected to fear their masters'.[50] This expectation of fear, the slave hearer would realize, would include the first two slaves: 'In the parable of the talents, the faithful slaves may be proud to advance owner's interests, but they should certainly be fearful of the punishment awaits them should they fail'.[51]

The response of third slave explains his reasoning with an account of the inner motivation that resulted in his mistaken course of action: 'Master, I knew that you were a harsh man, reaping where you did not sow, and gathering where you did not scatter seed; so I was afraid, and I went and hid your talent in the ground. Here you have what is yours' (vv. 24-25). Harrill has cautioned that slave psychology cannot be easily discerned from the parables due to the stereotypical portrayals of slaves as stock characters in these stories, e.g., stark polarities of 'faithful' versus 'unfaithful' slaves (Matt. 24:45-47; Luke 12:42-44); the comedic motif of 'the abusive slave-"king" *absente ero*' (Matt. 18:23-27).[52] Harrill is correct in cautioning that, '[b]efore reconstructing the lives or, in this case, the psychology of ancient slaves from Jesus' parables, scholars should keep in mind the literary and rhetorical nature of all our sources before reading them as straightforward social description'.[53] The parables reflect the perspective of slaveholders, not slaves. This is where the memoirs of North American ex-slaves can be illuminating. Common themes in this literature are the constant effort on the part of slaves to discern the intentions of slaveholders, role-playing behaviours, and the god-like status of the master inculcated by the slaveholder, more or less successfully, in the minds of the enslaved.[54] Indeed, traditional readings of the parables where the 'master' represents God and 'slaves' represent his faithful or unfaithful human servants make this explicit. Slaveholding culture is not only assumed but reinforced.

There is ample evidence in the North American freedom narratives of enslaved persons' striving to please capricious slaveholders. Isaac Mason recalls that his 'utmost endeavor' was always to 'try and please' the master.[55] He recalls being introduced to a new master and mistress and trying to adjust to their changing demands:

> I found that my work was precisely the same as that I had performed at Dr. Hyde' s, my last place, so I got along for the first two weeks very nicely. I gave them satisfaction, as I thought; they, that is my master and his wife, appeared pleased. I concluded I was all right and was going to have a nice time at my new home. At this time there was not the dread of a daily whipping and the loss of one meal a day. It was not long before I was to learn that storms followed calms, and war came after peace.[56]

Louis Hughes remembers doing all he could to please 'Boss' simply because he was better clothed in a new household: 'I had known no comforts, and had been so cowed and broken in spirits, by cruel lashings, that I really felt light-hearted at this improvement in my personal appearance,

---

49 Glancy, 'Slaves and Slavery', 17, citing Saller, 'Corporal Punishment', 144-145.
50 Smith, *Insights*, 83.
51 Glancy, 'Slaves and Slavery', 75.
52 Harrill, 'Psychology of Slaves', 66-73.
53 Harrill, 'Psychology of Slaves', 73.
54 See Wyatt-Brown, 'Mask of Obedience', 1239, 1246, 1238; Ferguson, 'Christian Violence'.
55 Mason, *Life of Isaac Mason*, 34.
56 Mason, *Life of Isaac Mason*, 19.

although it was merely for the gratification of my master's pride'.[57] He further recalls his youthful dismay and resentment at being unable to read his new mistress's intentions:

> My heart sank within me. What good was it for me to try to please? She would find fault anyway. Her usual morning greeting was: 'Well, Lou, have you dusted the parlors?' 'Oh, yes,' I would answer. 'Have the flowers been arranged?'. 'Yes, all is in readiness,' I would say. Once I had stoned the steps as usual, but the madam grew angry as soon as she saw them. I had labored hard, and thought she would be pleased. The result, however, was very far from that. She took me out, stripped me of my shirt and began thrashing me, saying I was spoiled. I was no longer a child, but old enough to be treated differently. I began to cry, for it seemed to me my heart would break. But, after the first burst of tears, the feeling came over me that I was a man, and it was an outrage to treat me so—to keep me under the lash day after day.[58]

Frederick Douglass speaks of the elation rural slaves felt when they were ordered to run errands to the home plantation:

> Few privileges were esteemed higher, by the slaves of the out-farms, than that of being selected to do errands at the Great House Farm. It was associated in their minds with greatness. A representative could not be prouder of his election to a seat in the American Congress, than a slave on one of the out-farms would be of his election to do errands at the Great House Farm. They regarded it as evidence of great confidence reposed in them by their overseers; and it was on this account, as well as a constant desire to be out of the field from under the driver's lash, that they esteemed it a high privilege, one worth careful living for. He was called the smartest and most trusty fellow, who had this honor conferred upon him the most frequently. The competitors for this office sought as diligently to please their overseers, as the office-seekers in the political parties seek to please and deceive the people.[59]

In addition, there is ample evidence in these sources that the inevitability and desirability of the system of slavery was upheld in the theology of Christian slaveholders.[60] An example from the memoir of Solomon Northrup underlines this:

> Like William Ford, his brother-in-law, Tanner was in the habit of reading the Bible to his slaves on the Sabbath, but in a somewhat different spirit. He was an impressive commentator on the New Testament. The first Sunday after my coming to the plantation, he called them together, and began to read the twelfth chapter of Luke. When he came to the 47th verse, he looked deliberately around him, and continued—'And that servant which knew his lord's *will*,'—here he paused, looking around more deliberately than before, and again proceeded—'which knew his lord's *will*, and *prepared* not himself'—here was another pause— '*prepared* not himself, neither did *according* to his will, shall be beaten with many *stripes*.'

> 'D'ye hear that?' demanded Peter, emphatically. '*Stripes*,' he repeated, slowly and distinctly, taking off his spectacles, preparatory to making a few remarks.

> 'That nigger that don't take care—that don't obey his lord—that's his master—d'ye see?—that 'ere nigger shall be beaten with many stripes. Now, "many" signifies a *great* many—forty, a

---

57   Hughes, *Thirty Years a Slave*, 63-64.
58   Hughes, *Thirty Years a Slave*, 73-74.
59   Douglass, *Life of Frederick Douglass*, 12-13. See also Wyatt-Brown, 'Mask of Obedience', 1237.
60   See, e.g., Wilson Hartgrove, *Reconstructing the Gospel*.

hundred, a hundred and fifty lashes. *That's* Scripter!' and so Peter continued to elucidate the subject for a great length of time, much to the edification of his sable audience.[61]

As Sally Ann Ferguson remarks, North American slaves were often critical of the conflation of God and slaveholder: 'When not intimidated by violence, slaves know that the "Almighty God" and "Lord" the reverend urges them to worship is the slaveowner himself. Harriet Jacobs writes in *Incidents* that after "Pious Mr. Pike" preached in this way one evening, "We went home highly amused"'.[62] Early Christian slaves might have concurred.

In contrast to the slaveholders in the early Christian *ecclesia*, who may well have been contented with the stereotyped contrast between faithful and unfaithful slaves, slave-hearers of the parable might have responded with a complex array of emotions: envy of the successful slaves, sympathy and fear for the third slave, identification with all three slaves' wish to 'please the Boss' ('enter into the joy of your master', Matt. 25:21, 23), despite the vagueness of his instructions. Some may have been angered at the master's harsh dismissal of the third slave's efforts: 'You wicked and lazy slave! You knew, did you, that I reap where I did not sow, and gather where I did not scatter? Then you ought to have invested my money with the bankers, and on my return I would have received what was my own with interest. So take the talent from him, and give it to the one with the ten talents' (Matt. 25:26-28). Others may have admired the third slave's speech to the slaveholder, recognizing it as a veiled criticism of his venality and brutality, wrapped in the guise of servility: 'Master, I knew that you were a harsh man, reaping where you did not sow, and gathering where you did not scatter seed; so I was afraid, and I went and hid your talent in the ground. Here you have what is yours' (Matt. 25:24-25). Or, they might have viewed his failure in terms of 'shame paralysis': 'shame-awareness of incompetence in any sphere, whether growing from self-observation or information from others—may arouse so much anxiety as to inhibit further the person's competence'.[63] Both slaves and slaveholders would have recognized the command to throw the 'worthless slave [...] into the outer darkness, where there will be weeping and gnashing of teeth' (Matt. 25:30) as a reference to torture (cf. Matt. 18:34).[64] Even though both slaves and slaveholders might have been expected to identify with the *douloi* in the parable relative to the ultimate divine *kyrios*, slaveholders would perceive the parable in terms of their voluntary spiritual acquiescence to conditions of dishonour, as opposed to the slaves, whose slavery was involuntary, very real and likely permanent.[65] Both would see the alignment between the divine master and human slaveholders (cf. Eph. 6.5; Col. 3.22).

In the case of the two 'faithful' slaves, their good performance does not earn them the coveted reward of manumission, but additional responsibility. As Glancy notes:

> Both in practice and in literature many faithful slaves achieved manumission; both in practice and in literature, many faithful slaves did not achieve manumission. The parabolic reward of the faithful slave—additional responsibility rather than freedom—is neither distinctive nor countercultural. To assure smooth functioning of their households, masters relied on skillful

---

61 Northrup, *Twelve Years a Slave*.
62 Ferguson, 'Violence and the Slave Narrative', 308, citing Jacobs, *Incidents*, 69.
63 Wallace, *Culture and Personality*, 182-183.
64 See Glancy, 'Slaves and Slavery', 67; Smith, *Insights*, 85-90.
65 See Briggs, 'Can an Enslaved God Liberate?', 146; Briggs's argument concerning the depiction of Christ in the Philippians hymn is reminiscent of the stance of slaveholders vis-à-vis the parable: 'When they are reduced to slavery, they are essentially not slaves, but they do not resist their role as slaves. Instead, they are exemplary in their obedience and their moral superiority to their servile status is expressed not through an attempt to claim the honor, which is intrinsically theirs, but their acquiescence in their conditions of dishonor'.

slaves. In turn, as they undertook increasing responsibility, slaves often accrued personal funds and even personal influence. Such rewards were a strong incentive to fidelity.[66]

Slave-hearers might imagine that the successful slaves wished not only to earn the 'joy of the master' (vv. 21, 23), but to use their doubled *peculium*, along with their enhanced status in the slaveholder's estate, to eventually buy their freedom. Gamauf observes that, '[f]or a slave starting from scraps and aspiring to freedom, there was little chance to realise a sufficient peculium without his willingness to put it at high risk. By timid saving he could hardly gain what was needed'.[67] Slave-hearers might imagine the despair of the third slave, deprived of his talent and consigned to torture, with no such hope: 'For to all those who have, more will be given, and they will have an abundance; but from those who have nothing, even what they have will be taken away' (Matt. 25:29).

A Freedman's Parable

In contrast to the abundant North American freedom narratives,[68] literary evidence of ancient slaves' experience and perspectives is scarce,[69] and evidence of slave reception of the parables might be expected to be nonexistent. However, a well-known piece of early Christian literature attributed to a formerly enslaved person, the freedman Hermas (Herm. *Sim.* 1.1), contains an otherwise unattested parable with many similarities to those in the Gospels, including Matt. 25:14-30 (Herm. *Sim.* 5.2-11).[70] As with the other similitudes in the *Shepherd*, the parable is not attributed to Jesus, but to an angelic revealer,[71] who mediates most of the revelations in the apocalypse to the visionary Hermas.

In the parable, before embarking on a journey, a wealthy slaveholder instructs a trusted slave to build an enclosure around a vineyard—and nothing else—until his return (5.2.2). The slaveholder promises the slave that if he obeys, he will manumit him on his return. The slave not only builds the fence but takes the initiative to weed and dig the vineyard, to its great improvement (5.2.4). When the slaveholder finally returns, he is not angry at the slave's disregard of his instruction *only* to build the fence; rather, he is delighted (5.2.5). The slaveholder consults his beloved son and heir, along with some trusted advisors, who all approve not only of his plan to manumit the worthy slave, but also of his astonishing wish to adopt the slave as co-heir with the son—a course of action that the beloved son and heir enthusiastically endorses (5.2.8).[72]

Compared to the Gospel parables, this ending would be astonishing enough, but Hermas' similitude continues with an equally unexpected sequel:

> After some few days, his master made a feast, and sent to him many dainties from the feast. But when the servant received [the dainties sent to him by the master], he took what was sufficient for him, and distributed the rest to his fellow servants.

---

66 Glancy, 'Slaves and Slavery', 79.
67 Gamauf, 'Slaves Doing Business', 336.
68 Extensive collections of these materials are available online, e.g., <http://docsouth.unc.edu/neh/texts.html> [accessed 12 April 2018].
69 Harrill cites Epictetus and the fables of Aesop as possible sources of ancient slaves' point of view (*Manumission*, 19-21).
70 Osiek lists Mark 12:1-12, par Matt. 21:33-46 and Luke 20:9-19 (see also *Gos. Thom.* 65); Matt. 13:24-30; 24; 24:45-51, par Luke 12:41-46; Mark 13:34; Matt. 25:14-30; Luke 12:27; *Gos. Phil.* 52.2-15; cf. Isa 5:1-11 (*Shepherd of Hermas*, 171 n. 1).
71 Holmes, *Apostolic Fathers*, 199.
72 For a fuller discussion, see Beavis, 'Parable of the Slave'.

And his fellow-servants, when they received the dainties, rejoiced, and began to pray for him, that he might find greater favor with the master, because he had treated them so handsomely. All these things which had taken place his master heard, and again rejoiced greatly at his deed. So the master called together again his friends and his son, and announced to them the deed that he had done with regard to his dainties which he had received; and they still more approved of his resolve, that his servant should be made joint-heir with his son (5.2.9-11).[73]

Jennifer Glancy has remarked on the contrast between this parable and the somewhat similar Markan parable of the tenants, which has a decidedly less optimistic outcome (Mark 12:1-11).[74] She further notes that Hermas' parable is unique in that 'a faithful slave not only receives manumission but also joins the slaveholder's son as co-heir of the vineyard, *a reward for faithful service that was both distinctive and countercultural*'.[75] However, Glancy does not make the connection between Hermas' early life in slavery and the unexpected turns in the plot. Despite its many echoes of Gospel slave parables, this parable, filtered through the experience of a freedman, bristles with differences:

> The trustworthy slaves of Matt 24-25 are rewarded by added responsibilities, not by manumission and adoption. The unfaithful slaves with whom the trustworthy ones are contrasted are harshly punished; they are 'cut in pieces' (24:51), and thrown 'into the outer darkness' where there is 'weeping and gnashing of teeth' (25:30). [...] There is no hint in the similitude of the routine brutality of the synoptic parables where slaves are abused, shamed and killed. The social distance between the son and the adopted co-heir recedes; there is no hint of rivalry or antagonism between freeborn son and adopted slave (cf. Luke 15:25-31; John 8:35-36; Gal. 3:26–4:11). Unlike the ill-fed slaves in Gos. *Phil.*, the freedman of the *Shepherd* is offered a banquet that he shares with the household slaves.[76]

Hermas' parable shares with Matt. 25:14-30 the motif of a master entrusting a slave with a task to be completed by the time of his return. Readers familiar with the harsh outcome of the Matthean parable might well be anxious for the diligent slave who disregards his master's express instruction to fence the vineyard, and only that, in his absence (5.2.2), but decides on his own initiative to dig, weed and improve it (5.2.4). Would the master withdraw his promise of manumission, or even subject the slave to corporal punishment for his disobedience?[77] Hermas, however, as a formerly enslaved interpreter of the parable tradition, was able to imagine what the slaveholding perspective of the synoptic slave parables could not: a slave rewarded for his hard work and enterprise not merely by the slaveholder's praise and added responsibility, but by manumission and adoption that enables him to generously share his good fortune with other slaves.

Mary Ann Beavis
St Thomas More College
Saskatoon, Canada

---

73 Lightfoot translation; <www.earlychristianwritings.com/text/shepherd-lightfoot.html> [accessed 11 April 2018].
74 Glancy, *Slavery*, 105.
75 Glancy, *Slavery*, 118, italics added.
76 Beavis, 'Parable of the Slave'.
77 Sojourner Truth remembered the propensity of slaveholders to promise slaves that they would be emancipated on a certain date to encourage them to work harder, only to withdraw the offer on some pretext when the time came; <http://digital.library.upenn.edu/women/truth/1850/1850.html#14> [accessed 11 April 11 2018].

References

Arbesman, R., E.J. Daly and E.A. Quain (trans.), *The Fathers of the Church: Tertullian—Disciplinary, Moral and Ascetical Works* (Washington, DC: Catholic University of America, 2008).

Beavis, M.A. 'The Parable of the Slave, Son and Vineyard: An Early Christian Freedman's Narrative (Herm., *Sim.* 5.2–11)', *CBQ* 80.4 (2018). Forthcoming.

Beavis, M.A. 'Ancient Slavery as an Interpretation Context for the New Testament Slave Parables, with Special Reference to the Unjust Steward (Luke 16:1-8)', *JBL* 111 (1992), 37-54.

Bradley, K. 'Engaging with Slavery', *Biblical Interpretation* 21 (2013), 533-46.

Bradley, K. *Slavery and Society at Rome* (Cambridge: Cambridge University Press, 1994).

Briggs, S. 'Can an Enslaved God Liberate? Hermeneutical Reflections on Philippians 2:6-11', *Semeia* 47 (1989), 137-53.

Schlabach, G.W. (ed.) 'Celsus' View of Christians and Christianity', www.bluffton.edu/courses/humanities/1/celsus.htm [accessed 11 April 2018].

Derrett, J.D.M. *Law in the New Testament* (London: Darton, Longman, & Todd, 1970).

Douglass, F. *Narrative of the Life of Frederick Douglass, An American Slave* www.gutenberg.org/files/23/23–h/23–h.htm [accessed 11 April 2018].

EDB 'Talent', *Eerdmans Dictionary of the Bible* (ed. David Noel Freedman; Grand Rapids: Eerdmans, 2000), 1272

Elliott, S.M. *Family Empires, Roman and Christian, Volume 1: Roman Family Empires, Household, Empire, Resistance* (Salem, OR: Polebridge Press, 2018).

Ferguson, S.A.H. 'Christian Violence and the Slave Narrative', *American Literature* 68.2 (1996), 297-320.

Gamauf, R. 'Slaves Doing Business: The Role of Roman Law in the Economy of a Roman Household', *European Review of History—Revue européenne d'histoire* 16 (2009), 331-46.

Glancy, J. 'Slaves and Slavery in the Matthean Parables', *JBL* 119 (2000), 67-90.

Glancy, J. *Slavery in Early Christianity* (Minneapolis: Fortress, 2006).

Harrill, J.A. 'The Psychology of Slaves in the Gospel Parables: A Case Study in Social History', *Biblische Zeitschrift* 55 (2011), 63-74.

Harrill, J.A. *The Manumission of Slaves in Early Christianity* (Tübingen: J.C.B. Mohr [Paul Siebeck], 1995).

Herzog, W.R. *Parables as Subversive Speech: Jesus as Pedagogue of the Oppressed* (Louisville: Westminster John Knox, 1994).

Holmes, M.W.H. *The Apostolic Fathers in English* (Grand Rapids, MI: Baker Academic, ³2006).

Hughes, I.	*Thirty Years a Slave: From Bondage to Freedom.* http://docsouth.unc.edu/fpn/hughes/hughes.html [accessed 11 April 2018].
Hurtado, L.W.	*Destroyer of the Gods: Early Christian Distinctiveness in the Roman World* (Waco, TX: Baylor University Press, 2016).
Jacobs, H.	*Incidents in the Life of a Slave Girl, Written by Herself* (1861; repr. Cambridge: Harvard University Press, 1987).
Jeremias, J.	*Parables of Jesus* (New York: Scribner, 1954).
Lightfoot, J.B. (trans.).	*The Shepherd of Hermas* www.earlychristianwritings.com/text/shepherd–lightfoot.html [accessed 11 April 2018].
Mason, I.	*Life of Isaac Mason as a Slave.* <http://docsouth.unc.edu/fpn/mason/mason.html [accessed 11 April 2018].
Moxnes, H.	'The Beaten Body of Christ: Reading and Empowering Slave Bodies in 1 Peter', *Religion & Theology* 21 (2014), 125-41.
Munro, W.	*Jesus, Born of a Slave* (Studies in the Bible and Early Christianity 37; Lewiston/Queenston/Lampeter: Edwin Mellen, 1998).
Northrup, S.	*Twelve Years a Slave: Narrative of Solomon Northrup, a Citizen of New York, Kidnapped in Washington City in 1841, and Rescued in 1853.* http://docsouth.unc.edu/fpn/northup/northup.html [accessed 11 April 2018].
Osiek, C.	*The Shepherd of Hermas* (Hermeneia; Minneapolis: Augsburg Fortress, 1999).
Osiek, C.	'What We Do and Don't Know About Early Christian Families', in Beryl Rawson (ed.), *A Companion to Families in the Greek and Roman Worlds* (Oxford: Blackwell, 2011), 198-213.
Patterson, O.	*Slavery and Social Death* (Cambridge & London: Harvard University Press, 1982).
Powery, E.B. & R.S. Sadler, Jr.	*The Genesis of Liberation: Biblical Interpretation in the Antebellum Narratives of the Enslaved* (Louisville, KY: Westminster John Knox, 2016).
Reid, B.E.	*Taking up the Cross: New Testament Interpretations through Latina and Feminist Eyes* (Minneapolis: Fortress, 2007).
Rohrbaugh, R.	'Biblical Views: Reading the Bible Through Ancient Eyes', *Biblical Archaeology Review* 42 (2016), 22-24.
Saller, R.P.	'Corporal Punishment, Authority, and Obedience in the Roman Household', in Beryl Rawson (ed.), *Marriage, Divorce, and Children in Ancient Rome* (Oxford: Clarendon, 1991): 144-65.
Schlabach, G.W. (ed.)	'Celsus' View of Christians and Christianity', www.bluffton.edu/courses/humanities/1/celsus.htm [accessed 11 April 2018].

Schottroff, L.	*Lydia's Impatient Sisters: A Feminist Social History of Early Christianity* (Louisville, KY: Westminster John Knox, 1995).
Scott, B.B.	*Hear Then the Parable: A Commentary on the Parables of Jesus* (Minneapolis: Fortress, 1990).
Shaner, K.A.	'The Religious Practices of the Enslaved: A Study of Roman Ephesos' (Th.D. Dissertation, Harvard Divinity School, 2012).
Smith, M.J.	*Insights from African American Interpretation* (Minneapolis: Fortress, 2017).
Starling, M.A.	*The Slave Narrative: Its Place in American History* (Washington, DC: Howard University Press, ²1988).
EDB	'Talent', *Eerdmans Dictionary of the Bible* (ed. David Noel Freedman; Grand Rapids: Eerdmans, 2000), 1272.
Truth, S.	*Narrative of Sojourner Truth: A Northern Slave, Emancipated from Bodily Servitude by the State of New York in 1828* http://digital.library.upenn.edu/women/truth/1850/1850.html#14 [accessed 11 April 2018].
Viviano, B.T.	'The Gospel according to Matthew', *The New Jerome Biblical Commentary* (ed. R.E. Brown, J.A. Fitzmyer and R.E. Murphy; Englewood Cliffs, NJ: Prentice-Hall, 1990), 630-74.
Wallace, A.F.C.	*Culture and Personality* (New York: Random House, 1961).
Wyatt-Brown, B.	'The Mask of Obedience: Male Slave Psychology in the Old South', *American Historical Review* 93 (1988), 1228-52.

The woman with the 'flow of blood' (Mark 5:25-34) and disability in the ancient world

LOUISE GOSBELL

Abstract[1]

Scholars addressing the Markan pericope of the woman with the 'flow of blood' have often focused on the issue of the woman's ritual impurity with little or no attention given to how the woman's illness would have been understood against the background of the ancient medical sources. This article assesses the woman with the flow of blood in terms of the impact of her particular illness—a long-term 'flow of blood'—on her social standing in the ancient world. In addition, the woman's illness is addressed in terms of current research on disability in the ancient world and focuses not only on the physical condition but also the social limitations the woman would have experienced as a result of her particular disabling illness.

1. Introduction

In her 2010 article on the woman with the flow of blood entitled *The Man with the Flow of Power:*

Porous Bodies in Mark 5:25-34, Candida Moss contends that scholarship on this pericope has focused its attention on the apparently gender-specific nature of the woman's condition 'to the neglect of her disability'.[2] While Moss notes that the woman's illness would have rendered her disabled,[3] Moss does not elaborate on the reasons for interpreting the woman as such nor the social and cultural implications of such a disability for a woman in the first century. The aim of this article is to build upon Moss' contention that the woman with the flow of blood should be considered disabled, as well as to consider the social implications of such a disabling condition within the woman's first-century milieu.

This article begins with some introductory comments about the methods of defining disability and the hazards associated with such definitions, as well as the challenges of finding a definition that is suitable for the ancient biblical texts. Following this is an outline of some of the most common interpretations of the woman with the flow of blood to date. The article then outlines the way in which

---

1 This article is an abbreviated version of a chapter which appears in my PhD thesis now published through Mohr Siebeck: Gosbell, 'The Poor, the Crippled, the Blind, and the Lame', 230–77.

2 Moss, *Man with the Flow of Power*, 509.

3 Moss, *Man with the Flow of Power*, 511.

long-term bleeding such as experienced by the woman in Mark 5:25-34 would have been interpreted in light of Greek medical literature. The social and familial consequences of both the illness itself and the likely subsequent infertility will also be considered. The article will conclude with some considerations and implications of reading the woman with bleeding as an example of a woman with a disability in the first-century Greco-Roman world.

While the healing of the woman with the flow of blood appears in all three Synoptic Gospels,[4] this article addresses only the version as it appears in Mark's Gospel. In addition, while the story of the woman with bleeding exists as part of a conjoined healing account with that of Jairus' daughter, and there are some important (and deliberate) parallels and contrasts between the woman with the flow of blood and Jairus' daughter, this article will only address the elements of the story which relate to the woman with the flow of blood.[5]

2. Definitions of Disability

In order to be able to determine that the woman with the flow of blood in Mark 5:25-34 can be considered disabled within her first-century context, we must first outline an understanding of disability that can be applied to the ancient biblical texts without anachronism. However, determining one clear definition for disability even in the 21st century proves challenging. This is because, as noted by the World Health Organization, disability is a 'complex phenomenon, reflecting the interaction between features of a person's body and features of the society in which he or she lives'.[6] In this sense, disability is a combination of factors that are both physical (or mental/intellectual) as well as social. In their definition of disability, the World Health Organization describe disability as 'an umbrella term' referring to a combination of three separate elements: (1) impairments; (2) activity limitations; and (3) participation restrictions.[7] Impairment refers to 'a problem in body function or structure' while an activity limitation refers to the extent to which a person with an impairment can execute or complete a task or action on their own without assistance. Finally, participation restrictions refer to the limitations experienced by people with impairments in attempting to navigate the social world within which they live.[8]

In order to understand the interplay between these various factors, an example of these three elements follows. A friend of mine has Cerebral Palsy. Her Cerebral Palsy is such that it impairs her body in a number of ways, for example, she is unable to walk unassisted and so requires the use of a wheelchair. As a result of the Cerebral Palsy, there are some functions that are difficult for her to perform. Although she has a car that has been modified for her needs and is able to manoeuvre herself in and out of the vehicle, lifting objects is difficult for her due to muscle weakness, and she requires assistance with getting her wheelchair in and out of her vehicle. As her Cerebral Palsy impacts her fine motor skills, she also has difficulty at times with using cutlery, pouring water from the kettle, or drinking out of a glass without a straw. In this sense, she experiences 'activity limitations' as a result of her condition. Also as a consequence of her condition, although she is an incredibly social and gregarious woman, dining out can prove problematic due to her wheelchair. Many buildings are inaccessible for wheelchair users and even when she does find a restaurant with ramps and accessible bathrooms, manoeuvring her wheelchair between closely-packed chairs and tables can prove difficult. If she wishes to attend a concert or a sporting event, careful

---

4 Mark 5:25-34, Matt. 9:20-2, Luke 8:43-8.
5 For more on this see Gosbell, 'The Poor, the Crippled', 230-77.
6 World Health Organization, 'Disabilities', n.p.
7 World Health Organization, 'Disabilities', n.p.
8 World Health Organization, 'Disabilities', n.p.

planning must be done in order to ensure she can not only access the venue but that suitable bathrooms will be close by. In many cases, venues are simply not accessible, and she is forced to miss out on attending the event. These are the 'participation restrictions' that are associated with her condition. While it is her Cerebral Palsy which is the root cause of her impairments and which impacts the functionality of her body, she is also limited in a number of ways not as a direct result of her condition but as a result of living in a society which has not been built to accommodate people using wheelchairs. For this reason, disability is considered to be composed of both a physical as well as a social component.

Disability scholars thus contend that while disability is a 'universal experience of humanity',[9] concepts of disability are socially and culturally located and are a direct reflection of any culture's particular expectations of the body. Consequently, disability advocate Michael Oliver contends that 'the kinds of disabling restrictions and the experience of disabled people, both individually and collectively, have varied from society to society and from age to age'.[10] In order to be able to assess the woman with the flow of blood as disabled, we must first evaluate the kinds of conditions that would have been considered disabling within the Greco-Roman world of the first century.

Based on the World Health Organization's tripartite definition of disability, one of the values of the human body in the *modern* world is the emphasis on individual autonomy and the ability to execute tasks independently. In contrast, Martha L. Edwards in her work on disability in ancient Greece suggests that concepts of disability would have been much more community orientated in the ancient world. Edwards determines that the kinds of impairments that would have been most disabling were those that inhibited a person's ability to 'fulfill the tasks of membership in the community'.[11] For men, these 'tasks of membership' would have been in the form of civic duties including various military, religious, financial, judicial, and political obligations.[12] For women, 'tasks of membership' were defined primarily by marriage and child-bearing as well as the maintenance of the household.[13] For this reason, the most disabling illnesses for women in the ancient world would have been those conditions that prevented women from fulfilling their domestic duties. Although a protracted uterine bleed may not be considered a form of disability in the modern world, it is apparent from our ancient medical sources that such long-term bleeding was known to cause a range of health concerns including tiredness, weakness, and even infertility.[14] The impact of such long-term bleeding on the woman's ability to fulfill her social duties in caring for the household and her potential to produce offspring, therefore, cannot be underestimated. As such, as is the case with modern definitions of disability, we can consider disability in the ancient world a combination of factors that include both a bodily component as well as a social one.

While the writers of antiquity did not possess an overarching word for disability such as exists in the modern world, and especially not one that encompassed the same 'medical, social, economic and political connotations' as our modern label of 'disability',[15] it is apparent our ancient sources express some

---

9   Shakespeare, 'Social Model of Disability', 221.
10 Oliver, *Politics of Disablement*, 17–8.
11 Edwards, 'Constructions of Physical Disability', 35.
12 Sinclair, *Democracy and Participation in Athens*, 53.
13 For women in wealthier families, the maintenance of the *domus* consisted of supervision of household affairs and slaves. In the case of poorer families, the women were required to carry out these household tasks themselves. For detailed information about the role of women in antiquity, particularly in relation to the *domus*, employment, citizenship, and social status, see Pomeroy, *Goddesses, Whores, Wives and Slaves*, passim.
14 E.g. Hipp. *Mul.* 1.5.
15 Edwards, 'Women and Disability', 6.

understanding of illness having both a physical as well as a social component.

3. Previous Interpretations of the Woman with the 'flow of blood'

It has been noted by Mary-Rose D'Angelo that the conjoined story of the woman with the flow of blood with that of Jairus' daughter 'has become an important locus in feminist interpretation of the Gospel of Mark'.[16] The reason for this is that not only are the two primary characters requiring healing in the story women, but in addition, the woman with the flow of blood appears to be experiencing a gynecological, and therefore gender-related, illness. Rather than focusing on the social consequences of the woman's illness, interpreters of this Markan pericope instead often focus on a number of other issues in the text. For many scholars, the issue of faith is foregrounded in this pericope as both the woman with bleeding and Jairus openly place their trust in Jesus for healing.[17] This interpretation was particularly important in patristic reflections of the pericope where the woman's faith is juxtaposed with the lack of faith of Peter, for example.[18] Other scholars focus on the issue of Jesus' power to heal and raise the dead which is demonstrated in the passage.[19]

The aspect most commonly addressed by interpreters of this pericope, however, is in relation to ritual purity.[20] Both women in the conjoined story are usually considered by scholars to be ritually impure according to the Levitical purity system.[21] In the case of the woman, this is as a result of her long-term uterine bleeding. In the case of the girl, it because she died before Jesus' arrival at her home.[22] Commentators often note that while Jesus should have been rendered unclean through his physical contact with both the woman with the flow of blood as well as the 'dead' girl, this does not appear to be the case.[23] Many commentators also note that while Jesus was aware of the impurity of the women based on the Levitical purity code, he shows no concern about the possibility of either woman passing on their contagion to him.[24]

Numerous scholars suggest that the woman's flow of blood would have meant she was ritually unclean at the time of her healing and as a result, she would have been restricted in her ability to touch and be touched by others.[25] In this respect, by entering the

16   D'Angelo, 'Gender and Power', 83.
17   Boring even says that the original story was laden with magical undertones and that Mark has turned this narrative instead into being about faith (Boring, *Mark*, 160); cf. Reid, *Choosing the Better Part?*, 136.
18   E.g. Origen (Matt. 14:28-33); Origen, *Comm. Matthew*, trans. Patrick, ANF 9, 10.19.5291.
19   Calduch-Benages, *Perfume of the Gospel*, 18; Collins, *Mark*, 283; D'Angelo, 'Gender and Power', 85, 91; Guelich, *Mark 1–8:26*, 294.
20   E.g. Holmén, 'Jesus and the Purity Paradigm', 3:2716; Selvidge, 'Mark 5:25-34 and Leviticus 15:19-20', 619–23; Selvidge, *Woman, Cult and Miracle Recital*, passim. Miller sees purity as a primary concern of the passage (*Women in Mark's Gospel*, 55).
21   E.g. Boring, *Mark*, 158–9; Calduch-Benages, *Perfume of the Gospel*, 27; Focant, *Gospel According to Mark*, 212; Guelich, *Mark 1–8:26*, 297; Love, 'Jesus Heals the Hemorrhaging Woman', 91; Marcus, *Mark 1–8*, 357; Miller, *Women in Mark's Gospel*, 57; Witherington, *Gospel of Mark*, 187. France says that while the issue of purity isn't made explicit in chapter 5, it serves as a precursor to the more specific discussion of purity that takes place in chapter 7 (France, *Gospel of Mark*, 235).
22   Taylor suggests that Jesus is being literal in his declaration that the girl was not dead and thus no resurrection actually takes place here (*Gospel According to St. Mark*, 295).
23   Witherington, *Gospel of Mark*, 190.
24   Guelich, for example, suggests that Jesus acts like the purification rite described in Leviticus 12:7 following the birth of a child through which a woman shall be declared 'ceremonially clean from the flow of her blood (τῆς πηγῆς τοῦ αἵματος αὐτῆς)' (Mark 1–8:26, 297).
25   E.g. Focant, *Gospel According to Mark*, 211; Guelich, *Mark 1–8:26*, 296; Marcus, *Mark 1–8*, 357. In contrast, in discussing the Lukan version of the same healing account, Annette Weisenrider states that 'Jesus was not risking contamination being touched by the hemorrhaging woman, since the Levitical text in question makes a distinction between the contamination of people and of objects when referring to irregularly bleeding women' (*Images of Illness*, 239–40).

crowd, the woman was jeopardising not only the purity of those in the crowd but also the purity status of Jesus himself.[26] Her 'trembling with fear' (v. 33) in speaking to Jesus is considered by numerous scholars a sign that she knows that her presence in the crowd is inappropriate.[27] For many scholars, the fact that Jesus disregarded the purity regulations which should have prevented his contact with the women is evidence of Jesus' rejection of the allegedly oppressive purity regulations of the Torah.[28] This view is exemplified in the work of Marla Selvidge for whom purity is the primary interpretive key to the passage.[29] Selvidge, among others, argues that this passage is evidence of Jesus' dismissal of the Levitical purity system thus giving permission to the members of the Jesus movement to make a firm break with the ritual rigours of Judaism and its ostracism of menstruating women and others deemed ritually impure.[30] For Selvidge, the Gospel writers retained this story of the healing of the woman with the flow of blood in order to 'free early Christian women from the social bonds of [...] "banishment" during a woman's menstrual period'.[31]

While there has certainly been a number of recent works which seek to counter the purity interpretation of this Markan pericope,[32] the emphasis on ritual purity is still favoured by many commentators. While purity is undoubtedly of some importance in the pericope,[33] by focusing solely on this issue, traditional scholarship has failed to address the significance of the woman's condition in light of ancient medical sources on faulty menstrual cycles and the social consequences experienced by women in this position. The following section will address the nature of the woman's condition in light of Greek medical imagery.

4. Uterine Bleeding in the Greek Medical Literature

4.1 The woman's 'flow of blood' as Uterine Bleeding

Commentators addressing the pericope of the woman with bleeding in Mark 5:25-34 often comment on the source of the woman's bleeding. Although it is not stated explicitly in the Markan text, scholars regularly suggest that the woman was experiencing uterine bleeding.[34]

---

26 For example, Calduch-Benages says the woman knew she was impure and was willingly put Jesus as risk (*Perfume of the Gospel*, 27) even if the woman only touched Jesus cloak (e.g., Guelich, *Mark 1–8:26*, 297; Marcus, *Mark 1–8*, 357).

27 E.g. Calduch-Benages, *Perfume of the Gospel*, 27; Selvidge, *Woman, Cult and Miracle Recital*, 87.

28 Selvidge, 'Mark 5:25-34 and Leviticus 15:19-20', 619–23; Kinukawa, *Women and Jesus in Mark*, 44–5; Miller, *Women in Mark's Gospel*, 53.

29 Selvidge, 'Mark 5:25-34 and Leviticus 15:19-20', 619–23; Selvidge, *Woman, Cult and Miracle Recital, passim.*

30 Selvidge, 'Mark 5:25-34 and Leviticus 15:19-20', 622; Selvidge, *Woman, Cult and Miracle Recital*, 30.

31 Selvidge, *Woman, Cult, and Miracle Recital*, 30.

32 E.g. D'Angelo ('Gender and Power', 84), Kahl ('Jairus und die Verlorenen Töchter Israels', 69), and Etzelmüller and Weissenrieder ('Illness and Healing', 282) all note that the woman with bleeding seeks and receives healing (σώζω [*sōzō*]/ἰάομαι [*iaomai*]) not cleansing (καθαρίζω [*katharizō*]) such as is the case with the man with leprosy in Mark 1:40–5. Charlotte Fonrobert argues that while the woman with a flow of a blood may well have been impure, previous scholars have exaggerated the extent to which this woman's life would have been impacted by her impurity (Fonrobert, 'Woman with a Blood-Flow', 131).

33 E.g. Haber acknowledges that we 'cannot dismiss the significance of (the woman's) impurity within the narrative', however, the primary interpretation of the passage should shift from being about purity to that of health and illness (Haber, 'Woman's Touch', 173).

34 Some scholars refer to the woman's condition as 'uterine' bleeding (Collins, *Mark*, 280) while others refer to it as 'vaginal' bleeding (Boring, *Mark*, 159; Marcus, *Mark 1–8*, 357; Witherington, *Gospel of Mark*, 187) or others the less specific 'menstrual disorder' (France, *Gospel of Mark*, 236). Other commentators seem unwilling to even mention the taboo topic and simply refer to the bleeding as 'ritually defiling' without stating the origin of the bleeding (e.g., Guelich, *Mark 1–8:26*, 296).

While there is certainly good evidence for this in the text of Mark 5:25-34, often this detail is proffered without any explanation for how this conclusion has been reached.[35]

In Mark 5, the woman's experience is described as her being long-term 'in a flow of blood' (ἐν ῥύσει αἵματος [en rusei haimatos]) without any specific mention of the location of the bleeding. The phrase ῥύσις αἵματος (rusis haimatos) in itself is not specific to gynecological bleeding but rather is a phrase used throughout the Hippocratic corpus and other ancient medical texts to refer to significant bleeding from any part of the body. But in addition to this, the same phrase, ῥύσις αἵματος (rusis haimatos), also appears in the LXX in Leviticus 15 in a section addressing the various discharges of both men and women. In the Hebrew text, Leviticus 15:25 refers to two different categories of women: a woman was experiencing regular uterine bleeding, whom the text calls a *niddah*, and a woman with irregular uterine bleeding, that is, bleeding outside of her regular menstrual cycle who is referred to as a *zavah*.[36] As Leviticus 15:25 is clearly referring to uterine bleeding, it seems likely that Mark's adoption of this same phrase is in order to situate the woman's bleeding within the realms of the bodily discharges referred to in Leviticus 15.

In addition to the linguistic link between Mark 5:25 and Leviticus 15:25 and the use of the phrase '[in] flow of blood' ([ἐν] ῥύσει αἵματος [rusei haimatos]), Mark also uses a second significant phrase from Leviticus though it is often overlooked by commentators of Mark. Chapter 12 of Leviticus discusses the impurity associated with childbirth. Here the LXX refers to this postpartum flow of blood as the 'πηγὴ τοῦ αἵματος αὐτῆς' (pēgē tou haimatos autēs) which Mark repeats verbatim in 5:29 to describe the woman's 'fountain of blood'.[37] This same phrase is also used in the LXX translation of Leviticus 20:18 which speaks of menstruation. Thus, Annette Weissenrieder contends that the phrase 'πηγὴ τοῦ αἵματος αὐτῆς' (pēgē tou haimatos) is 'the equivalent of the uterus in those Hebrew texts that also deal with medical problems'.[38] These semantic parallels with Leviticus 12 and 15 thus render the woman's bleeding in Mark 5 clearly within the framework of a gender-specific flow of blood.

4.2 Forms of Illness in the Greek Medical Literature

But what evidence do we have from the ancient world that uterine bleeding would have been considered a form of illness by the ancient hearers of Mark's Gospel? Before addressing this question, it is first necessary to outline what exactly would have been considered illness in the ancient world. Since the work of John J. Pilch in the 1990s and other social scientists addressing the biblical texts, it has been commonplace for scholars to differentiate between *disease* and *illness*.[39] The suggestion of Pilch and others addressing medical anthropology in relation to the New

---

35 E.g. France, *Gospel of Mark*, 236; Guelich, *Mark 1–8:26*, 296.

36 While the Masoretic text distinguishes clearly between a woman experiencing regular uterine bleeding (*niddah*) and the one experiencing bleeding outside of the regular menstrual cycle (*zavah*), the same Greek phrase 'ῥύσει αἵματος' ([*rusei haimatos*] flow of blood) is used to describe both states of bleeding in the LXX. The only differentiation made between these conditions in the LXX are the phrases 'in (the time of) her menstruation' (ἐν τῇ ἀφέδρῳ αὐτῆς [*en tē aphedrō autēs*]; Lev. 15:19) and '*not* in the time of her menstruation' (οὐκ ἐν καιρῷ τῆς ἀφέδρου αὐτῆς [*ouk en kairō tēs aphedrou autēs*]; Lev. 15:25).

37 Gerburgis Feld contends that although English translations often render this phrase in Levitcus 'flow of blood', it is better translated as 'source/fountain of blood' as a metaphor for the uterus being not just the source of bleeding but also the source of life ('Leviticus: The ABC of Creation', 62).

38 Weissenrieder, *Images of Illness*, 251.

39 Pilch, 'Sickness and healing in Luke-Acts', 181–209; Pilch, *Healing in the NT, passim*; Malina and Rohrbaugh, *Social Science Commentary*, 210.

Testament[40] is that while the terms disease and illness are interchangeable in English in the modern western world, we must differentiate between the meaning of these words in order to understand the language of illness and healing in the New Testament texts. Pilch argues that the concept of disease is one connected purely with 'Western, scientifically-oriented cultures' whereby disease is analysed in terms of etiology, that is, the scientific causes of diseases.[41] These, he argues, can only be tested by means of blood tests, urine samples, X-rays, CT scans and other modern medical techniques. However, Pilch argues that in 'cultures that are not scientifically oriented, therapies are symptomatic, that is, aimed at alleviating or managing the symptoms'.[42] Illness then, according to Pilch, specifically refers not to medical diagnoses but to the overarching experience of a lack of wholeness and the experience of being in a socially devalued state.[43]

While Pilch's work has been highly influential among New Testament scholars,[44] there has been a pushback against the extent to which Pilch stretches this differentiation between disease and illness. Pilch claims, for example, that 'in the Bible there is no interest at all in disease '.[45] Pilch also claims that Jesus is not concerned with the curing of disease, but rather, was focused only on healing whereby healing is considered to be the process of removing the negative social experience associated with illness.[46] However, such a hypothesis clearly overlooks the obvious medical language that is used throughout the Gospels in relation to people's illnesses especially in the Gospel of Luke.[47] In the case of the woman with the flow of blood, for example, although her socially devalued position is an important element of the text (this will be discussed further in section 5.1 below), what is also significant is that on two occasions, the Markan author refers to her condition as a 'plague' (μάστιξ [$mastix$])[48] which is a word used metaphorically in the Gospels to refer to disease, for example, in Mark 3:10: 'For he had healed many, so that those with diseases (μάστιξ [$mastix$]) were pushing forward to touch him'. Indeed, the two-step nature of the woman's healing by Jesus in Mark 5:24-35 also highlights that Jesus addresses both the medical condition itself as well as the social consequences of such an illness. This will be discussed in more detail in section five below.

Such a differentiation between disease and illness also ignores the reality that throughout the Gospel texts Jesus is seen as removing the visible markers of a range of clearly medical conditions. As Jason Meggitt has noted: 'Jesus' healings were regarded by his contemporaries as unexpectedly efficacious with tangible consequences: the blind, it is claimed, received their sight, the lame walked, people with leprosy were cleansed, and the deaf heard'.[49] Jesus did not simply eradicate the negative social consequences for a person living with a physical or sensory disability but removed the actual bodily condition as well. And thus Meggitt, Weissenrieder, and Craffert, among others, all argue that such a staunch dichotomy between disease and illness cannot be so

---

40 Pilch, *Healing in the NT, passim*; Horsley, 'Jesus and Empire', *passim*.
41 Pilch, *Healing in the NT*, 13.
42 Pilch, *Healing in the NT*, 13, cf. Kleinman, *Patients and Healers*, 82.
43 Pilch, *Healing in the NT*, 13–4, cf. Kleinman, *Patients and Healers*, 265.
44 Calduch-Benages notes this exact dichotomy in relation to the healing of the woman with bleeding (*Perfume of the Gospel*, 19).
45 Pilch, *Healing in the NT*, 76.
46 Pilch, *Healing in the NT*, 13.
47 Weissenrieder argues that this language of illness in a medical sense is particularly dominant in Luke's Gospel (*Images of Illness*, 250–1).
48 Although the word μαστιγόω ($mastigoō$) is used in a literal sense to mean scourging, beating, or punishment in other places in the NT (e.g. Matt. 10:17, 23:34), it is used in both a literal sense and figurative sense throughout the LXX, for example, it is used in the sense of plague in Psalm 91:10.
49 Meggitt, 'The Historical Jesus and Healing', 23.

easily made.[50] What is important to recognise, however, is that health itself is not a universal concept but one that is socially located within specific cultural and social groups.[51] Each cultural and social group determines the parameters of what is considered a healthy body and what is considered an ill body. While we might not be able to diagnose the precise medical condition the woman was experiencing in terms of modern biomedical language,[52] we can make an attempt to understand how a long-term uterine bleed would have been understood and interpreted within the social and cultural framework of the Greek medical literature.

4.3 Inter-Menstrual Bleeding as Illness in the Greek Medical Literature

Annette Weissenrieder contends that one of the difficulties of interpreting the story of the woman with bleeding in the twenty-first century is that 'an issue of blood no longer exists as an image of illness in modern medicine'.[53] As a consequence of this, many scholars 'attach no importance whatsoever'[54] to the implications of such a condition for a woman in the first century and the impact on her social and familial relationships. In general, scholars who make considerations with respect to the illness are often limited in their analysis to mere retrospective diagnosis, that is, attempting only to 'diagnose' the woman's condition with some form of modern medical terminology.[55] However, such medical terminology does little to help us to understand better the status of an ill woman within the social and cultural milieu of the first century. Instead, we need to address theories of medicine that were predominant in the first-century Greco-Roman world to understand how a condition of such long-term bleeding would have been interpreted at the time Mark's Gospel was written.

One of the most influential systems of categorising health and illness in antiquity was the humoral theory developed initially by the Hippocratic writers in the fifth and fourth centuries BCE. Although the humoral theory was developed over time and is expressed in various manifestations across the range of Hippocratic texts as well as in Galen, in general, the theory proposed that the human body is made of four distinct fluids or humors: phlegm, blood, yellow bile, and black bile.[56] Health was the state of balance or equilibrium in the body when all the humors were in equal measure. Illness was thus the result of humoral imbalance.[57]

According to the Greek medical writer Galen writing in the 2nd century C.E., summarising the theories from the Hippocratic corpus, 'Health is a sort of harmony […] For in every instance, health is a due proportion of moist, dry, warm, and cold […] but always we function in our parts through their due proportion'.[58] A healthy body then is one which is in perfect proportion in terms of humors, temperature, and moisture. In the instance that a body was out of balance in any aspect, the treatment would be the

---

50 Weissenrieder, *Images of Illness*, 12–3; Meggitt, 'The Historical Jesus and Healing', 23; Craffert, 'Medical Anthropology', 1–2.
51 King, 'Women's Health', 160.
52 Some scholars have made attempts at 'diagnosing' the woman's illness—along with other references to illness throughout the Gospels—but this process of retrospective diagnosis is unhelpful because while there is certainly medical language in the Gospels, they are not medical texts. In addition, as noted by Heike Peckruhn, this approach ignores 'the different and changing cultural values attached to certain conditions' ('Disability Studies', 102).
53 Weissenrieder, *Images of Illness*, 229.
54 Weissenrieder, *Images of Illness*, 230.
55 For example, in his commentary on Matthew, Keener posits that the woman may have experienced 'menorrhagia' (Keener, *Gospel of Matthew* 303).
56 Hipp. *Nat. Hom.* 5. An earlier version exists in the Hippocratic work *On Diseases* where the four humors are described as phlegm, blood, bile, and water (4.35); cf. Galen, *In Hipp. De nat. hom. comm.* 1.11 (CMG V).
57 Hipp. *Nat. Hom.* 5; Galen, *hipp. De nat. hom. Comm.*, 1 prooem. 11: CMG V cf. Hipp. *Morb.* 4.
58 Galen, *San. Tuend.* 1.3 (trans. Green).

application of the opposing element. For example, the Hippocratic text *Aphorisms* states that 'diseases caused by repletion are cured by depletion; those caused by depletion are cured by repletion'.[59] For example, the body that is considered too moist must be brought back into balance through a process of drying out.

However, according to the Greek medical writers, health was not considered a static state but something that needed to be worked at in order to maintain it.[60] This was especially the case for women whose bodies were considered to be pathologically out of balance. Aristotle, for example, believed that women were simply 'deformed males'[61] who had 'never achieved the heat, dryness or impermeability that make up healthy bodies'.[62] Thus women, in general, were considered to be too cold, soft, wet, and porous.[63] Men's bodies, through physical activity and exercise, had the capacity to turn excess fluids into semen in order to maintain humoral balance.[64] Women's bodies, on the other hand, did not have the same capacity.[65] A woman's pathological tendency towards moistness was exacerbated by women's lifestyles which were characterised as sedentary and inactive.[66] Menstruation was thus considered a therapeutic evacuation that was vital for women in order to dispose of excess fluids and maintain balance, that is, as much as it was possible for a woman's body to be balanced. Disruptions in this evacuation of fluids—either too much or not enough menstrual bleeding—were of great concern to medical writers as the result would be that a woman's body would then stay in a state of imbalance which was considered highly dangerous and potentially life-threatening.

Due to the serious impact of such imbalance in a woman's body, this topic is addressed on numerous occasions throughout the extant Greek medical literature. The medical sources address menstrual suppression, excessive menstrual bleeding as well as inter-menstrual bleeding such as that experienced by the woman in Mark 5:25-34. While menstrual suppression appears with greater frequency in the medical literature,[67] the seriousness of excess menstrual bleeding and inter-menstrual bleeding is also considered. Lesley Dean-Jones suggests that the reason that menstrual suppression appears more frequently in the medical literature is connected with what the ancient medical writers considered was an acceptable amount of blood loss during menstruation.[68] This figure is so much higher than what is considered normal blood loss by modern standards—indeed, even 'seven to eight times what is considered the normal amount today'[69]—that it would have required an exceedingly heavy or prolonged bleed for the ancient medical writers to consider the condition serious. Given this, when the Hippocratics did address cases of excessive menstrual or inter-menstrual bleeding, we can assume that such cases would have been very serious knowing the amount of blood loss considered 'normal' by the Greek medical writers. Hearers of Mark's Gospel would thus know that for a woman's bleeding to be such that she had endured it continuously for twelve years, her condition must have been

---

59 Hipp. *Aph.* 2.20 (Jones LCL).
60 Cf. King, 'Women's Health', 155.
61 Arist. *Gen. an.* 737a26-30; 728a.
62 Moss, 'Man with the Flow of Power', 513.
63 Hippoc. *Mul.* 1.1; Hipp. *Nat. puer.* 15.
64 E.g. 'the female, in fact, is female on account of inability of a sort [...] it lacks the power to concoct semen out of the final state of the nourishment [...] because of the coldness of its nature' (*Gen. an.* 728a [Peck, LCL]).
65 Hipp. *Salubr.* 6 advises that women should hold to a diet of dry food because of their tendency towards too much moisture.
66 Arist. *Gen. an.* 728a (Peck, LCL).
67 For a discussion on Jairus' daughter representing the body that was the opposite of the woman with bleeding, that is, too dry, and therefore experiencing menstrual suppression, see D'Angelo 'Gender and Power', 83-109, and Gosbell, 'The Poor, the Crippled', 272-5.
68 The Hippocratic text lists 'two Attic cotyls' as the normal amount of blood loss in 2-3 days of menstruation which is around 475 mls (Hipp. *Mul.* 1.6).
69 Dean-Jones, *Women's Bodies*, 89.

very serious indeed.

In his medical writings, Galen refers to a range of 'abnormal fluxes' and relates a story of healing a woman from her prolonged 'female flux'.[70] Second-century medical writer Soranus also features a section in his *Gynecology* entitled 'On the Flux of Women' where he differentiates between two different forms of irregular menstrual bleeding: the first he refers to as a 'haemorrhage of the uterus' and the second a 'menstrual flux'. In respect to the 'haemorrhage of the uterus'. Soranus notes that this can occur as the result of a 'difficult labor, or miscarriage, or erosion by ulceration, or a porous condition, or from the bursting of blood vessels'.[71] In this instance, Soranus notes that the bleeding is a 'sudden and excessive rush of blood' and the results are that 'patients become weak, shrunken, thin, pale, and if the condition persists, suffer from anorexia'.[72] Soranus also describes a range of different menstrual fluxes, but that symptoms for all of these conditions are that 'the patient is pale, wastes away, lacks appetite, often becomes breathless when walking and has swollen feet'.[73]

Likewise, the Hippocratic text *The Diseases of Women* also notes the physiological effects of a prolonged uterine bleed describing a patient as becoming pallid as well as experiencing fever and loss of appetite leading to emaciation, weakness, and perpetual exhaustion.[74] The Hippocratic author notes that experiencing such a condition long-term can lead to infertility and notes that 'if some other disease should attack her at the same time, she could die'.[75]

According to the Greek medical literature then, a protracted uterine bleed was considered to be a serious illness.[76] Upon hearing of a woman with such long-term bleeding, Mark's audience would have understood the significance of such humoral imbalance. Mark's hearers would have been aware of the seriousness of the woman's condition and understood the symptoms of such a condition would be such as those outlined by the Hippocratic corpus: weakness, fatigue, fever, and weight loss. Ancient audiences also would have understood the impact that such symptoms would have had on a woman's ability to fulfill her domestic functions in the household.

4.4 Infertility Connected with Uterine Bleeding in the Greek Medical Literature

In addition to poor general health, one of the other side-effects the Greek medical writers associated with a long-term uterine bleed was infertility. While the possibility of the woman being infertile is only mentioned by a small number of commentators of Mark,[77] this would have been of serious concern to ancient hearers of the text. While we cannot know for certain whether the woman's bleeding would have rendered her infertile, we can be certain that it was known to be a side-effect of such long-term bleeding and that in itself would have been enough to reduce her likelihood of marriage.

Although infertility is not considered a

---

70 Galen, *Praecog.* 14.641–7K.
71 Sor. *Gyn.* 3.10.40 (trans. Temkin).
72 Sor. *Gyn.* 3.10.43 (trans. Temkin).
73 Sor. *Gyn.* 3.11.43 (trans. Temkin).
74 Hipp. *Mul.* 5.
75 Hipp. *Mul* 1.5 (trans. Whitely).

76 The Hippocratic text *On Epidemics* refers to the duration of an illness often noting the direct correlation between the length of the condition and its severity. Thus, Weissenreider observes that the number of weeks, months, or years (though often conditions do not last as long as to be able to be measured in years) 'are seen as signs of intensification of the illness and of the immenence of death'. Weissenreider goes on to say regarding the woman with the flow of blood that 'In light of this understanding, an illness lasting twelve years would signal incurability and approaching death' (*Images of Illness*, 253).
77 The issue of infertility as a result of the woman's condition has only been noted by a small number of commentators and exegetes e.g., Boring, *Mark*, 158; Gench, *Back to the Well*, 29; Rosenblatt, 'Gender, Ethnicity', 153; Wassen, 'Jesus and the Hemorrhaging Woman', 644.

disability in the modern scientific world, writers on disability in antiquity consider infertility a particularly significant disability. In the Ancient Near East, infertility appears alongside lists of other illnesses and disability such as blindness and lameness implying some commonality between the conditions.[78] In the Hebrew Bible, infertility is also described as an illness that people petition God to be healed from in the same way people request healing from other illnesses and disabilities.[79] Indeed, in their work on disability and the Hebrew Bible, both Jeremy Schipper and Rebecca Raphael contend that infertility is the most significant and frequently appearing disability in the Hebrew Bible.[80] Raphael goes on to suggest that infertility is 'the defining female disability in the Hebrew Bible'.[81]

The reason that infertility can be considered a disability within the ancient context is that infertility hit at the very heart of a woman's identity and purpose in the ancient world. If a woman's primary role was centered around conception and childbearing,[82] then any woman unable to fulfill these duties would have been considered disabled according to their own society's expectations of women.[83] For this reason, Johannes Stahl in his work on disability in the Roman world suggests that:

> infertility in women amounted, for all intents and purposes, to a disability, and was treated as such. Thus, the reportedly first case of divorce in the Roman Republic, initiated by a certain Sp. Carvilius Ruga, was founded on the inability of his wife to provide him with children (Gell., *NA* 4.3.2; 17.21.33).[84]
> 146/5864/1136

The issue of infertility is often raised by Aristotle and the Hippocratic writers. In the Hippocratic text *The Diseases of Women*, the writer explains a number of reasons why a woman may be unable to bear children. The author outlines a range of possible causes of infertility including mechanical issues with the shape or size of the uterus as well as too much or not enough menstrual bleeding. The Hippocratic writer goes onto outline a list of measures that can be taken to counter this failure to conceive.[85] In this sense, both Aristotle and the Hippocratic writers considered infertility a state that had the potential to be reversed, but the longer a woman remained 'unhealthy', the more likely it was that she would become permanently infertile, that is, barren.[86] Both Aristotle and the Hippocratic writers list heavy menstrual or inter-menstrual bleeding as a possible cause for infertility.[87]

Given the severity and longevity of her condition, it is highly likely that the woman with bleeding in Mark 5 would have been considered to be infertile, and as a result of this assumed infertility, she would not have been able to fulfill her socially prescribed roles as wife and mother. As such, she could never achieve the full status of a γυνή ([*gynē*] woman) within her ancient context. Although the Greek word γυνή (*gynē*) is often just translated as 'woman' in many ancient texts, including the New Testament,[88] Helen King suggests that there is much more to being a γυνή (*gynē*) than one's gender.[89] To be a γυνή (*gynē*), King insists, was not simply a matter of transitioning from

---

78 Cf. Schipper, *Disability and Isaiah's Suffering Servant*, 21. See, for example, the Sumerian myth of Enki and Ninmah (*COS* 1.159:518) as well as a rabbinic commentary on Isaac's birth in Genesis 21:2 (*Gen. Rab.* 53:8); cf. Walls, "Origins of the Disabled Body," 16–9.
79 E.g. Hannah (1 Sam. 1). Cf. Schipper, 'Disabling Israelite Leadership', 105; Avalos, *Illness and Health Care*, 248–9.
80 Schipper, *Disability and Isaiah's Suffering Servant*, 21–2; Raphael, *Biblical Corpora*, 57–8.
81 Raphael, *Biblical Corpora*, 57–8. *Italics mine*.
82 Edwards, 'Women and Physical Disability', 3–9.
83 Edwards, 'Women and Physical Disability', 3–9.
84 Stahl, 'Physically Deformed and Disabled People', 719.
85 Hipp. *Mul.* 1.6; 3.213.
86 Hipp. *Mul.* 1.6.
87 Hipp. *Mul.* 1.6; Arist. *HA* 281.
88 In the New Testament, the word γυνή (*gynē*) is translated as 'woman' (e.g. Matt. 9:20; Acts 5:14) but also as 'wife' (e.g. 1 Cor. 7:3-4; Eph. 5:22).
89 King, 'Bound to Bleed', 112.

childhood into adulthood: a young woman's transformation into a γυνή (*gynē*) in its fullest sense was also connected closely with the social acts of marriage and childbearing.[90] Any woman who was unable to fulfill any or all of these elements was not only relegated to a state of permanent illness but also to some extent, to a status of an incomplete woman. A permanently ill woman was not a complete woman but only a subcategory of womanhood whereby the standard norm was a woman who was able to be both wife and mother.[91]

Marriage and motherhood were the expected norms for women according to both Jewish writers Philo and Josephus, with Philo specifically stating that men who knowingly marry women unable to bear children are simply 'destroy(ing) the procreative germs with deliberate purpose'.[92] Josephus likewise states that the primary purpose of marriage is procreation and suggests that sexual intercourse during menstruation was a capital offence.[93] His rationale for this is not based on the Levitical purity system, but rather, it is because a woman is unable to fall pregnant while she is menstruating.[94] A rabbinical text from the Babylonian Talmud recalls that 'Four are considered dead: a poor person, a leper, a blind person and a childless one'.[95] These views, however, were not limited to Jewish writers. Stoic philosopher Musonius Rufus reportedly stated that sexual intercourse should only be 'indulged in for the purpose of begetting children', and was thus unlawful for 'mere pleasure-seeking, even in marriage'.[96]

While scholars have debated the extent to which purity issues are at play in the account of the woman with the flow of blood, it seems more apparent that it is her illness and the social and cultural consequences of this disabling condition that was as much, if not a more, significant factor in her stigmatisation and marginalisation. It was not simply that the woman was ritually unclean and could pass on this contagion to others in the crowd—a situation that would be quickly remedied—but her protracted illness prevented her from participating in her role as a γυνή (*gynē*); she was perpetually existent as a παρθένος (*parthenos*), a maiden; essentially, the same status as that of Jairus' dying daughter.[97] Her illness would have relegated her virtually unmarriageable.

5. Implications of Considering the Woman with the flow of blood as 'disabled'

5a The Social Status of the Woman with the 'flow of blood'

In their expositions of this pericope, many scholars comment on the social status of the woman with the flow of blood. Numerous scholars see in Mark's description of the woman a social outcast who serves as a foil for the high-status Jairus with whom the pericope begins. Indeed, the Markan author appears to stress the paradox between the social status of the woman and Jairus: Jairus is a male synagogue ruler of significant status, and one of the rare characters who is named in Mark's Gospel, who was seeking healing on behalf of his sick daughter and whose home was surrounded by a crowd of

---

90 King, 'Bound to Bleed', 112.
91 King refers to one Hippocratic citation which refers to a woman's recovery after an illness and which states that the woman on her recovery 'will be healthy, but sterile' (Hipp. *Mul.* 1.2). King says that the word 'but' implies that 'female health would normally be thought to include fertility' ('Women's Health', 157).
92 Philo, *Spec. Leg.* 3.34 (Colson, LCL).
93 Joseph., *Ant.* 3.275; cf. Lev. 20:18.
94 Joseph., *War* 2.161.
95 BT *Ned.* 64b.

96 Musonius Rufus, frag. 12 (in Stobaeus, *Anth.* 4.22.90 [trans. Lutz]).
97 Although Jairus' daughter is not referred to by the term παρθένος (*parthenos*) or maiden in the Markan text, she is referred to by the term κοράσιον (*korasion*) is 'scarcely different' in meaning from παρθένος (*parthenos*; Dowden, *Death and the Maiden*, 2).

mourners (5:38). In contrast, the woman with the flow of blood is described as being alone in the crowd with no one to seek healing on her behalf and who had been economically drained as a result of medical professionals who could bring her no healing (5:26). Ched Myers thus states on this paradox that 'Mark [...] portrays the two main characters in this episode as archetypical opposites in terms of economic status and honor'.[98]

One particular detail in Mark's account serves as an indicator of the woman's status in her ancient community: her solo appearance in the crowd. In antiquity, health was considered to be under the control of the head of the household, the paterfamilias or οἰκοδεσπότης (*oikodespotēs*).[99] It was the duty of the *paterfamilias* to seek out healing for anyone in the household—family members or servants—who required medical intervention whether that was herbal remedies, professional healers or petitions to God/the gods. It is, for this reason, most petitions to Jesus for healing come via someone other than the ill person themselves in the Gospel.[100] The only two characters to actively seek healing for themselves in Mark's Gospel are Bartimaeus[101] and the woman with the flow of blood. Indeed, part of Mark's contrast between Jairus' daughter and the bleeding woman is that the daughter has her father Jairus—the head of the household—seeking healing on her behalf. In comparison, the woman with bleeding appears to have no *paterfamilias*, no father or husband, to petition for her healing. The woman's low social status seems to be further underlined by Mark in his reference to her financial status. Although it appears she may have been a woman of some means in her past,[102] Mark recalls that prior to seeking healing from Jesus, the woman 'had spent everything she had' (5:26) on medical professionals to no avail.

While numerous scholars comment on the woman's marginal status, what is not explained by Markan commentators is why long-term bleeding would lead to social marginalisation in the ancient world. France, for example, states that the woman's bleeding was the cause of her 'social and religious isolation'[103] but without further explanation. Likewise, Guelich argues that the woman would have been 'personally, socially and spiritually cut off' as a result of her condition but again does not elaborate on why her bleeding would lead to such disenfranchisement.[104] Other scholars make their case more clearly, for example, Marla Selvidge who states that a woman with a long-term flow of blood would have been 'restricted (in her) movement in cult, society, and the home' because of her ritual impurity.[105] Selvidge contends that all Jewish women in the midst of menstrual or inter-menstrual bleeding were 'banished' from the community until seven days after the bleeding had ceased as a means of protecting others in the community from the women's contagion.[106]

Selvidge maintains that strict adherence to the Levitical purity laws was still considered normative in the first century and argues that Josephus' writes about the purity laws regarding menstruation as though they were still current practice in his time.[107] Other scholars, however, are not so convinced. Mary Rose D'Angelo, for example, contends that as the healing of the woman with the flow of blood took place in Galilee and not within

---

98 Myers, *Binding the Strong Man*, 200.
99 E.g. Cato, Agr. 156-8.
100 E.g. Simon and Andrew seek healing on behalf of their mother (Mark 1:29-31); Jairus seeking healing on behalf of his daughter (Mark 5:21-43). In many instances, we are told that 'some people' brought an ill person to be healing (e.g. Mark 2:1-12; 7:31-37; 8:22-26 etc.).
101 Mark 10:46-52.
102 Malina and Rohrbaugh say that professional healers were limited to the elite and so the fact that the woman first appealed to professional healers probably indicates her original social status (*Social Science Commentary*, 210).
103 France, *Gospel of Mark*, 236.
104 Guelich, *Mark 1-8:26*, 296.
105 Selvidge, 'Mark 5:25-34 and Leviticus 15:19-20', 619.
106 Selvidge, 'Mark 5:25-34 and Leviticus 15:19-20', 619.
107 Selvidge, *Woman, Cult and Miracle Recital*, 47-90, 83-91; cf. See Joseph., *Wars* 5.227; *Ant*. 3.261; AA 2.103.

close proximity to the temple, it 'makes the issue of contracting ritual impurity whether from the dead girl or the woman, more or less irrelevant'.[108] Similarly, Shaye J. D. Cohen argues that issues of purity were only a matter of concern 'in the Temple and in proximity to persons and objects bound for the Temple', but in all other circumstances, 'the purity laws could be ignored'.[109]

While the Markan author does seem to align the woman's condition with the intermenstrual bleeding addressed in Leviticus 12 and 15, and this seems to have a bearing on the woman's stealthy approach to Jesus, it is much more likely that her disenfranchisement as it is depicted in the pericope is as a result of her illness rather than her purity status. A long-term flow of blood as experienced by the woman would have been isolating because of the impact the illness would have had on her ability to fulfill her social duties. As a result of such a significant long-term bleed, the woman would have been without the markers of marriage and childbearing that gave women identity and value in the ancient world. Not only this, but the severity of her illness would have impacted all her relationships. In emphasising that the woman was alone in the crowd in her search for healing, Mark is highlighting the glaring absence of any *paterfamilias*. She apparently had no father nor husband to venture into the crowd on her behalf with no apparent prospects for this circumstance to change. Being without a *paterfamilias* would have meant she had no one to provide for her financially and would have been akin to the widow of Nain in Luke's Gospel who was likewise left without a *paterfamilias* to provide for her needs.[110] Life with an exhausting, physically debilitating illness in addition to the complex social implications of such an illness certainly marked the woman as socially marginalised and disabled. Indeed, the impact of her illness would have been far more detrimental than any exclusion from the temple or any other limitations that may have arisen from being ritually unclean.

6a The Physical and Social Contexts of the Woman's Healing

In section 2 above, we considered the World Health Organization's definition of disability and its applicability to concepts of disability in the ancient world. In both modern as well as ancient contexts, it is evident that in cases of significant illness or impairment, it is not only the physical condition itself which is important but also its impact on one's social interactions. What is particularly significant about Jesus' encounter with the woman with bleeding in Mark 5:24-35 is that more than any of Jesus' other healings, this healing story shows Jesus addressing both the physical as well as the social components of the woman's illness.

At the outset of the passage, Mark relays the woman's thoughts as she attempted to make contact with Jesus: 'For she said, "If I can just touch His robes, I'll be made well (σῴζω [*sōzō*])!"' (5:28). While the word σῴζω (*sōzō*) is often translated as 'to heal',[111] the word has a wider semantic range than just physical healing. Σῴζω (*sōzō*) does not just indicate a physical release from symptoms but has a broader concept of wellbeing akin to the concept of *shalom* in the Hebrew Bible.[112] It is for this reason that σῴζω (*sōzō*) is also translated as 'to save', in a literal sense, as well as in a Christological sense of salvation in Christ,

---

108 D'Angelo, 'Gender and Power', 91.
109 Cohen, 'Purity and Piety', 106.
110 Luke 7:1-17.

111 E.g. Mark 6:56; 10:52.
112 Foerster and Fohrer suggest that "The choice of the word (σῴζω [*sōzō*]) leaves room for the view that the healing power of Jesus and the saving power of faith go beyond the physical life. This is particularly clear in the fact that ἡ πίστις σου σέσωκέν σε, which perhaps finds its original locus in the story of the woman with a bloody flux, is also said to the woman who is a great sinner in Lk. 7:50 even though there has been no preceding cure in this case' (Foerster and Fohrer, 'σῴζω, σωτηρία, σωτήρ, σωτήριος', 990).

THE WOMAN WITH THE 'FLOW OF BLOOD' (MARK 5:25-34)

throughout the Synoptic Gospels.[113] Thus at the outset of the pericope, Mark relates that what the woman was seeking was actually wholeness or wellbeing. Mark then goes on to relate the woman's encounter with Jesus describing the way the bleeding ceased at the moment the woman touched Jesus' cloak. While the NIV states simply that the woman's 'bleeding stopped', the Greek text states that ἐξηράνθη ἡ πηγὴ τοῦ αἵματος αὐτῆς (*ezēranthē ē pēgē tou haimatos autēs*), that is, that the bleeding 'dried up'. This language of drying up is important as it shows Jesus physically healing the woman in a way deemed consistent with humoral system. As the woman was too wet due to her excess bleeding, the bleeding needed to not only just cease, but the woman's body required drying out in order to bring her back into equilibrium according to the humoral system.[114] But despite the medical significance of stemming the blood flow, Mark states that at the moment the woman touched Jesus, it was not σωτηρία (*sōtēria*) she received from Jesus but she is described as being ἴαται ἀπὸ τῆς μάστιγος (*iatai apo tēs mastigos*), 'healed of her affliction' (5:29).

Although the woman's bleeding ceased, her encounter with Jesus did not immediately come to an end. Jesus could have allowed the woman to continue her retreat anonymously back into the crowd, but instead, Jesus requested from the crowd the identity of the person who touched him. Although some scholars consider Jesus' question an indication of his limited human knowledge,[115] it is far more likely that Mark shows Jesus deliberately drawing the woman out of anonymity. Unlike many of the other healing accounts in Mark's Gospel, this woman's illness was invisible. There was nothing in her healing that would have been apparent immediately to those around her. This is in stark contrast to the healing of others in Mark whose physical bodies were markedly different following their healing by Jesus.[116] For this reason, even with the cessation of the bleeding, the woman would have continued to carry the stigma of her illness even though her bleeding had stopped.

The woman's public acknowledgment that it was her who had touched Jesus is thus significant in Mark's account. By coming forward and telling the 'whole truth' about her illness and search for healing, the news of her healing was announced publicly allowing her to not only be 'freed from her suffering' (5:29) but it also aided in the removal of the associated stigma of her illness. The long-term nature of the woman's illness, as well as the gender-specific nature of her condition, would have made it difficult for her to discuss the healing publicly herself and difficult to remove the stigma associated with her condition. However, by Jesus prompting her to announce her healing in such a public setting, the message of the woman's healing could begin to circulate among the people present and thus begin to remove her long-standing stigmatisation. In this sense, the woman's healing took place in two stages: firstly, the woman experienced the physical release from her 'affliction' which occurred at the moment she touched Jesus' cloak. The second stage of the healing commenced with the woman's

---

113 The word σῴζω (*sōzō*) is used to refer to salvation throughout Mark (e.g. Mark 3:4; 8:35; 10:26; 13:20; 15:30; 16:16).

114 Candida Moss and Joel Baden suggests that the 'drying up' of the uterus here happens to such an extent that the woman's uterus would have been completely withered and useless (*Reconceiving Infertility*, 203-6). Moss and Baden say that we can assume that the process of healing dries her up and brings her back into balance but actually, they state that, 'we do not *know* this. The language employed by Mark is the language of sterility' (*Reconceiving Infertility*, 205). However, this interpretation does not seem viable in light of the concept of healing as a balance of the humoral system. If the woman was too wet, healing would come through being brought back into balance not being sent from one extreme of being 'too wet' to the other extreme of being 'too dry.'

115 E.g. France, *Mark*, 237-8.

116 E.g. The man with a mobility impairment (Mark 2:1-12) the demon possessed man (Mark 5:1-20); Blind Bartimaeus (Mark 10:46-52).

public declaration of her healing. This second and social component of the woman's healing is marked by Jesus in his statement: 'Daughter, your faith has healed (σῴζω [sōzō]) you. Go in peace and be freed from your suffering' (5:34). While the touch of Jesus' cloak brought the woman healing in the physical sense, indicated by Mark by the word ἰάομαι (iaomai) for healing,[117] Jesus' declaration following the woman's confession brought her healing in a wider context: the fullness of wellbeing she was seeking at the outset of the passage. This is evident in Jesus' repetition of the word (σῴζω [sōzō]); the very word the woman was seeking at the beginning of the pericope. The social component of the woman's healing is also signaled through Jesus' use of the word 'daughter' in speaking to the woman. While the passage began with her alone in the crowd with no head of the household to petition for healing on her behalf, Jesus now placed himself in the position of her *paterfamilias* and welcomed her into his spiritual family being generated from people who were willing to put their faith in him. What we see taking place here then, as Weissenrieder has noted, is that 'Jesus functions as a "healer" of both physical and social bodies'.[118]

6. Conclusion

Although there was no overarching term for disability in the ancient world, the medical literature from antiquity clearly shows the ancients had an understanding of the impact illness could have upon a person's ability to function in society and on their familial and other social relationships. In Mark's account of the woman with the 'flow of blood' in 5:25-34, Mark describes the woman as experiencing an incredibly disabling illness. The long-term nature of the woman's condition would have marked her illness as serious and possibly even life-threatening. Such long-term bleeding would have had an adverse effect on the woman's ability to function in the way her society expected of her. The lethargy and weakness associated with such long-term bleeding would have made handling the daily tasks of running a household particularly difficult, if not impossible. Not only this, but those who knew of the woman's condition, and those who would have heard her story through Mark's narrative of Jesus, would likely have assumed that the condition would have rendered the woman infertile and therefore unable to fulfill one of the primary functions of women in antiquity.

While the woman's impurity does have some bearing on the woman's situation in Mark 5:25-34, by focusing solely on the issue of purity, scholars have failed to address the woman's illness and the disabling nature of such a condition. While she was unclean and may have been able to pass on this contagion, it was a situation that would have been easily remedied for anyone who came into contact with her. In contrast, the severity and longevity of the woman's illness would have had serious ramifications on the woman's financial position and her social standing in her society. Not only would she have struggled in maintaining a household but her condition would have reduced her likelihood of marriage and the possibility of childbearing: the primary markers of usefulness and identity for women in the ancient world.

Jesus' healing of the woman occurs in two stages which address both the physical and social concerns of the woman's illness. With her touch of Jesus' cloak, the woman's 'fountain of bleeding' did not simply cease but 'dried up'. This drying out of the too-wet woman's body would have been deemed wholly consistent with the medical literature from the ancient world and the widely accepted humoral theory. Through the process of drying out, the woman's body was being restored to its right balance and

---

117 The word ἰάομαι (iaomai) is only used once in Mark's Gospel. On other occasions in Mark, the Gospel writer uses the word θεραπεύω (therapeuō; 1:34; 6:5, 13; 3:1) as well as σῴζω (sōzō; 6:56; 10:52) to refer to healing.
118 Weissenrieder, 'Plague of Uncleanness', 207.

equilibrium. Jesus' ability as a physical healer is contrast with that of the physicians who were not able to stem the woman's flow of blood. However, Jesus' healing of the woman was not limited to her physical affliction. While Jesus could have allowed the woman to slip quietly back into the crowd, he instead had her declare her healing publicly to begin her transition back into the social networks from which she had been disconnected. Through her confession, the woman's journey to reintegration had commenced as the stigma she had carried for twelve years could finally begin to dissipate. But Jesus' ultimate message of social restoration comes through the woman's inclusion into the family of faith. While her illness had rendered her isolated and disabled, Jesus' declaration of 'daughter' aligned himself in the role of her *paterfamilias* who would be in the position of caring for her needs, not necessarily in a physical sense but certainly in a spiritual one. Mark's account of the woman with the flow of blood thus represents Jesus as a complete healer: not only does he have the ability to bring an end to physical suffering but he is also able to restore people to the fullness of life in its broadest sense. For Mark, this woman's healing and social restoration are depicted as a foretaste of the complete and permanent healing available through Jesus in the eschaton.

Dr. Louise Gosbell
Mary Andrews College
louisegosbell@mac.edu.au

Primary Sources

Aristotle.	*Generation of Animals.* Translated by A. L. Peck. LCL. Cambridge: Harvard University Press, 1942.
Galen.	*On Diseases and Symptoms.* Translated, with introduction and notes by Ian Johnston. Cambridge: Cambridge University Press, 2006.
Galen.	*A Translation of Galen's Hygiene (De sanitate tuenda).* Translated by Robert Montraville Green. Springfield: Charles C. Thomas, 1951.
Hippocrates.	*Diseases of Women 1.* Translated by K. Whiteley. Masters diss., University of South Africa, 2003.
Hippocrates.	*Nature of Man. Regimen in Health. Humours. Aphorisms. Regimen 1–3. Dreams. Heracleitus: On the Universe.* Vol 4. Translated by William H. S. Jones. Loeb Classical Library. Cambridge: Harvard University Press, 1931.
Hippocrates.	*Epidemics 2, 4–7.* Vol. 7. Edited and translated by W. D. Smith. Loeb Classical Library. Cambridge: Harvard University Press, 1994.
Musonius Rufus.	*The Roman Socrates.* Vol. 10. Yale Classical Studies. New Haven: Yale University Press, 1947.
Origen.	*Origen's Commentary on the Gospel of Matthew.* Translated by J. Patrick. Ante-Nicene Fathers, 1896.
Philo.	*On the Decalogue. On the Special Laws 1–3.* Vol. 7. Translated by F. H. Colson. Loeb Classical Library. Cambridge: Harvard University Press, 1937.
Pliny the Elder.	*Natural History.* Translated by H. Rackham, W. H. S. Jones, and D. E. Eichholz. 10 vols. Loeb Classical Library. Cambridge: Harvard University Press, 1938–1963.
Soranus.	*Gynecology.* Translated with an introduction by O. Temkin. Baltimore: Johns Hopkins Press, 1956.

Secondary Sources

Avalos, H.	*Illness and Health Care in the Ancient Near East: The Role of the Temple in Greece, Mesopotamia and Israel.* Atlanta: Scholars Press, 1995.
Beavis, M. A.	*Mark.* Grand Rapids: Baker Academic, 2011.
Boring, M. E.	*Mark: A Commentary.* Louisville: Westminster/John Knox, 2006.
Calduch-Benages, N.	*Perfume of the Gospel: Jesus' Encounters with Women.* Translated by P.-D. Nau. Theologia 8. Rome: Gregorian & Biblical, 2012.
Cohen, S. J. D.	'Purity and Piety: The Separation of Menstruants from the Sancta'. Pages 103–15 in *Daughters of the King: Women and the Synagogue.* Edited by Susan Grossman and Rivka Haut. Philadelphia: Jewish Publication Society, 1993.
Collins, A. Y.	*Mark: A Commentary.* Hermeneia. Minneapolis: Fortress, 2007.

Craffert, P. F.   'Medical anthropology as an antidote for ethnocentrism in Jesus research? Putting the illness–disease distinction into perspective'. *HTS Teologiese Studies/Theological Studies* 67.1. (2011). Art. #970. DOI: 10.4102/hts.v67i1.970

D'Angelo, M.-R.   'Gender and Power in the Gospel of Mark: The Daughter of Jairus and the Woman with Flow of Blood'. Pages 83–109 in *Miracles in Jewish and Christian Antiquity: Imagine Truth*. Edited by J. C. Cavadini. Notre Dame: University of Notre Dame Press, 1999.

Dean-Jones, L.   *Women's Bodies in Classical Greek Science*. Oxford: Clarendon, 1994.

Dowden, K.   *Death and the Maiden: Girls' Initiation Rites in Greek Mythology*. Routledge Revivals. Abingdon: Routledge, 1989.

Edwards, M. L.   'Constructions of Physical Disability in the Ancient Greek World: The Community Concept'. Pages 35–50 in *The Body and Physical Difference: Discourses of Disability*. Edited by D. T. Mitchell and S. L. Snyder. Ann Arbor: University of Michigan Press, 1997.

–.   'Women and Physical Disability in Ancient Greece'. *The Ancient World* 29 (1998): 3–9.

Etzelmüller, G., and A. Weissenrieder. 'Illness and Healing in Christian Tradition'. Pages 263–305 in *Religion and Illness*. Edited by A. Weissenrieder and G. Etzelmüller. Eugene: Cascade Books, 2016.

Feld, G.   "Leviticus: The ABC of Creation." Pages 51–67 in *Feminist Biblical Interpretation: A Compendium of Critical Commentary on the Books of the Bible and Related Literature*. Edited by Luise Schottroff and Marie-Therese Wacker. Grand Rapids: Eerdmans, 2012.

Focant, C.   *The Gospel According to Mark: A Commentary*. Translated by L. R. Keylock. Eugene: Pickwick Publications, 2012.

Foerster, W. and G. Fohrer. 'σῴζω, σωτηρία, σωτήρ, σωτήριος'. Pages 965–1024 in *Theological Dictionary of the New Testament*. Translated by Geoffrey W. Bromiley. Edited by G. Kittel and G. Friedrich. Vol. 7. Grand Rapids: Eerdmans, 1971.

Fonrobert, C.   'The Woman with a Blood-Flow (Mark 5.24-34) Revisited: Menstrual Laws and Jewish Culture in Christian Feminist Hermeneutics'. Pages 121–41 in *Early Christian Interpretation of the Scriptures of Israel: Investigations and Proposals*. Edited by C. A. Evans and J. A. Sanders. JSNTSS 148. Sheffield: Sheffield Academic, 1997.

France, R. T.   *The Gospel of Mark*. NIGTC. Grand Rapids: Eerdmans, 2002.

Gench, F. T.   *Back to the Well: Women's Encounters with Jesus in the Gospels*. Louisville: Westminster/John Knox, 2004.

Gosbell, L.   *'The Poor, The Crippled, the Blind, and the Lame': Physical and Sensory Disability in the Gospels of the New Testament*. WUNT II 469. Tübingen: Mohr Siebeck, 2018.

Guelich, R. A.	*Mark 1–8:26*. Word Biblical Commentary. Waco: Word, 1989.
Haber, S.	'A Woman's Touch: Feminist Encounters with the Hemorrhaging Woman in Mark 5.24-34'. *JSNT* 26.2 (2003): 171–92.
Holmén, T.	'Jesus and the Purity Paradigm'. Pages 2709–44 in *The Historical Jesus*. Vol. 3 of *Handbook for the Study of the Historical Jesus*. Edited by T. Holmén and S. E. Porter. Leiden: Brill, 2011.
Horsley, R. A.	'Jesus and Empire'. Pages 75–96 in *In the Shadow of Empire: Reclaiming the Bible as a History of Faithful Resistance*. Edited by R. A. Horsley. Louisville: Westminster John Knox, 2008.
Kahl, B.	'Jairus und die Verlorenen Töchter Israels: Sozioliterarische Überlegungen zum Problem der Grenzüberschreitung in Mk 5,21–43'. Pages 61–78 in *Von Der Wurzel Getragen: Christlich-Feministische Exegese in Auseinandersetzung Mit Antijudaismus*. Edited by L. Schottroff and M.-T. Wacker. Leiden: Brill, 1996.
Keener, C. S.	*The Gospel of Matthew: Socio-Rhetorical Commentary*. Grand Rapids: Eerdmans, 2009.
King, H.	'Bound to Bleed: Artemis and Greek Women'. Pages 109–27 in *Images of Women in Antiquity*. Edited by A. Cameron and A. Kuhrt. Abingdon: Routledge, 1983.
–.	'Women's Health and Recovery in the Hippocratic Corpus'. Pages 150–61 in *Health in Antiquity*. Edited by H. King. Abingdon: Routledge, 2005.
Kinukawa, H.	*Women and Jesus in Mark: A Japanese Feminist Perspective*. Maryknoll: Orbis Books, 1994.
Kleinman, A. M.	*Patients and Healers in the Context of Culture: An Exploration of the Borderland between Anthropology, Medicine and Psychiatry*. Comparative Studies of Health Systems and Medical Care. Berkeley: University of California Press, 1980.
Krötzl, C., K. Mustakallio, and J. Kuuliala (eds.).	*Infirmity in Antiquity and the Middle Ages: Social and Cultural Approaches to Health, Weakness and Care*. Farnham: Ashgate, 2015.
Love, S.	'Jesus Heals the Hemorrhaging Woman'. Pages 85–101 in *The Social Setting of Jesus and the Gospels*. Edited by W. Stegemann, B. J. Malina, and G. Theissen. Minneapolis: Fortress, 2002.
Malina, B. J., and R. L. Rohrbaugh.	*Social-Science Commentary on the Synoptic Gospels*. Minneapolis: Fortress, 1992.
Marcus, J.	*Mark 1–8: A New Translation with Introduction and Commentary*. AB. New York: Doubleday, 2000.
Meggitt, J.	'The Historical Jesus and Healing: Jesus' Miracles in Psychosocial Context'. Pages 17–43 in *Spiritual Healing: Scientific and Religious Perspectives*. Edited by Fraser Watts. Cambridge: Cambridge University Press, 2011.
Miller, S.	*Women in Mark's Gospel*. London: T&T Clark, 2004.

Moss, C. R. 'Man with the Flow of Power: Porous Bodies in Mark 5:25-34'. *JBL* 129.3 (2010): 507–19.

Moss, C. R., and J. S. Baden. *Reconceiving Infertility: Biblical Perspectives on Procreation and Childlessness*. Princeton: Princeton University Press, 2015.

Myers, C. *Binding the Strong Man: A Political Reading of Mark's Story of Jesus*. 25th Ann. ed. New York: Orbis Books, 2008.

Oliver, M. *The Politics of Disablement*. London: MacMillan Education, 1990.

Peckruhn, H. 'Disability Studies'. Pages 101–11 in *Oxford Encyclopedia of the Bible and Gender Studies*. Edited by J. M. O'Brien. Oxford: Oxford University Press, 2014.

Pilch, J. J. 'Understanding Biblical Healing: Selecting the Appropriate Model'. *BTB* 18.2 (1988): 60–6.

–. 'Sickness and Healing in Luke-Acts'. Pages 181–209 in *The Social World of Luke-Acts: Models for Interpretation*. Edited by J. H. Neyrey. Peabody: Hendrickson, 1991.

–. *Healing in the New Testament: Insights from Medical and Mediterranean Anthropology*. Minneapolis: Fortress, 2000.

Pomeroy, S. B. *Goddesses, Whores, Wives and Slaves: Women in Classical Antiquity*. New York: Schoken, 1975.

Raphael, R. *Biblical Corpora: Representations of Disability in Hebrew Biblical Literature*. LHB/OTS 445. London: T&T Clark, 2008.

Reid, B. E. *Choosing the Better Part? Women in the Gospel of Luke*. Collegeville: Liturgical, 1996.

Rosenblatt, M.-E. 'Gender, Ethnicity, and Legal Considerations in the Haemorrhaging Woman's Story, Mark 5:25-34'. Pages 137–61 in *Transformative Encounters: Jesus and Women Re-viewed*. Edited by I. R. Kitzberger. Leiden: Brill, 2000.

Schiefer Ferrari, M. '(Un)gestörte Lektüre von Lk 14,12–14: Deutung, Differenz und Disability.' Pages 13–47 in *Gestörte Lektüre: Disability als hermeneutische Leitkategorie biblischer Exegese*. Edited by Wolfgang Grünstäudl and Markus Schiefer Ferrari. Behinderung – Theologie – Kirche 4. Stuttgart: Kohlhammer, 2012.

Schipper, J. 'Disabling Israelite Leadership: 2 Samuel 6:23 and Other Images of Disability in the Deuteronomistic History'. Pages 103–14 in *This Abled Body: Rethinking Disabilities in Biblical Studies*. Edited by H. Avalos, S. J. Melcher, and J. Schipper. Semeia Studies 55. Atlanta: Society of Biblical Literature, 2007.

–. *Disability and Isaiah's Suffering Servant*. Biblical Refigurations. Oxford: Oxford University Press, 2011.

Selvidge, M. J. 'Mark 5:25-34 and Leviticus 15:19-10: A Reaction to Restrictive Purity Regulations'. *JBL* 103 (1984): 619–23.

—.	*Woman, Cult and Miracle Recital: A Redactional Critical Investigation on Mark 5:24-34.* London: Associated University Press, 1990.
Shakespeare, T.	'The Social Model of Disability'. Pages 214–21 in *The Disability Studies Reader.* Edited by L. J. Davis. New York: Routledge, 1997.
Sinclair, R. K.	*Democracy and Participation in Athens.* Cambridge: Cambridge University Press, 1988.
Taylor, V.	*The Gospel According to St. Mark: The Greek Text.* 2nd ed. London: Macmillan, 1966.
Wassen, C.	'Jesus and the Hemorrhaging Woman in Mark 5:24-34: Insights from Purity Laws from the Dead Sea Scrolls'. Pages 641–60 in *Scripture in Transition: Essays on Septuagint, Hebrew Bible and Dead Sea Scrolls in Honour of Raija Sollamo.* Edited by A. Voitila and J. Jokiranta. Supplement to the Journal for the Study of Judaism 126. Leiden: Brill, 2008.
Weissenrieder, A.	*Images of Illness in the Gospel of Luke: Insights of Ancient Medical Texts.* WUNT II 164. Tübingen: Mohr Siebeck, 2003.
—.	'The Plague of Uncleanness? The Ancient Illness Construct Issue of Blood in Luke 8:43-48'. Pages 207–22 in *The Social Setting of Jesus and the Gospels.* Edited by W. Stegemann, B. J. Malina, and G. Theissen. Minneapolis: Fortress, 2002.
Witherington III, B.	*The Gospel of Mark: A Socio-Rhetorical Commentary.* Grand Rapids: Eerdmans, 2001.
World Health Organization.	'Disabilities'. No pages. Cited 11 March 2014. Online: http://www.who.int/topics/disabilities/en/.

A Study of Mark 16:6-8
Hope in the Midst of Failure

FRANCIS J. MOLONEY, SDB, AM, FAHA

Scholarly debate over the ending of the Gospel of Mark must cover a number of critical questions. Did the Gospel originally end at 16:8? If not, do any of the other endings available in the manuscript traditions provide a possible original conclusion, or has it been lost? What is the relationship between 16:7, where the young man in the tomb tells the women that Jesus is going before them into Galilee, and 14:28, where Jesus spoke almost these exact words to the disciples at the last meal? Most of all, however, if the Gospel ends at v. 8, why does Mark report that the women fled from the tomb, full of fear, and said nothing to anyone? Surely the promise of an encounter with the risen Lord, promised in 14:28 and 16:7 could not be thwarted by the silence of the women?[1] There is one truth, however, that cannot be contested, and where all scholars agree. This briefest, and probably earliest, of the Four Gospels was received by a Christian community late in the first Christian century. Only recently has its subtle power been recognized,[2] but the Gospel of Mark has been read, and is still read, within the context of the believing Christian Community. Without a community of Christian readers and listeners, over the centuries, this Gospel would have slipped off the shelves of Christian literature. It is upon this uncontested and obvious truth that I would like base my interpretation of Mark 16:6-8.[3]

The study that follows will suggest that the literary utterance of the Gospel of Mark, for all its incongruence for modern Gospel scholarship and a contemporary reader, was crafted to both

---

[1] This question is heightened by the fact that the very last word in v. 8 is γάρ ("for"), a most unusual ending for a complete document: ἐφοβοῦντο γάρ ("for they were afraid"). However, the strangeness of this ending is sometimes exaggerated. For a correction of this exaggeration see Robert H. Lightfoot, *The Gospel Message of St Mark* (Oxford: Clarendon Press, 1950), 80-97. More recently, see Kelly R. Iverson, "A Further Word on the Final Γάρ (Mark 16:8)," *CBQ* 68 (2006): 79-94.

[2] On the reception of the Gospel of Mark over the centuries, see Brenda D. Schildgen, *Power and Prejudice: The Reception of the Gospel of Mark* (Detroit: Wayne State University Press, 1999). On its dating at c. 70 CE, see Francis J. Moloney, *The Gospel of Mark. A Commentary* (Grand Rapids: Baker Academic, 2012 [reprint of 2002 original]), 2-4.

[3] The importance of this question motivates the current essay. I have addressed this issue twice in earlier publications: Francis J. Moloney, "'He is going before you into Galilee.' Mark 16:1-8 and the Christian Community," in *Be My Witnesses. Essays in Honour of Dr Sebastian Karotemprel SDB*, eds. Jose Varickassiril and Matthew Kariapuram (Shillong: Vendrame Institute Publications, 2001), 108-21, and Idem, *Mark*, 339-54. I am using the occasion of this publication to take into account the significant recent commentaries of Joel Marcus, *Mark* (2 vols., The Anchor Yale Bible 27-27A; New York/New Haven: Doubleday/Yale University Press, 2000-2009), and Adela Yarbro Collins, *Mark* (Hermeneia; Minneapolis: Fortress, 2007).

comfort and provoke its readership.[4] One of the several reasons for the fascination of this Gospel is its *direct appeal* to a believing, yet struggling, community of Christian believers. The author of the Gospel closed his Gospel with an Easter message to the women at the tomb, and an enigmatic flight in silence and fear, to challenge and comfort the Christian community.

Mark 16:8 as the Original Ending

The problem we are facing emerged in the earliest days of Christian tradition. Once the written Gospel texts were passed on from generation to generation, scribes began to provide more satisfactory endings to make the Gospel of Mark conform to the concluding stages of the Gospels of Matthew, Luke, and John. In Matthew and Luke, women receive the Easter message and report it to the disciples (Matt 18:1-10; Luke 24:1-12). In the Gospel of John, there is only one woman, Mary of Magdalene, but the story of the empty tomb is reported to Peter and the Beloved Disciple (John 20:1-3). Most English editions of the Gospel of Mark print either a longer ending (Mark 16:9-20) or a shorter ending (16:9-10). Some provide both. The imaginative gathering of a number of Easter appearance stories from the other Gospels, and the Acts of the Apostles generated the longer ending. The shorter ending merely affirms that the women reported the message, and from then on salvation was proclaimed from east to west. However, these are only two of four major textual traditions that have come down to us, and none of them have any claim to authenticity. They are clearly the work of troubled scribes, unhappy with the silence of the woman in v. 8.[5] The *textual* problem was created by a *theological* problem. The early scribes asked whether it was possible that, for Mark, the Easter message was not proclaimed by the women, with the result that the relationship between Jesus and the faltering disciples was never restored, as in Matthew, Luke and John.

Only one solution remains for those who would like to claim that the original Gospel of Mark did not end at 16:8: the ending was lost. Many have suggested that this was the case, unable to accept that Mark could changed the tradition of the women's announcing of the Easter message.[6] It is so crucial to the Christian story, especially in the light of the promise of a future encounter in Galilee (v. 7), that there must have been a further page to resolve the tension created by vv. 7-8. Physically, it is quite possible that a page of a codex or the final inches of a papyrus scroll could be lost through the wear and tear generated by heavy usage. However, the suggestion of a lost ending creates more difficulties than it resolves. The "lost ending" solution depends upon a number of well-nigh impossible hypotheses. The first hypothesis is that the original ending was contained in a self-standing page in what I have just called a "codex." A codex is an ancient form of a book, with pages sewn together, as we bind a modern book. But it is unlikely that the Gospel of Mark was originally written in a codex. That form used for the preservation of texts came into Christian

---

4   Significant evidence for this "incongruence" is found in the Roman Catholic Sunday Lectionary. In Year B, when Mark 16 is read at the Easter Vigil, only 16:1-7 is proclaimed. Avoiding all problems, the proclamation ends: "But go, tell his disciples and Peter that he is going before you to Galilee; there you will see him, just as he told you" (v. 7). Such a reading misses Mark's Easter message of hope to people who fail.

5   For a succinct treatment of the textual traditions, see Bruce M. Metzger, *A Textual Commentary on the Greek New Testament* (2nd ed.; Stuttgart: Deutsche Bibelgesellschaft, 1994), 102-107.

6   See, for example, Vincent Taylor, *The Gospel According to St Mark* (London: Macmillan, 1966), 609-10; Charles E. B. Cranfield, *The Gospel According to Saint Mark* (2nd ed., The Cambridge Greek New Testament Commentary; Cambridge: Cambridge University Press, 1963), 470-71; Eduard Schweizer, *The Good News According to Mark* (trans. David H. Madvig; London: SPCK, 1971), 365-67; Eta Linnemann, "Der (wiedergefundene) Markusschluss," *ZTK* 66 (1969): 255-87.

usage very early, but probably not for the original autographs of the New Testament texts.[7] It is thus more than likely that the very first "Gospel of Mark" was written on a scroll, not a codex.[8] The use of the codex for transmitting the Gospels began as the need to preserve and facilitate the use of the early Church's emerging sacred texts increased.

Secondly, is it possible that the full resurrection account of the original manuscript was torn off, as the last page of a codex might have become detached? Although more difficult than losing the last page of a codex, wear and tear of a much-used scroll may have damaged its final several inches. It is certainly physically possible that this could happen. As with modern books, with wear and tear, the first or last page of our favourite book might become detached. This also happens regularly with certain textbooks used day in and day out in the classroom. In the more likely case that the original Gospel of Mark existed as a papyrus scroll, the same physical possibility exists. But we must then consider the possibility that the loss of the closing section of the scroll would have taken place *with the original autograph of the Gospel of Mark*. Would such a loss be regarded as so unimportant to the community which received the original scroll containing the Gospel of Mark that the ending was simply allowed to disappear? That is most unlikely. Heavy consultation and much handling of the codex would have been the cause of a lost final page, or the wear and tear of the final few inches of the scroll. This document must have been very precious for the Christian community in which it was created and where it was regularly used.

It is very difficult to imagine that before there existed even a single copied version of the original Gospel of Mark, the ending of that original was inadvertently torn off, and nothing was done to retrieve it. It would only take a few copies of the original Mark, one or other of which would have contained the so-called "lost ending," to be in existence for something of that ending to be present in some ancient manuscripts. There is no such evidence, as our present endings all come from a later period, and are attempts to harmonize Mark 16:1-8 with the ending of Matthew, Luke and John, with some help from the Acts of the Apostles.[9] A single conclusion imposes itself: the original Gospel of Mark ended at 16:8. If that is the case, then it is the responsibility of the interpreter to identify, in so far as that is possible, Mark's literary and theological reasons for

---

[7] There is some discussion concerning the use of the scroll and the codex in the early Church. Most argue (as above) that the autographs would have been on scrolls, but that Christians used the codex very early, perhaps even toward the end of the first century. See, for example, Bruce M. Metzger, *The Text of the New Testament. Its Transmission, Corruption, and Restoration* (2nd ed.; Oxford: Clarendon Press, 1968), 5-8; Jack Finegan, *Encountering New Testament Manuscripts. A Working Introduction to Textual Criticism* (London: SPCK, 1975), 27-29. See, however, Kurt and Barbara Aland, *The Text of the New Testament. An Introduction to the Critical Editions and to the Theory and Practice of Modern Textual Criticism* (trans. Erroll F. Rhodes; Grand Rapids: Eerdmans, 1987), 75: "Apparently from the very beginning Christians did not use the scroll format for their writings, but rather the codex." See also pp. 101-102.

[8] It was not called "The Gospel of Mark" at that stage. The titles ascribing authors to the Gospels are generally regarded as coming from the second century, although Martin Hengel, *Studies in the Gospel of Mark* (trans. John Bowden; London: SPCK, 1985), 64-84, disputes this. He claims that once more than one "Gospel" existed, they were attached to an author. Thus "according to Mark" would have been attached to the title before the end of the first Christian century. However, even for Hengel, the Gospel titles did not belong to the original autographs.

[9] As Taylor, *St Mark*, 610, admits: "How the original ending disappeared is ... obscure." The definitive study of the composition, history, and theology of 16:9-20 is James A. Kelhoffer, *Miracle and Mission. The Authentication of Missionaries and their Message in the Longer Ending of Mark* (WUNT 2.112; Tübingen: Mohr Siebeck, 2000). See also Collins, *Mark*, 798-801.

closing his Gospel with the fear, flight and silence of the women (16:8).[10]

An Ending which Returns to a Beginning?

The story of Jesus, as we have it in the Gospel of Mark, is determined by a logic that leads inevitably toward the cross. The story opens with great promise (1:1-13), but the reader is led further into a story whose ending is known,[11] yet is surprised on the way—and in the very last verse! The plot is shot through with hints that look forward to the end of the story. The Gospel of Mark is unique among the Gospels because, unlike most narratives (including Matthew, Luke and John), the crises that emerge during the course of the narrative are not resolved through a *dénouement* at the end of the story (Mark 16:1-8). Much is resolved, but a further crisis emerges which cannot be resolved by the story itself. This suggests that it might be resolved in the lives of the people reading or hearing the story. We should recall that in a good story the audience is told enough to be made curious, without ever being given all the answers. Narrative texts keep promising the great prize of understanding—later.[12] Given the perplexing failure of the women to so what they are told *within the narrative of the Gospel*, the "later" generated by the Gospel of Mark, I will suggest, is the "now" of the Christian reader, *among those who receive the Gospel*.

The audience meets a number of significant turning points in the story. The Gospel begins (1:1), Jesus opens his ministry in Galilee (1:14-15), he announces his forthcoming death and resurrection for the first time (8:31), he enters Jerusalem (11:1-11), a decision is made that Jesus must be arrested and killed (14:1-2), and women discover an empty tomb (16:1-4).[13] As has been obvious since the days of William Wrede, Karl-Ludwig Schmidt, Martin Dibelius, and Rudolf Bultmann, this "framework" was devised by the Evangelist Mark. Its appearance as the "plot" of

---

10 Many of the scholars who insist that there must have been a lost ending (see above, note 4) are reacting against the suggestions of Ernst Lohmeyer, *Das Evangelium des Markus* (17th ed., Meyers Kommentar; Göttingen: Vandenhoeck & Ruprecht, 1967), 355–58, that the ending points to a Markan community waiting in Galilee for the parousia. This claim has been further developed by Willi Marxsen, *Mark the Evangelist. Studies in Redaction Criticism* (trans. James Boyce and Others; Nashville: Abingdon Press, 1969), 75–92, and a number of more recent redaction critics in the USA who have accepted the conclusions of Lohmeyer and Marxsen (e.g., Norman Perrin, Theodore J. Weeden, and Werner Kelber). This position, which stresses a community living in the absence of Jesus and waiting for the parousia, does not do justice to the message of the Gospel as a whole. See especially Jack D. Kingsbury, *The Christology of Mark's Gospel* (Philadelphia: Fortress, 1983), and the summary of Marcus, *Mark*, 75–79. Although they reject the Lohmeyer proposal, Kingsbury and Marcus rightly insist that the original Gospel closed with 16:8. Marcus (pp. 1088–1096) accepts that there may have been a longer ending, but we must interpret what Mark has left us.
11 Accepting that the Gospel was primarily written for a Christian community whose members knew that Jesus had been crucified, and who gathered because they believed that he had been raised. On this, see Adela Yarbro Collins, *The Beginning of the Gospel. Probings of Mark in Context* (Minneapolis: Fortress, 1992), 1–38; Marcus, *Mark*, 25–28
12 See Schlomith Rimmon-Kenan, *Narrative Fiction: Contemporary Poetics* (New Accents; London: Methuen, 1983), 125.
13 This paragraph depends upon a literary design composed of a prologue directed to the audience (1:1-13), a Galilean ministry during which the puzzle of Jesus' person and role is acted out (1:14–8:30), the journey to and through the cross, where Jesus is shown to be Son of God and Son of Man (8:31–15:47), and an epilogue directed to the audience (16:1-8). See further, Moloney, *Mark*, 16-22. For a fine overview of scholarly attempts to determine the composition and structure of Mark's Gospel, see Collins, *Mark*, 85–93.

the first early Christian "Gospel" was intentionally a theological statement.[14] *Whatever the first readers knew of the life-story of Jesus of Nazareth was subverted by the Markan story. Jesus' presence in Galilee, his single journey to Jerusalem to be rejected, tried and crucified, the resurrection and the surprising silence of the women was not familiar.* Such a "plot" saw the light of day *for the first time* when Mark invented it. It is this *radical newness* of the Markan story that must be kept in mind.[15] It is an original way of telling the story of Jesus, and its author must be credited with an equally original understanding of why he plotted the story in this way. Attempts to "improve" upon its ending by making it conform to the endings of other early Christian narratives that tell the story of Jesus betray Mark's originality.

Mark's plot is a God-designed sequence of time and events designed to lead the reader to a surprising re-telling of the story of death and resurrection of Jesus to which she or he could not remain indifferent. On the basis of the turning points we have identified, one can trace the following God-designed temporal and geographical strategies. In 1:1-13 Mark provides *the audience* with a great deal of information about God's beloved Son in a prologue to the Gospel. Across the first half of the narrative, 1:14–8:30, the words and deeds of Jesus' ministry increasingly force the question: who is this man (see 1:27, 45; 2:12; 3:22; 4:41; 5:20; 6:2-3, 48-50; 7:37)? During his Galilean ministry, some accept Jesus, some are indifferent and many oppose him, but the question behind the story is: can he be the Messiah? In 8:29, Peter, in the name of the disciples, resolves the problem by confessing: "You are the Messiah." The guessing has come to an end, but further questions emerge. Surprisingly, Jesus warns Peter not to tell anyone of his recognition of Jesus as the Messiah. The Petrine confession of faith may not make known the whole truth about Jesus, as Mark understands it.

Although never entirely absent (see as early as 2:19-20), the theme of the death and resurrection of Jesus looms large across 8:31–15:47. Jesus journeys to Jerusalem (8:22-52), returning systematically to tell his disciples of his oncoming death and resurrection (8:31; 9:31; 10:32-33), something the disciples cannot and will not accept. He enters Jerusalem (11:1-11), brings all Temple practice to an end (11:12-24), encounters and silences Israel's religious authorities (11:27–12:44), and prophesies the end of the Holy City and the world (13:1-37). The ministry is over as Jesus enters his passion and death (14:1–15:47). The steady procession to Jerusalem reported in 8:31–13:39 certainly forms a "second half" for Mark's literary and theological presentation of the story of Jesus. If 1:14–8:30 made it clear that Jesus is the Messiah (8:29), but suggested that this may not be the whole truth (8:30), on arrival at 13:37 the audience has been informed that Jesus is a suffering Messiah, the Son of Man (8:31; 9:31; 10:32-33).

---

14 In the middle of the nineteenth century, once scholars accepted that Mark was the earliest Gospel, many (especially Heinrich J. Holzmann) concluded that the simple story-line of Mark provided what they called a "framework" for the life of the historical Jesus. This widely accepted "framework" was shown to be the theological creation of the Evangelist Mark by William Wrede in 1901 (ET: *The Messianic Secret* [trans. J. C. G. Grieg; Cambridge and London: James Clark, 1971], and Wrede's work became a point of departure for the founders of Form Criticism, Karl-Ludwig Schmidt, Martin Dibelius, and Rudolf Bultmann from 1919–21. For a survey of this period, with full bibliographical details for the work of the above-mentioned scholarly giants, see Francis J. Moloney, *Beginning the Good News. A narrative approach* (Collegeville: The Liturgical Press, 1992), 19–24.

15 See the important essay by Eduard Schweizer, "Mark's Theological Achievement," in William Telford (ed.), *The Interpretation of Mark* (Issues in Religion and Theology 7; Philadelphia: Fortress Press, 1985), 42-63. Werner H. Kelber, *The Oral and Written Gospel. The Hermeneutics of Speaking and Writing in the Synoptic Tradition, Mark, Paul and Q* (Philadelphia: Fortress, 1983), pushes this to the limit. He rightly argues that Mark took a vivacious and living oral tradition and created something quite different with his "writing" (see pp. 44–139). But he argues that the movement from oral tradition to written Gospel created a written text which was a contradiction of what went before. The thesis is overstated, but rightly highlights the radical newness of the Gospel of Mark.

Despite the apparent theological contradiction that the Messiah must go to Jerusalem to die (8:31; 9:31; 10:32-34), the audience has heard that such must be the case from the most authoritative voice in the Gospel: Jesus. However, *the audience* has experienced the Prologue (1:1-13) and must listen to the voice of the Christ, the Son of God (1:1, 11. See 9:7: "This is my beloved Son. Listen to him"). But *the disciples* have not experienced the authorial introduction of Jesus in 1:1-13. They remain perplexed, and do not accept that the Messiah must suffer, die, and be raised from the dead.

During the passion account (14:1–15:47), Jesus publicly accepts that he is the Christ, the Son of God and the Son of Man (14:62). Throughout the Gospel he has avoided any such public confession or recognition. That period of "messianic secrecy" is over, as in and through the events of the passion Jesus makes known, in word and deed, that God's Messiah is a suffering and crucified Messiah. The Markan description of Jesus' suffering and death is relentless in portraying his anguish and his suffering. In prayer before his arrest, Jesus begs his Father to let this chalice pass from him (14:36). In death he asks his God why he has abandoned him (15:34), and he hands over his spirit with a loud scream (15:37). But the disciples witness none of this. They have fled (14:50), naked in their nothingness (14:51-52).[16] They are absent as Jesus' messianic status is proclaimed in word and deed. Apart from the demonic characters across the Gospel, who have access to the secret of Jesus (see 1:24; 3:11; 5:7), no character in the narrative has recognised Jesus.[17] As Jesus dies, seeing how he died, a Roman centurion confesses: "Truly this man was God's Son!" (15:37). The suffering Son of Man is truly the Son of God.

Many questions raised by the story remain unresolved. The question Jesus asks of God as he does (15:34) question is resolved in the concluding story of women visiting an empty tomb. In 16:1-8 the reader learns that God has not forsaken his Son. He has been raised (see 16:6). But a solution to the problem of failing disciples lies in the future. They are to go into Galilee, there they will see him (v. 7). The women, frightened by all that they have seen and heard, flee and say nothing to anyone (v. 8). Mark 16:1-8 asks questions of the experience of *the believing reader*.

The beginning (1:1-13) and the end (16:1-8) of the Gospel of Mark address the audience. The prologue to the Gospel (1:1-13) is unashamedly full of confessions of faith in the person of Jesus of Nazareth. However, only *the audience* heard these confessions. The characters from the story are not standing by, listening. The narrator tells audience that Jesus is the Christ, the Son of God (v. 1), the Lord (v. 3), the mightier one (v. 7), the one who will baptize with the Holy Spirit (v. 8), the beloved Son in whom God is well pleased (v. 11). Only the audience recognizes that Jesus' presence in the wilderness, with the wild animals and served by angels, recalls God's original design for humankind, told in the story of Adam and Eve. God's original created order has been

---

16 The strange account of the "young man" (νεανίσκος) who was following, but who fled in fear, leaving his only clothing, a linen cloth, behind in 14:51–52 has been the source of much speculation. For the discussion, and the suggestion that he is a "model" of the disciples, fleeing in fear, now without any association with Jesus (see 3:14), see Moloney, *Mark*, 299–300. See below, n. 23.

17 Since the time of William Wrede (1901), the insistence in the Gospel of Mark (repeated to some extent in Matthew and Luke) that his messianic deeds, and any confession of Jesus as the Messiah, was to be kept "secret," has been seen as a creation of the early Church to explain why some did not recognise Jesus of Nazareth as the Messiah. If such was the case, then (at least in the Gospel of Mark) it is the worst kept secret in the history of secrecy. Despite his requests, who he is and what he does is widely proclaimed (see, for example, 1:44-45; 5:19-20). Most likely, there are at least two motives for the so-called "messianic secret." Initially, Jesus was unwilling that he be known as a Messiah, as such a figure was widely (but not only) understood as a military figure. Secondly, as indicated above (and accepting Wrede's suggestion that Mark uses it for his own ends), Mark turns this into a literary technique so that the narrative proclamation of Jesus as Messiah and Son of God does not happen until the end of the story. He is Christ and Son of God on the cross (see 14:62; 15:29-32, 39). See Moloney, *Mark*, 4–5, 335-36.

restored in the person of Jesus of Nazareth (vv. 12-13).[18]

By the time the reader has arrived at the end of the story, some doubts may have arisen about the confessions of faith that marked its beginnings. A feature of the Gospel of Mark is the disciples' steady movement away from an original enthusiastic following of Jesus (see 1:16-20), to their last appearance in the story in Gethsemane: "And they all forsook him and fled" (14:50). Only two disciples remain active: Judas who betrays Jesus (14:43-45) and Peter who denies him three times (14:66-72).[19] Jesus' cry of dereliction on the cross, "My God, my God, why have you abandoned me?" (15:34) rings in the reader's and the listener's mind and heart. If this is what happens to the Son of God, what sort of God and what sort of Son are we dealing with? The audience, aware of the traditions associated with the women, the disciples and the Easter appearances (see 1 Cor 15:3-7),[20] expects the story of a glorious resurrection to resolve the question. But 16:1-8 proves to be something of a let down! The young man in the tomb announces an Easter message (v. 6), but there is no appearance of Jesus; only the promise of one (v. 7). The women deliver neither the Easter message of v. 6 nor the promise of v. 7. They join the disciples in fear and flight, as the Gospel comes to an end (v. 8).

The audience that received the Gospel of Mark was given privileged access to who Jesus was, and what he was to do as Christ and Son of God in the Prologue (1:1-13). Is it possible that the Epilogue to the book (16:1-8) is also directed to a privileged group of believers? The splendid Christology outlined in the Prologue has been tested by the events reported in the story. The Messiah should not die by crucifixion (see 1 Cor 1:23-25). The audience is asked to retain the beliefs communicated to them in the Prologue as they hear of—and perhaps identify with—the failure of the women. What are they to make of the promise Jesus made to his frail disciples in 14:20, taken up by the young man: "He is going ahead of you to Galilee; there you will see him, just as he told you" (16:7)? Who is being addressed by the "you" in the words of the young man: the characters *in the story* or the audience *of the story*?

---

18 On the links between 1:12-13 and God's original creative design, see Moloney, *Beginning the Good News*, 43–71.

19 The steady movement of the disciples away from Jesus, until they leave him, betray him and deny him, has been the subject of much research. For some (e.g. Theodore J. Weeden, *Mark—Traditions in Conflict* [Philadelphia: Fortress, 1971]), they represent an incorrect understanding of Jesus, the heresy that occasioned the writing of the Gospel of Mark. At the other end of the scale, others (the majority) see Mark's use of the disciples as an attempt to develop characters in the story who embody the failure of all disciples. See especially Robert C. Tannehill, "The Disciples in Mark: the Function of a Narrative Role," in William Telford (ed.), *The Interpretation of Mark* (Issues in Religion and Theology 7; Philadelphia: Fortress, 1985), 134–57. See also Francis J. Moloney, *Mark. Storyteller, Interpreter, Evangelist* (Grand Rapids: Baker Academic, 2004), 159–81.

20 Historical analyses of "what happened" at the tomb have recourse to Mark 16:1-8 is the earliest narrative account of an empty tomb, and go from there to discuss what may or may not have happened. See Collins, *Mark*, 781–82. Many use Mark's account to suggest that the notion of a physical resurrection of Jesus is a Christian invention. However, well before Mark (c. 70 CE), in about 54 CE Paul passes on to the Corinthians a tradition he had received about Jesus' death, burial, and appearances to many, possibly including the women (see 1 Cor 15:3-7). As well as that very old tradition, the oral narratives that eventually formed Matthew 28, Luke 24, and John 20-21 would have been part of the widespread Christian understanding of "what happened." Mark 16:8 is "out of tune" with this well-known tradition. For further discussion of this important matter, among many see Francis J. Moloney, *The Resurrection of the Messiah. A Narrative Commentary on the Resurrection Accounts of the Four Gospels* (New York: Paulist, 2015), 138–48. Further details of this perennial and important discussion can be found there.

Mark 16:6-8

A number of tensions exist in the Markan report of Easter day (Mark 16:1-8). They cannot detain us here, as we are concerned with vv. 6-8, but some odd features must be noted. The women bringing spices mentioned in v. 1 (Mary Magdalene, Mary the mother of James, and Salome) is the same group that stood looking upon the crucifixion from afar in 15:40-41. Although articulated differently, two of them appear watching the location of the burial of Jesus in 15:47. Mary Magdalene and Mary the mother of Joses saw where the body of Jesus was laid.[21] Female followers of Jesus (see 15:40-41) remain with him at the cross, see where he is buried, and come to the empty tomb. There is a marked contrast between their performance and that of the disciples who have moved gradually into ignorance and failure to stay with Jesus, until the point where they flee in fear (14:50), betray and deny him (14: 43-45 [Judas], 66-72 [Peter]). The theme of the anointing of Jesus' body seems somewhat superfluous, after three days, and also after the symbolic anointing of Jesus body at Bethany by the unnamed women in 14:3-9. It serves as a reason for the women's visit to the tomb, and also indicates that they journey to the tomb expecting to find a dead body.[22] There is no hint of Easter faith as the narrative opens, although the indication that the sun had risen (v. 2) introduces the believing audience to the hope that follows.[23] However, wonder is generated in the story as the women ask who will roll away the stone, which is very large ... only to find that it has been rolled away (ἀποκεκύλισται ὁ λίθος) (vv. 3-4). Critics claim that this is clumsy, as the women should have thought of the problems of anointing a body that had been dead for three days, and the problem of rolling back a large stone, before they set out for the tomb.[24] Such questions miss the point of the narrative.[25] The use of the passive voice ("had been rolled back") indicates that third party has entered the story. Perhaps an answer to the agonized question asked by Jesus of God in 15:34 is emerging.[26] The answer becomes explicit in the appearance of the

---

21 This issue is somewhat clouded by the different names in 15:40 and 15:47. Accepting that "Mary the mother of James" and "Mary the mother of Joses" are the same person, the three women who saw the crucifixion (15:40-41) are reduced to two at the tomb (15:47), yet return to the original three on Easter Sunday morning. The confusion over the names need not detain us. It is the result Mark's respect for the traditions surrounding Jesus' death and resurrection that came to him. He accepts the tradition by repeating the names exactly as they came to him. But Mark also wishes to show that women who had been with him in Galilee (15:41) were at the cross (15:40), at the grave (15:47), and then at the empty tomb (16:1). See Joachim Gnilka, *Das Evangelium nach Markus* (5th ed., 2 vols., Evangelisch-Katholischer Kommentar zum Neuen Testament II/1–2; Zürich/Neukirchen-Vluyn: Benziger Verlag/Neukirchener Verlag, 1999), 2:338. The lack of identity between the groups of women has created a textual problem. For the details, and the discussion, see Collins, *Mark*, 779–80.
22 See Collins, *Mark*, 794. Already within the Synoptic tradition this superfluity is noticed. Luke 24:1 reports that they took the spices that had prepared, but does not explicitly state that they set out to anoint the dead body of Jesus. Matt 28:1 omits all references to spices and anointing.
23 See Marcus, *Mark*, 1083–84.
24 See, for example, Walter Grundmann, *Das Evangelium nach Markus* (6th ed., Theologischer Handkommentar zum Neuen Testament 2; Berlin: Evangelische Verlagsanstalt, 1973), 320–21. Marcus, *Mark*, 1079–80, offers possible historical reasons for their oversight.
25 As Collins, *Mark*, 795, rightly points out.
26 As Marcus, *Mark*, 1084, comments: "An action of God, then, has accomplished what was beyond the women's capacity."

young man, seated on the right side of the tomb, dressed in a white robe.[27]

The Easter proclamation is carefully constructed, showing that the God of Jesus has never abandoned his Son (see 1:11; 9:7; 15:39). The young man tells the women that they are seeking the one they had once known and accompanied: "Jesus the Nazarene the crucified one" (v. 6a: Ἰησοῦν ζητεῖτε τὸν Ναζαρηνόν).[28] The burial of Jesus was the last act in a series of seeming victories for Jesus' opponents, but the young man instructs them, "He is not here. See the place where *they* laid him" (v. 6c: ἔθηκαν αὐτόν). The two affirmations cannot stand side by side. Jesus is the crucified one (v. 6a), but he is not in the place where those who crucified him had lain the dead body (v. 6c). What has happened? The definitive answer to Jesus' question to God in 15:34 appears in the passive verb of v. 6b: "He has been raised" (ἠγέρθη).[29] God has entered the story of the crucified one, and raised him from death. His enemies (those who crucified him and laid him in the tomb) have been overcome; the empty tomb is a symbol of God's victory. The reader recalls Jesus' prophecies of his forthcoming death *and* resurrection as he journeyed with the increasingly obdurate disciples toward Jerusalem (see 8:31; 9:31; 10:33-34). *What Jesus said would happen, has happened.*

What of the disciples? The promise of the restoration of the failed disciples was first made by Jesus to his disciples as they walked away from their last meal: "After I am raised up, I will go before (future tense: προάξω) you into Galilee" (14:28). A hint that this promise was to be realized was found in the presence of a young man in the empty tomb (16:5), reversing the parabolic comment upon the fleeing disciples (see 14:50) in the episode of the young man who fled in fear, naked (14:51-52). The future tense of 14:28 is now rendered as a present tense in the young man's instruction to the women. They are to tell the disciples of Jesus ("his disciples") and Peter that "he is going (προάγει) before you into Galilee, as he told you" (v. 7).[30] The stage is set for an encounter in Galilee where failure will be overcome and discipleship restored. They will see him there, as Jesus had promised (14:28).

But this is thwarted by the very last line of the Gospel: "And they went out and fled from the tomb; for trembling and astonishment had come upon them; and they said nothing to anyone, for they were afraid" (v. 8). Does this mean that there is, in Mark's view of things, no vision of the resurrected Jesus, and that the disciples are still waiting for his return?[31] Or is the fear and flight an indication of holy awe in the face of the wonder of the resurrection.[32]

---

27 This young man (νεανίσκος) is generally regarded as an angel, especially on the basis of the white clothing. See, for example, Morna D. Hooker, *The Gospel According to St Mark* (Black's New Testament Commentaries; London: A. & C. Black, 1991), 584–85; Marcus, *Mark*, 1080; Collins, *Mark*, 795–96. Collins sees the angel as the "interpreting angel" of the apocalypses and other such works. As such, he explains the situation. But he also recalls the young man (νεανίσκος) of 14:51-52. In a tiny parable, commenting on the flight of the disciples in v. 50, the author tells of a young man who, like the disciples, fled when those who had come to take Jesus laid hands upon him. He leaves his linen cloth behind, and—a symbol of the disciples—flees naked. See above, n. 15. The appearance of a young man "clothed" (περιβεβλημένον [another passive]) is a symbolic first hint of the future restoration of the failed disciples. See, Harry Fledderman, "The Flight of a Naked Young Man," *CBQ* 41 (1979): 412–18; Moloney, *Mark*, 345–46. For a contrary opinion, see Marcus, *Mark*, 1124–25.

28 See Marcus, *Mark*, 1085.

29 Many translations render the verb "he has risen." On the importance of the passive, see Marcus, *Mark*, 1080, but in favor of an active translation "He is risen," see Collins, *Mark*, 796.

30 A number of commentators regard the explicit mention of Peter as an indication of Jesus' reaching out to the disciple who has denied him three times. See, for example, Collins, *Mark*, 797.

31 This is the position of Lohmeyer, followed by a number of contemporary scholars. See above, note 10.

32 This is the traditional solution to the problem, generally with reference back to the fear of the disciples at the Transfiguration (see 9:6). See, for example, Marie-Joseph Lagrange, *Évangile selon Marc* (Études Bibliques; Paris: Gabalda, 1920), 418; Taylor, *St Mark*, 609; William L. Lane, *Commentary on the Gospel of Mark* (NICNT; Grand Rapids: Eerdmans, 1974), 590–91; Collins, *Mark*, 801; Schweizer Marcus, *Mark*, 1081–82. On p. 1087, Marcus suggests that "perhaps" the message is aimed at the Gospel's audience, but focusses upon the theme of fearful silence and flight.

The Christian Community

The ending of the Gospel of Mark must be understood in the light of the story as a whole. The reader was provided with all the information necessary to understand who Jesus was, and what he was doing for humankind in the prologue (1:1-13). Throughout the story the reader has followed the disciples, as they steadily fell further from the design God had for his Son, and for those who follow him (see 8:34–9:1). They have now abandoned him (14:50), betrayed him (14:43-45) and denied him (14:66-72). Only the women, who have been with him since his days in Galilee (see 15:41) have been present at the cross (15:40-41), at the burial (15:47) and at the empty tomb (16:1-7). But in the end, in the very last line of the Gospel, they too join the disciples in their trembling, astonishment, fear and flight (v. 8. See 14:50). Does this mean that the information provided in 1:1-13 is wrong?

Mark 16:8 is the masterstroke of a story-teller who has relentlessly presented the gradual movement to failure of all the male disciples. The evidence of the tradition (as reported by the Gospels of Matthew, Luke and John) indicates that, historically, women were the first witnesses of the Easter event, and reported an Easter message to the unbelieving and discouraged disciples.[33] This was well known by members of early Christian communities. In this, Matthew, Luke and John (each in their own way) have it right. *But Mark has changed the story.* Why has Mark taken a well-known tradition and altered it so radically? There is something profoundly Pauline in what Mark is trying to do.[34] As with the promises of Jesus' forthcoming death and resurrection (8:31; 9:31; 10:33-34), the promise of 16:7 will be fulfilled. *What Jesus said would happen, will happen*, but it does not take place within the limitations of the plot of the Markan story. It cannot, because the women do not obey the missionary command of the young man (vv. 7-8). They, like the disciples, fail. As with the disciples, they flee in fear (see 14:50-52 where the same expressions appear: flight, fear and trembling).

When and how does Jesus' meeting with the failed disciples, women and men, take place? The answer to that question is not found *in the story*, but the very existence *of the story* tells the reader that *what Jesus said would happen, did happen*. The Gospel of Mark, with its faith-filled prologue (1:1-13) addressing a believing community, indicates that the disciples and Peter did see Jesus in Galilee, as he had said (14:28; 16:7). If the promise of 14:28 and 16:7 had been thwarted, there would be no Christian community, and thus no Gospel of Mark, read and heard within that community. The reason for the enigma of 16:8 lies in Mark's desire to teach his readers that the encounter between the risen Jesus and the failed disciples did not take place because of the success of the women. In the end, *all human beings fail* ... but God succeeds. God has raised Jesus from the dead (16:6). The Father has not abandoned the Son (15:34). The same God will also raise

---

33 See Edward L. Bode, *The First Easter Morning: The Gospel Accounts of the Women's Visit to the Tomb of Jesus* (Analecta Biblica 45; Rome: Biblical Institute Press, 1970) on the traditional witness. Elizabeth Struthers Malbon, "Fallible Followers: Women and Men in the Gospel of Mark," *Semeia* 28 (1983): 104–30, argues persuasively in support of Mark's portrayal of failing disciples *in the story* in order to address the fragile Christian situation of the audience *of the story*.

34 Fundamental to Pauline thought is the belief that God has saved sinful humankind by his free gift of grace, made available in and through the death and resurrection of Jesus Christ (see Rom 3:21-26). It is not so much a question of how good the believer might be, or how well he or she performs (although a life modeled on that of Jesus is demanded [see what has been called the "ethical excursus" of Rom 5:1–8:39]). What ultimately changes the relationship between God and the human story, lost since the fall of Adam, is the boundless goodness of God (Rom 5:12-21), made visible in Jesus Christ (see Rom 8:31-39). For an excellent analysis of the similarities between Pauline and Markan thought, without suggesting literary dependence, see Marcus, *Mark*, 73–75. See also Joel Marcus, "Mark—Interpreter of Paul," *NTS* 46 (2000): 473–87. See further the recent collection of studies in Oda Wischmeyer and David Sim (eds.), *Paul and Mark. Two Authors at the Beginnings of Christianity* (Berlin: Walter de Gruyter, 2014).

the disciples, men and women, from their failure. They will see the risen Lord in Galilee. That event took place because of the initiative of God, and not the success of the men *or the women*. The Christian community that produced and received the Gospel of Mark exists because of the initiative of God.

Conclusion

The unique conclusion to the Markan Gospel maintains its relevance. The Easter proclamation, the promise that Jesus was going before his disciples into Galilee, and the failure of the women to speak to anyone because they, like the disciples before them, fled in fear (16:6-8. See 14:50), point beyond the limitations of the Markan story to the existence of a believing Christian community. The Gospel of Mark has been received and proclaimed in such communities, despite their experiences of fear and flight, for 2000 years. What Jesus said would happen (14:28; 16:7), has happened, and continues to happen.

Christian communities and the Christian Church have their *raison d'être* in the attempt to follow Jesus. An honest reading of Christian history, and in a particular way the history of the encounter between European Christianity and the Christianity emerging in worlds where more ancient religions have determined culture, is instructive. Has the figure of the Son of Man who came to serve and not to be served, to lay down his life for all (see 10:45), the one who has saved others, and has no intention of coming down from the cross to save himself (see 15:30-31), always been the Christological model that directs the life and mission of Christian churches? There has been much heroism, marked by fear and trembling (see 10:32), but this witness has been damaged by arrogance and sin.[35] Yet, despite our ambiguity, like the many Christian communities which preceded us, we continue to celebrate Eucharist (see 6:31-44; 8:1-9). We continue our commitment to discipleship (see 8:22–10:52), we strain to preach the gospel to all nations (see 13:10), aware that it is not the success stories of human beings, men or women, that make Christian discipleship and the Christian Church an effective presence of God and his word in the world. Mark 16:6-8 proclaims a message hope and of fundamental importance for the fragile Christian community: God always has, and always will, make sense of our nonsense.

---

35 There is no need to list examples of this arrogance and sin across the centuries in the encounter between Christianity and the traditional religions of the new world, often associated with a biblically motivated approval of widespread slavery. Nor need I list the horror of the abuse of minors in our institutions. A remark on the inner-Christian scandal, especially in this journal committed to ecumenical scholarship, is in place. Across the year of 2017, the 500th anniversary of the formal beginning of the Protestant Reformation, I have read widely. Always aware of this tragic moment in Christian history, my more intense reading has been overwhelming. The details of the hatred, violence, and sheer stupidity on all sides of these divisions defies reasonable explanation. The divisions continue, and they render the face of Christianity deeply ambiguous. Popes and their court would not accept legitimate differences of opinion; simple people spat at the elevated host at Mass; icons, vestments and sacred objects were smashed and burnt; a Pope authorized the murder of Elizabeth I; wholesale slayings in warfare and public executions took place on all sides. Significant recent studies are: Heinz Schilling, *Martin Luther. Rebel in an Age of Upheaval* (trans. Rona Johnston; Oxford: Oxford University Press, 2016); Diarmaid MacCulloch, *All Things Made New. Writings on the Reformation* (London: Allen Lane, 2016); Carlos M. N. Eire, *Reformations. The Early Modern World. 1450-1650* (New Haven: Yale University Press, 2016); Eamon Duffy, *Reformation Divided. Catholics, Protestants and the Conversion of England* (London: Bloomsbury, 2017); Peter Marshall, *Heretics and Believers. The History of the English Reformation* (New Haven: Yale University Press, 2017). I express my gratitude to the Knights of the Southern Cross, Bulli, NSW, Australia, who have generously made these precious books my companions across 2017.

The Historical Jesus as 'Social Critic'
An Investigation of Luke 6:27-36

JAMES R. HARRISON

1. Jesus and the Graeco-Roman Reciprocity System

In antiquity reciprocity was fundamental to relationships involving beneficence. It created networks of obligation that spanned the divine and human world.[1] Modern sociological studies have afforded New Testament scholars insight into the way that the ethos of reciprocity shaped a range of relationships in the Gospels.[2] However, as useful as this approach is, there has been insufficient analysis of the ancient evidence regarding reciprocity rituals in the ministry of the historical Jesus. Few scholars have explored the extent to which the documentary and literary evidence throws light on Jesus' critique of the reciprocity system in Luke 6:27-36, especially as articulated in vv. 31-36.[3] Does this pericope represent Luke's own redaction of Q

---

1 On reciprocity in the ancient world, see C. Gill, et. al., ed., *Reciprocity in Ancient Greece* (Clarendon Press: Oxford, 1998); D.E. Briones, *Paul's Financial Policy: A Socio-Theological Approach* (London and New York: Bloomsbury T&T Clark, 2013), 26-41. For a helpful coverage of what exchange theorists have said regarding reciprocity in the sociological and psychological literature from the 1900's until our century, see L.M. Molm, 'The Structure of Reciprocity', *Social Psychology Quarterly* 73.2 (2010), 119-31. I will adopt the general definition of reciprocity provided by R. Seaforth ('Introduction', in Gill, *Reciprocity*, 1): 'Reciprocity is the principal and practice of voluntary requital, of benefit for benefit (positive reciprocity) or harm for harm (negative reciprocity)'.

2 H. Moxnes, *The Economy of the Kingdom: Social Conflict and Economic Relations in Luke's Gospel* (Philadelphia: Fortress Press, 1988); idem, 'Patron-Client Relations and the New Community in Luke-Acts', in *The Social World of Luke-Acts*, ed. J.H. Neyrey (Peabody: Hendrickson, 1991), 241-68; B.J. Malina and R.L. Rohrbaugh, eds., *Social-Science Commentary on the Synoptic Gospels* (Minneapolis: Fortress Press, 1992), 325. For assessments of 'reciprocity' studies in New Testament, see D.A. deSilva, 'Patronage and Reciprocity: The Context of Grace in the New Testament', *ATJ* 31 (1999), 32-84; E.D. MacGillivray, 'Re-Evaluating Patronage in Antiquity and New Testament Studies', *JGRCh* 6 (2009), 37-81.

3 See W.C. Van Unnik, 'Die Motivierung der Feindesliebe in Lukas VI 32-35', NovT 8.2 (1966), 284-300; G. Theissen, 'Nonviolence and Love of Our Enemies (Matthew 5:38-48; Luke 6:27-38)', in *Social Reality and the Early Christians: Theology, Ethics, and the World of the New Testament,* idem, tr. M. Kohl (Edinburgh: T&T Clark, 1992), 115-56; H.D. Betz, *The Sermon on the Mount: A Commentary on the Sermon on the Mount, including the Sermon on the Plain (Matthew 5:3-7:27 and Luke 6:20-49)* (Minneapolis: Fortress, 1995), 590-614, A. Kirk, '"Love Your Enemies," the Golden Rule, and Ancient Reciprocity (Luke 6: 27-35)', *JBL* 122.4 (2003), 667-81; J. Marshall, *Jesus, Patrons, and Benefactors: Roman Palestine and the Gospel of Luke* (Tübingen: Mohr Siebeck, 2009), 193-247. For other studies on reciprocity in Luke-Acts, see Brian Capper, 'Reciprocity and the Ethic of Acts', in *Witness to the Gospel: The Theology of Acts*, ed. I.H. Marshall and D. Peterson (Grand Rapids: Eerdmans, 1998), 499-518; M.P. Knowles, 'Reciprocity and "Favour" in the Parable of the Undeserving Servant', *NTS* 49 (2003), 256-60; D. H. Bertschmann, 'Hosting Jesus: Revisiting Luke's "Sinful Woman" (Luke 7:36-50) as a Tale of Two Hosts', *JSNT* 40.1 (2017): 30-50.

traditions—whether oral or written—or are we dealing here with an independent historical tradition regarding Jesus as a social critic, notwithstanding its Lucan redaction?[4] Moreover, we run the risk of simplifying the complexity of ancient reciprocity rituals when we view them through a sociological lens.[5] In neglecting the ancient evidence, we overlook contemporary critiques of the benefaction system that provide a useful backdrop against which we can assess Jesus' criticism of the reciprocity system.

By the first-century B.C., the Graeco-Roman reciprocity system had taken firm hold in Palestine and its conventions were well known to the Judaean elite, in its Herodian and imperial expression.[6] According to Josephus, Herod the Great—a client of Augustus and a benefactor of international

---

4   D. Lührmann ('Liebet eure Feinde: Lk 6:27-36; Mt 5:39-48', *ZTK* 69.4 [1972]: 412-38, esp. 413-15) has argued that the Sermon on the Mount and the Sermon on the Plain have significant parallels throughout and that the order of the subject matter is the same in each Gospel. Similarly, R. A. Piper, *Wisdom in the Q Tradition: The Aphoristic Teaching of Jesus* (Cambridge: Cambridge University Press, 1989), 193, cf. 77-82. On this basis many scholars, including W.E. Arnal (*Jesus and the Village Scribes: Galilean Conflicts and the Setting of Q* [Minneapolis: Fortress Press, 2003], 168), conclude that Q was a written document. G. Theissen (*Social Reality and the Early Christians: Theology, Ethics, and the World of the New Testament* [Edinburgh: T&T Clark, 1993], 141 n. 52) argues more cautiously. He suggests that Luke and Matthew reproduce 'a common tradition, probably a written source, even though it is impossible to see all the divergences between Matthew and Luke as editorial changes'. However, J. Piper ('*Love Your Enemies': Jesus' Love Command in the Synoptic Gospels and the Early Christian Paraenesis* [Cambridge; Cambridge University Press, 1979], 49-51) has warned against assuming that there existed a definitive form of Q upon which Luke and Matthew relied. Piper moves in the right direction in acknowledging the speculative nature of much Q scholarship, but he does not sufficiently reckon with the possibility that Jesus taught some of these materials (e.g. Matt 5:43-48; Luke 6:27-36), adapted to different contexts (e.g. 6:32-36), on two or more different occasions. See our discussion in §3.1 below. For excellent discussion of the critical options, see D.L. Bock, *Luke. Volume: 1:1-9:50* (Grand Rapids: Baker, 1994), 553-56. On the reliability of the oral forms behind the Gospels, see B. Gerhardsson, *Memory and Manuscript with Tradition and Transmission in Early Christianity* (Grand Rapids: Eerdmans, 1998); H. Wansbrough, ed., *Jesus and the Oral Gospel* (Sheffield: Sheffield Academic Press, 1991); C.S. Keener, *A Commentary on the Gospel of Matthew* (Grand Rapids: Eerdmans, 1999), 27-29. Whether Q was just an oral source rote memorized in Christian communities, or a single source written in either Greek or Aramaic and derived from a *specific* Christian community, or—in a more chaotic model of Q—tradition handed down from *different* Christian communities and written on wax tablets in Greek and Aramaic, will be bypassed here. See J.S. Kloppenborg, *The Formation of Q: Trajectories in Ancient Wisdom Collections* (Philadelphia: Fortress, 1987); M. Casey, *An Aramaic Approach to Q: Sources for the Gospels of Matthew and Luke* (Cambridge; Cambridge University Press, 2002). However, since I argue for the existence of independent Jesus traditions taught in several contexts and occasions, Casey's 'chaotic model of Q' (*ibid.*, 48) is highly attractive. Last, the attempt of M.S. Goodacre (*The Case Against Q: Studies in Markan Priority and the Synoptic Problem* [Harrisburg: Trinity Press International, 2002]) to dispense with Q altogether is unsuccessful. See J.S. Kloppenborg, 'On Dispensing with Q?: Goodacre on the Relation of Luke to Matthew', *NTS* 49 (2003), 210-36; D.R. Burkett, *Rethinking the Gospel Sources. Volume 2: The Unity or Plurality of Q* (Atlanta: SBL, 2009), 1-32.

5   See J.R. Harrison, *Paul's Language of Grace in Its Graeco-Roman Context* (Tübingen: Mohr Siebeck, 2003; rpt. Eugene: Wipf and Stock, 2017), 17-23.

6   For recent discussions of reciprocity and gift giving in ancient Israel and Second Temple Judaism, see T. Rajak, 'Benefactors in the Greco–Jewish Diaspora', in *Geschichte—Tradition—Reflexion: Festschrift für Martin Hengel zum 70. Geburtstag Band I: Judentum*, ed. H. Cancik *et al.* (Tübingen: Mohr Siebeck, 1996), 305–319; G. Stansell, 'The Gift in Ancient Israel', *Semeia* 87 (1999), 65-104; V. H. Matthews, 'The Unwanted Gift: Implications of Obligatory Gift Giving in Ancient Israel', *Semeia* 87 (1999), 91-104; S. Joubert, *Paul as Benefactor: Reciprocity, Strategy and Theological Reflection in Paul's Collection* (Tübingen: Mohr Siebeck, 2000), 93-99; Harrison, *Paul's Language of Grace*, 97-166; Marshall, *Jesus, Patrons, and Benefactors*, 24-124; S. Schwartz, *Were Jews a Mediterranean Society? Reciprocity and Solidarity in Ancient Judaism* (Princeton and Oxford: Princeton University Press, 2010); T. Novick, 'Charity and Reciprocity: Structures of Benevolence in Rabbinic Literature', *HTR* 105.1 (2012), 33-52; Y. Wilfred, *Poverty, Charity and the Image of the Poor in Rabbinic Texts from the Land of Israel* (Sheffield: Sheffield Phoenix Press, 2014), 255-59.

repute in his own right[7]—established and maintained bonds of reciprocity throughout his reign (*AJ* 15.18, 310-316; *BJ* 1.457-458).[8] Inscriptions from the Athenian Acropolis (*OGIS* 414, 427) and agora (*SEG* 12 [1955] 150) eulogise Herod for his beneficence to the city (εὐεργεσία) and emphasise his status as a friend of both the Romans (Φιλορωμαίος) and the Emperor (Φιλοκαίσαρ).[9] The Herodian dynasty was able to count on the return of favour from its clients, as the presence of a Herodian faction at the time of Jesus testifies (Mark 3:6; Matt 22:16).[10] The Herods were adept at appealing to the reciprocity system in their interactions with the imperial rulers. Philo's rendering of Herod Agrippa's letter to Gaius Caligula regarding the erection of his statue in the Temple is a case in point. The letter illustrates how a dependent might invoke loyalty to his patron as tool of persuasion in order to pressure him to change his policy.[11] The Roman Prefects were also dependent upon their imperial patrons and were vulnerable to threats of the withdrawal of Caesar's friendship, as the prefecture of Pilate amply demonstrates (John 19:12; Josephus, *BJ* 18.85-89; Philo, *Leg.* 299-305).[12]

While later Jewish writers were critical of the imperial reciprocity system,[13] the presence of a Phoenician honorific inscription from Greece—rendered in Semitic apart from the concluding reference in Greek to the Sidonian Council—confirms the presence of Hellenistic reciprocity rituals in the wider Semitic world. The Sidonian assembly awards Shama'baal, superintendent of the temple at Sidon and its buildings, a gold crown and erects an inscribed stele in his honour. Traditional reciprocity rituals are enunciated in the decision of the Sidonian assembly:

> —to crown Shama'baal son of MGN, who (had been) a superintendent of the community in charge of the buildings in the temple court and did all that was required of him by way of service;—that the men who are our superintendents in charge of the temple should write this decision on a chiseled stele, and should set it up in the portico of the temple before the eyes of men;—(and) that the community should be named as guarantor. For this stele the citizens

---

7   Two inscriptions, one from Jerusalem (*IEJ* 20 [1970], 97-98), the other from Ashdod (*ZPE* 105 [1995], 81-84), refer to Herod the Great as respectively 'Benefactor (εὐ[εργέτης]) and Friend of Caesar (φιλοκ[αίσαρος])' and 'pious (εὐσέβειας) and Friend of Caesar (φιλοκαίσαρος)'. For discussion, see P. Richardson, *Herod: King of the Jews and Friend of the Romans* (Columbia: University of South Carolina Press, 1996), 204. On the benefaction of the Herodian dynasty, see Marshall, *Jesus, Patrons, and Benefactors*, 125-73.
8   On Herod the Great as benefactor, see Richardson, *Herod*, 93-94, 127, 174-77, 272-73.
9   For discussion, see Richardson, *Herod*, 207-08.
10 The fact that Herod Antipas, like his father, cultivated and maintained client-patron relations with Greek cities overseas is evident from two inscriptions that honour Herod Antipas as 'guest and friend' (Cos: *OGIS* 416; cf. Luke 23:12) and which praise him 'on account of [his] piety and good' (Delos: *OGIS* 417). For discussion, see Richardson, *Herod*, 208-09.
11 Philo, *Leg.* 276-329, esp. 285-289, 294-298, 323-326. The boundaries that the imperial rulers could erect between themselves and their overly enthusiastic Jewish clients when occasion warranted is well illustrated by Claudius' letter to the Alexandrians (10th November A.D. 41: *CPJ* 2.153).
12 For Josephus' presentation of the operations of the imperial reciprocity system, see Harrison, *Paul's Language of Grace*, 138-40.
13 SibOr 8:52-55 (AD 185) speaks of Hadrian's benefactions and conquests thus: 'there will be a grey-haired prince with the name of a nearby sea, inspecting the world with polluted foot, giving gifts. Having abundant gold, he will also gather more silver from his enemies, and strip and undo them'. J.J. Collins discounts the possibility that this is another case of Christian interpolation in the Sibylline Oracles ('The Sibylline Oracles, Book 8', in *The Old Testament Pseudepigrapha: Apocalyptic Literature and Testaments Vol. 1*, ed. J.H. Charlesworth [Garden City NY: Double Day, 1983], 416): 'Jewish authorship of the remainder of the first section of the Sibylline Oracles 8 is supported by the animosity towards Hadrian in verses 50-59'. For criticism of Hadrian in the rabbinic literature, see *Tanh.*, Bereshit, §7, f.10b-11a (translated C.G. Montefiore and H. Loewe, eds., *A Rabbinic Anthology* [New York: Shocken Books, 1977], §13). See also SibOr 12.1-299 for an extended diatribe against the Roman imperial rulers. Notwithstanding the negative attitude to the imperial rulers in the Sibylline Oracles, SibOr 11:269-271 highlights the piety of the Roman people towards Julius Caesar at his funeral because of his friendship towards them.

of Sidon shall draw 20 drachmae sterling from the temple treasury. So may the Sidonians know that the community knows how to requite the men who have rendered service before the community.[14]

Similarly, while many Jewish inscriptions from Diaspora synagogues retain distinctive features that differentiate them to some extent from their eastern Mediterranean counterparts, there are inscriptions that operate according to traditional Greek models of reciprocity. For example, in a third-century A.D. decree from Phocaea, Tation is accorded conventional honours in the standard eulogistic vocabulary:

> Tation, daughter (or wife) of Straton, son of E(m)pedon, having erected the assembly hall and the enclosure of the open courtyard with her own funds (ἐκ τῶ[ν ἰδ]ίων), gave them as a gift (ἐξαρίσατο) to the Jews. The synagogue of the Jews honoured (ἐ[τείμη]σεν) Tation, daughter (or wife) of Straton, son of E(m)pedon, with a golden crown (χρυσῷ στεφάνῳ) and the privilege of sitting in the seat of honour (προεδρίᾳ).[15]

In the Gospels, however, Jesus is portrayed as one who criticised the rule of the Hellenistic and Roman Benefactor-Kings (Luke 22:25), along with their affluent Herodian clients in palaces (Matt 11:7-8; cf. Luke 13:32).[16] He castigated the synagogal benefactors for seeking public honours in recompense of their acts of generosity (Matt 6:2-4; contra, Luke 7:4-8). This (largely) negative attitude of Jesus towards the Jewish and Gentile representatives of the Graeco-Roman benefaction system was extended to its underlying social dynamic. Jesus, as depicted by Luke in 6:32-36, jettisoned the entire modus operandi of the reciprocity system, thereby setting himself against one of the most fundamental social conventions of antiquity.[17] But how do we account for (what seems

---

14 For a translation of the inscription (Piraeus: III. cent. B.C. or 96 B.C.), see J.C. Gibson, *Syrian Semitic Inscriptions Volume III: Phoenician Inscriptions Including Inscriptions in the Mixed Dialect of Arslam Tash* (Oxford; Clarendon Press, 1980), §41, 148-151. I am indebted to Dr. J.A. Davies for drawing this inscription to my attention. For discussion of the Greek model upon which the Syrian inscription is based, see Harrison, *Language of Grace*, 37-43.

15 B. Lifshitz, *Donateurs et Foundateurs dans les Synagogues Juives* (Paris: Gabalda, 1967), §13. Translated by B. J. Brooten, *Women Leaders in the Ancient Synagogue* (Atlanta: Scholars Press, 1982), Appendix §3. For discussion, *ibid.*, 143-44. For other examples, see *ibid.*, §6. For two inscriptions from Delos (150-50 B.C.) in which Samaritans honour their benefactors with the traditional coronal honours, see S.R. Llewelyn, ed., *New Documents Illustrating Early Christianity*, Vol. 8 (Grand Rapids: Eerdmans, 1998), §12.

16 For the historicity of the Matt 11:7 logion, see G. Theissen, *The Gospels in Context: Social and Political History in the Synoptic Tradition* (Minneapolis: Fortress Press, 1991), 26-42.

17 After the Second Jewish Revolt, a rabbinic tradition (b Shabbat 33[b]; cf. 'Abodah Zarah 2[b]) cynically exposes the self-centered motives that animated the gift-giving rituals of imperial and local Roman benefactors in the empire: 'How splendid are the works of this people', declared Rabbi Judah; 'they have built marketplaces, baths, and bridges'. … But Rabbi Simeon bar Yohai answered, 'Everything they have made they have made only for themselves—marketplaces, for whores; baths, to wallow in; bridges, to levy tolls'. Cited in N. Elliott, 'Paul and the Politics of Empire', in *Paul and Politics: Ekklesia, Israel, Imperium, Interpretation*, ed. R.A. Horsley (Harrisburg: Trinity Press International, 2000), 32. More generally, see N.R.M. de Lange, 'Jewish Attitudes to Roman Empire', in *Imperialism in the Ancient World*, ed. P.D.A. Garnsey and C.R. Whittaker (Cambridge: Cambridge University Press, 1978), 255-81; P. S. Alexander, 'The Family of Caesar and the Family of God: The Image of the Emperor in the Heikhalot Literature', in *Images of Empire*, ed. L. Alexander (Sheffield: Sheffield Academic Press, 1991), 276-97. However, we must not assume that such negative attitudes to Roman benefactors, including the ruler, were universal in post-A.D. 70 Judaism. One rabbinic commentator on Deuternomy 32:9 (Midrash Ha-Gaddol Deuteronomy 32:9: see §1.3.10 in M. Maas, *Readings in Late Antiquity* [London and New York: Routledge 2000]) speaks of the importance of choosing the imperial benefactor as a patron instead of his underlings because of his superior power: 'Some made of the governor their patron, some of the duke, some of the chief of the army. There was one clever fellow there. He said: All these people are under the authority of the king, and cannot prevent him from doing whatever he may wish to do. But he can prevent them from doing what they wish to. I shall choose as my patron none other than the king who can prevent all others from doing anything he objects to'.

to be) Jesus' ringing endorsement of reciprocity conventions in Luke 6:31?

Modern scholars have made much of v. 31 in discussion of the Lucan pericope, asserting that reciprocity was a key value in Jesus' exposition of his in-breaking Kingdom. Several examples will suffice. First, W.A. Meeks proposes that the charismatic movement of Jesus would reverse the social aggression that they encountered in their itinerant wanderings by means of the Q 'love your enemies' command. Although the Golden Rule (Luke 6:31) is a fundamental expression of human reciprocity, Luke interprets love for the enemy as the new hope and goal for social relationships.[18]

Second, R.A. Horsley divests Luke 6:27-36 of its purported anti-Roman polemic. He posits that the Jesus movement restored peasant practices of reciprocal generosity—and over against Theissen's 'itinerancy' thesis—in the *settled* context of households, villages and towns.[19]

Third, J.L. Reed has argued that Jesus rejected monetisation (e.g. Luke 12:33-34; 12:13-21; 15:8-9; 16:31; Matt 23:16-17) in favour of the ideal of reciprocity (Luke 6:27-35; 9:57-61). Reed believes that reciprocity found its expression not so much at the level of family and village life, as Horsley asserts, but more in the Kingdom of God.[20]

Fourth, W.E. Arnal has recently proposed that Herod Antipas' foundation of new cities in 20's Galilee brought vast social and economic changes that resulted in the loss of scribal independence.[21] As elite patronage increased, so village solidarity eroded. Therefore, the Herodian village scribes—who in Arnal's view were the originators of the Q tradition—espoused a state of idealized reciprocity that belonged to the past but which expressed the newness of the Kingdom of God in the present. In sum, Arnal views the Q 'love your enemies' speech (Q 6:27-35) as 'the pinnacle of an ethical revolution'.[22]

Fifth, H.D. Betz claims that Jesus' citation of the Golden Rule in v. 31 serves as an ethical principle which functions in precisely the same way as Greek ethical discussions did (*do ut des* ['I give so that you may give']).[23] Luke proceeds to refute incorrect understandings of the Golden Rule (vv. 32-34) and 'its misapplication to the commandments of Jesus' (v. 27).[24] The correct understanding of the Golden Rule is then enunciated in vv. 35-36. Thus, in Betz's view, v. 35 reflects general Hellenistic debates on beneficence, in which benevolence was not to be confused with business investments.[25] Conversely, in v. 36, the 'mercifulness of the deity was also a generally recognised

---

18 Theissen, 'Nonviolence and Love of Our Enemies', 121-25; idem, *The First Followers of Jesus: A Sociological Analysis of the Earliest Christianity* (London: SCM Press, 1978), 98-99. L.E. Vaage (*Galilean Upstarts: Jesus' First Followers According to Q* [Valley Forge: Trinity Press International, 1994], 121-27) considers Luke 6:27-35 to be general instruction on how to manage social conflict in antiquity, without any specific context.

19 R.A. Horsley, *Jesus and the Spiral of Violence: Popular Jewish Resistance in Roman Palestine* (San Francisco: Harper and Row, 1987), 255-75; idem, *Sociology and the Jesus Movement* (New York: Continuum, 1989), 125-26. Similarly, S. Freyne, 'The Geography, Politics, and Economics of Galilee and the Quest for the Historical Jesus', in *Studying the Historical Jesus: Evaluations of the State of Research*, ed. B. Chilton and C. A. Evans (Leiden-New York-Köln: Brill, 1994), 91. For Horsley's criticism of Theissen's arguments advocating an early Christian itinerant ethos, see his *Sociology and the Jesus Movement*, 116-29. For an extended critique of Theissen's position, see Arnal, *Jesus and the Village Scribes*, 1-95.

20 J.L. Reed, *Archaeology and the Galilean Jesus: A Re-examination of the Evidence* (Harrisburg: Trinity Press International, 2002), 97-98.

21 Arnal, *Jesus and the Village Scribes, passim*. Arnal builds upon the Q stratigraphy of J.S. Kloppenborg. However, the claim that one can chart a progression in Q from an early sapiental layer to a later eschatological layer, especially when we do not possess the original Q document (if there ever was one), creates a hypothetical reconstruction of early Christianity which we cannot possibly verify from our later documentary texts (Matthew, Luke) without being highly subjective in our judgements.

22 Arnal, *Jesus and the Village Scribes*, 58.

23 Betz, *The Sermon on the Mount*, 599.

24 Betz, *The Sermon on the Mount*, 604.

25 Betz, *The Sermon on the Mount*, 608.

element of Hellenistic religiosity',[26] as much as it was the case in Jewish covenantal piety.

Sixth, J. Marshall explores vv. 27-36 within the wider pericope of Luke 6:17-38.[27] He argues that the passage should be understood in light of Hellenistic reciprocity and benefaction rituals, operative in the Greek East, as opposed to the conventions of *patrocinium*, the Roman practice of benefaction, found in the Latin West. The rule of the Herod client-kings provides no real evidence for the evidence of *patrocinium* but rather for the Hellenised rituals of reciprocity, benefaction, and friendship flourished in Palestine.[28] While the Lukan portrait of Jesus demonstrate strong Jewish interpretative models (i.e. prophetic, Jubilee, Passover imagery),[29] Jesus, conversant with the benefaction system, does not reject the reciprocity system per se but only its improper adoption.[30] As Marshall observes, in Jesus' teaching 'new forms of reciprocity, friendship, and benefaction replace normal patterns which existed among the audience'.[31] Indeed, Jesus depicts God the Father as a generous Benefactor (Luke 6:35b) who reciprocates those who are generous to the marginalised (6:38).

But one wonders whether Marshall's tight distinction between 'Hellenised' and 'Romanised' models is overly prescriptive given the fluidity of intercultural contact that characterised the imperial world of the eastern Mediterranean basin. P.-S. Seo, for example, argues that Jesus' emphasis on loving the enemy in Luke 6:27-38 has the spiral of violence in the Roman Empire clearly in view.[32] While one would not want to restrict Luke 6:27-38 to a counter-imperial understanding, Jesus was nevertheless realistic about the threats and impositions wielded by the imperial rulers against their subjects (Luke 22:25a; 23:26), the violence of the Roman magistrates (13:1-3), and their Herodian clients (13:32; Matt 14:6-12; Mark 6:21-29) could bring to the rule of their subjects, even if they publicly projected the highly positive image of 'Benefactor' (22:25b: εὐεργέται καλοῦνται).[33] But imperial violence is only one aperture through which we can view the 'enemy' in our pericope: the enmity arising from the disruption of benefaction rituals, from the violation of φιλία, and from external enemies of the polis, among many other scenarios, are in view. Despite the differences in emphasis outlined above, many modern scholars believe that reciprocity is at the heart of the social revolution that Jesus is launching.[34] What Jesus intends is a revitalization or transformation of traditional reciprocity ethics, either as the dynamic of Judean village life or as the actualization of the Kingdom of God. What is unclear in this consensus, however, is the relation of v. 31 to vv. 27-30 and vv. 32-34. Does the Lucan Jesus endorse reciprocity only to undermine its operations subsequently in a searing exposé of the reciprocity system? Or is reciprocity a daring illustration of love for the enemy?

26 Betz, *The Sermon on the Mount*, 613.
27 Marshall, *Jesus, Patrons, and Benefactors*, 191-247.
28 Marshall, *Jesus, Patrons, and Benefactors*, 38-41, 44-49, 53-124, 331-33.
29 Marshall, *Jesus, Patrons, and Benefactors*, 239-43, 288-89.
30 Marshall, *Jesus, Patrons, and Benefactors*, 328-33.
31 Marshall, *Jesus, Patrons, and Benefactors*, 330.
32 P.S. Seo, *Luke's Jesus in the Roman Empire and the Emperor in the Gospel of Luke* (Eugene: Pickwick Publications, 2017), 147-55.
33 On 'Benefactor' see Marshall, *Jesus, Patrons, and Benefactors*, 286-323; Seo, *Luke's Jesus*, 96-115.
34 Not all scholars believe that reciprocity is at the core of Luke 6:31-36. Kirk ('"Love Your Enemies"', 667-86) argues that while the 'Love your enemy' command presupposes reciprocity rituals, Luke 6:32-34 challenges the ancient reciprocity system. In the view of Kirk, however, no new understanding of χάρις emerges. P. Ricoeur ('The Golden Rule: Exegetical and Theological Perplexities', *NTS* 36 [1990], 392-97) speaks of the presentation of a spirit of superabundant generosity and unilateral mercy in vv. 32-36 which empties reciprocity of its self-interest. For another 'non-reciprocal' interpretation, see J. Topel, 'The Tarnished Golden Rule (Luke 6:31): The Inescapable Radicalness of Christian Ethics', *TS* 59 (1998), 475-85.

Scholars have responded in vastly different ways to these issues.[35] Several scholars dismiss the authenticity of v. 31 in its present context. R.A. Piper posits that Luke 6:31 could be a 'floating unit of tradition', even though the consensus is that Matthew's placement of the Golden Rule (Matt 7:12) is redactional.[36] J.S. Kloppenborg proposes that because v. 31 interrupts the elaboration of vv. 27-30 by vv. 32-34, Luke 6:31 must be a later insertion, a position earlier articulated by R. Bultmann.[37] The Jesus Seminar rates v. 31 as grey ('Well, maybe') as far as authentic Jesus tradition. This is because, the Jesus Seminar asserts, the logion has a 'calculating egoism' and is widely attested in the ancient sources.[38]

Other scholars argue that v. 31 is correctly placed in its context, with vv. 32-35 clearly in view. A. Dihle considers v. 31 to be an instance of the general human behaviour which, as vv. 32-34 elucidates, must be surpassed,[39] a point which R. A. Piper—because of his indecisiveness over the issue[40]—is willing to concede.[41] Other scholars, while agreeing that v. 31 admirably fits its context, relate v. 31 to the preceding verses. R.C. Douglas, for example, states that v. 31 provides the rationale for vv. 27-30.[42] In a mediating position, J.B. Green argues that v. 31 is well integrated into the entire context of vv. 27-30 and vv. 32-35 by means of the repetition of the word 'do' throughout (ποιέω: vv. 27, 31 [2x], 33 [3x], 35).[43] C.S. Sunil also argues that the Golden Rule acts as a commentary both on Luke 6:27b-30 and 6:32-34. Its 'totally other-centred approach' in both pericopes is designed to 'reinforce the initial commands set forth in 6:27b-30: v. 32 recalls v. 27b (love your enemies), v. 33

---

35 Curiously, Piper ('*Love Your Enemies*', 54) does not address the issue. For an incisive coverage of the Golden Rule in Matthew and Luke, see Bock, *Luke*, 595.

36 Piper, *Wisdom in the Q Tradition*, 80.

37 Kloppenborg, *The Formation of Q*, 177; R. Bultmann, *History of the Synoptic Tradition* (Oxford: Basil Blackwell, 1963), 96. In my opinion, discussions as to which traditions in Luke 6:27-36 are either pre-Q, the work of the Q editor/community, or later than Q are precarious due to their inherent subjectivity. While the Q hypothesis is our best explanation of the similarities between Mathew and Luke, the absence of documentary evidence for Q renders our speculation about the pericope's tradition-history improbable. Note B.D. Ehrman's caustic evaluation (*Jesus: Apocalyptic Prophet of the New Millennium* [Oxford: Oxford University Press, 1999], 132) of the 'cottage industry' in Q studies that has risen out of a 'nonexistent source'. For stimulating discussions of the (proposed) tradition-history, see C. M. Tuckett, *Q and the History of Early Christianity* (Edinburgh: T&T Clark, 1996), 300-07; D. Catchpole, *The Quest for Q* (Edinburgh: T&T Clark, 1993), 101-34. Note, however, the correct observation of L. Schottroff ('Non Violence and the Love of One's Enemies', in *Essays on the Love Commandment*, idem et al. [Philadelphia: Fortress Press, 1978], 22) that the words 'bless those who curse you' (Luke 6:28) are 'substantially pre-Lukan' because they are alluded to in Rom 12:14.

38 R.W. Funk, et al., ed., *The Five Gospels: The Search for the Authentic Words of Jesus* (New York: Macmillan, 1993), 296.

39 A. Dihle, *Die Goldene Regel* (Göttingen: Vandenhoeck and Ruprecht, 1962), 113-14. Similarly, C.E. Evans, *Saint Luke* (London: SCM, 1990), 335. D.E. Oakman (*Jesus and the Economic Questions of His Day* [Lewiston: Edwin Mellen Press, 1986], 78-79) sees Luke 6:31 as a case of 'balanced reciprocity' where exchanges occur on a quid pro quo basis. However, Oakman (*ibid.*, 162-63) goes on to argue that Jesus undermines the notion of balanced reciprocity with the commands to love the enemy and to lend without expectation of return (Luke 6:32-35). As Oakman (*ibid.*, 163) observes, 'Loaning to enemies or strangers without the expectation of repayment goes against village commonsense'.

40 Rightly, Vaage, *Galilean Upstarts*, 127.

41 Piper, *Wisdom in the Q Tradition*, 80.

42 R.C. Douglas, '"Love Your Enemies": Rhetoric, Tradents, and Ethos,' in *Conflict and Invention: Literary, Rhetorical, and Social Studies on the Sayings Gospel Q*, ed. J. S. Kloppenborg (Valley Forge: Trinity Press International, 1995), 118. Similarly, J.A. Fitzmyer, *The Gospel According to Luke I-IX* (Garden City NY: Doubleday and Co., 1981), 639; R.H. Stein, *Luke* (Nashville: Broadman Press, 1992), 208. Catchpole (*The Quest for Q*, 114) says that the Q editor relates v. 31 more to vv. 27-28 than the 'detour' of vv. 29-30. L. E. Vaage ('Composite Texts and Oral Mythology: The Case of the "Sermon" in Q [6:20-49],' in Kloppenborg, *Conflict and Invention*, 82) concedes that v. 31 undergirds and elaborates by example the preceding instructions of vv. 27-30.

43 J.B. Green, *The Gospel of Luke* (Grand Rapids: Eerdmans, 1997), 273.

recalls v. 27c (do good) and v. 34 recalls v. 30 (give)'.[44] As such, Jesus' application of the Golden Rule in verse 31 'sharply overturns the principle of equal retribution (*lex talonis*)'.[45]

In contrast to the contextual approaches outlined above, there are scholars who argue that v. 31 is not clearly linked either with what precedes or follows. In this regard, V.P. Furnish writes that the Golden Rule in Luke 6:31 is '*separate* counsel *only generally illustrative* of the love command in vs.27'.[46]

Finally, scholars such as F.C. Downing interpret v. 31 against the backdrop of Cynic teaching on reciprocity.[47] Interestingly, L.E. Vaage entertains the possibility that v. 31—considered to be the *lectio difficilior* due to its inelegant placement—is authentic Jesus tradition. But he concludes that v. 31 is appropriately placed in its redactional context. For Vaage, the logion is a product of the Cynic-like 'Q' people, because it overturns customary ideas about 'how to manage social conflict in antiquity'.[48]

Clearly, the time is opportune for a re-appraisal of the complex issues raised by Luke 6:31-35. After examining select sources illustrating ancient reciprocity, the article addresses several questions. How far has Luke adapted Jesus' teaching in Luke 6.27-36 for his Hellenistic audience? What evidence is there that the historical Jesus critiqued Hellenistic reciprocity? How far does Jesus modify the traditional understanding of reciprocity in regard to divine beneficence and the return of favour? What alternative models of beneficence does Jesus promote?

I will argue that Jesus critiqued the ancient reciprocity system, subjecting its operations to his messianic appraisal. His intention was to establish a community of servant-benefactors—drawn in many cases (though not exclusively) from the marginalised subgroups of society—who would act beneficently as much towards their enemies as to their friends.

---

44 C.S. Ranjar, *Be Merciful Like the Father: Exegesis and Theology of the Sermon on the Plain (Luke 6:17-49)* (GBP: Roma 2017), 188-89.
45 Ranjar, *Be Merciful Like the Father*, 185 (cf. Exod 21:24; Lev 24:20; Deut 19:21).
46 V.P. Furnish, *The Love Command in the New Testament* (London: SCM, 1972), 57 (my emphasis). The contention of Vaage ('Composite Texts', 77) that Luke 6:31 finds a parallel in Gos. Thom 6:2 ('do not do what you hate') is overstated. It reflects the more negative formulations of the Golden Rule (e.g. Tobit 4:15; *b. Sabb.* 31a; '*Abot. R. Nat.* B. §26; *t. Ketub.* 7.6; Sir 31.15; *Ep. Arist.* 207; m. '*Abot* 2.10) rather than the positive rendering of Luke 6:31. J. D. G. Dunn (*Christianity Remembered. Volume 1: Jesus Remembered* [Grand Rapids: Eerdmans, 2003], 587) points out the same tendency is observed in the echo of the Golden Rule found in *P. Oxy.* 6546.2. Note the comment of I.H. Marshall (*Commentary on Luke* [Grand Rapids: Eerdmans, 1978], 262) regarding the negative form of the Golden Rule in contemporary Judaism: 'Jesus thus goes beyond the negative form, citing the rarer and more demanding form'. For a comprehensive coverage of the parallels to the Golden Rule, see Bock, *Luke*, 596-97.
47 F.G. Downing, *Christ and the Cynics* (Sheffield: JSOT Press, 1988), 27; Vaage, *Galilean Upstarts*, 40-54; idem, 'Deeper Reflections on the Jewish Cynic Jesus', *JBL* 117.1 (1998), 97-106. For criticism of the 'Cynic' Jesus thesis, see H.D. Betz, 'Jesus and the Cynics', *JR* 74.4 (1994), 453-75; P.R. Eddy, 'Jesus as Diogenes? Reflections on the Cynic Jesus Thesis', *JBL* 115.3 (1996), 449-69.
48 Vaage, *Galilean Upstarts*, 127; cf. also 104.

2. Luke 6:27-36 in Its Ancient Reciprocity Context

2.1 What Was the Social and Theological Ideology of Reciprocity in Antiquity?

How did reciprocity work between human beings in antiquity and what were its pitfalls?[49] A first-century A.D. decree from Cardamylae best represents orthodox first-century belief and practice regarding reciprocity. For five centuries prior to the Christian era, acts of beneficence by heads of state, public officials and private individuals had been celebrated in the stereotyped language of generosity and gratitude on the inscriptions. The key word of the inscriptions summing up the ethos of reciprocity is χάρις. It refers to the generosity of the benefactor—thus its meaning of 'favour, kindness, benefit'. Conversely it could designate the response of the person who had received the benefit, and be translated as 'gratitude, thankfulness', or the return of 'favour' to the benefactor. Note how this important inscription illuminates the ethos of reciprocity at a civic level:

> ... it was resolved by the people and the city and the ephors to praise Poseidippos (the son) of Attalos on account of the aforesaid kindnesses and also to bring never-ending gratitude (ἀτελῆ χάριν) in recompense of ([ἀμοι]βῆς) (his bestowal) of benefits; and also to give to him both the front seats at the theatre and the first place in a procession and (the privilege of) eating in the public festivals which are celebrated amongst us and to offer willingly (χαρ[ιζομέ]ους) all (the) honour (τειμήν) given to a good and fine man in return for (ἀντί) the many [kindnesses] which he provided, while giving a share of the lesser favour (ἐλάττονος χάριτος), (nevertheless) offering thankfulness (εὐχαριστίας) to the benefactors of ourselves as an incentive to the others, so that choosing the same favour (χάριν) some of them may win (the same) honours (τειμῶν). And (it was resolved) to set up this decree on a stone slab in the most conspicuous place in the gymnasium, while the ephors make the solemn procession to the building without hindrance, in order that those who confer benefits may receive favour (χάριν) in return for (ἀντί) love of honour (φιλοτειμίας), and that those who have been benefited, returning honours (ἀποδιδόντες τειμάς), may have a reputation for thankfulness ([εὐ]χαριστίας) before all people, never coming too late for the sake of recompense (ἀμοιβήν) for those who wish to do kindly (acts).[50]

Here we see a careful tabulation of the reciprocal benefits for the benefactor (Poseidippos) and his beneficiaries (the citizens of Cardamylae). Poseidippos receives 'favours' (public honours) in return for his 'love of honour' (his civic benefactions). Cardamylae receives the coveted reputation of gratitude in its return of honour to Poseidippos. The groveling reference to the 'lesser favour' on the part of the city underscores how city-states ensured that no touch of hubris could cause affront and spoil the smooth operation of the reciprocity system.[51] The ethos of reciprocity, as formulated in the Cardamylae decree, is striking for its calculation of the benefits to both parties.

---

49 This section draws upon a variety of genres of evidence from my book, *Paul's Language of Grace*. Far too many discussions of ancient reciprocity restrict their investigation of the ancient evidence exclusively to the popular philosophers or to the representatives of the major philosophical schools (e.g. Seneca, Aristotle), with the result that the complex social operations of the ancient 'pay-back' system are only discussed within specific ethical frameworks (e.g. Kirk, '"Love Your Enemies"'). For a sound social-scientific critique of the methodology of Kirk's article, see Z. A. Crook, 'Reflections on Culture and Social-Scientific Models', *JBL* 124.3 (2005), 515-32.
50 *SEG* 11(948).
51 For criticism of B. Malina's 'agonistic' model of social relations in the ancient honour system, see James R. Harrison, 'The Fading Crown: Divine Honour and the Early Christians', *JTS* 54.2 (2003), 494-95.

Furthermore, the decree is replete with the terminology of exchange. Apart from the obvious words 'recompense' (ἀμοιβῆς) and 'in return for' (ἀντί), χάρις shifts in its meaning as it moves its reference point from the beneficiary to the benefactor.

The ethos of reciprocity also operated in private patron-client relationships. Pseudo-Demetrius acknowledges that he returns the 'lesser' (ἔλαττον) thanks to his benefactor—the same terminology being employed as in the Cardamylae decree. Notwithstanding, the benefactor is encouraged to demand his rightful return (χάρις):

> I hasten to show in my actions how grateful I am to you for the kindness you showed me in your words. For I know that what I am doing for you is less (ἔλαττον) than I should, for even if I gave my life for you, I should not be giving adequate thanks (ἀξίαν ἀποδώσειν χάριν) for the benefits I have received. If you wish anything that is mine, do not write and request it, but demand a return (χάριν). For I am in your debt.[52]

We sense in Pseudo-Libanius the amazement that the ancients felt over the cardinal sin of ingratitude. It violated the principle of reciprocity where the benefactor was publicly recompensed with honours. More fundamentally, this negligence on the part of the beneficiary was an act of enmity since it deprived the benefactor of his prized status as a man of merit (ἀρετή):

> You have received many favours from us, and I am exceedingly amazed that you remember none of them but speak badly of us. That is characteristic of a person with an ungrateful (ἀχαρίστου) disposition. For the ungrateful (ἀχαρίστοι) forget noble men, and in addition ill-treat their benefactors as though they were enemies (ὡς ἐχθρούς).[53]

Seneca, too, comments on the problem of ingratitude towards the benefactor. The benefactor must carefully choose the recipients of his benefits.[54] However, the failure of a client to return a favour should not necessarily discourage the benefactor from beneficence. In a saying reminiscent of Matt 5:45, Seneca reminds his readers of the undiscriminating beneficence of the gods towards the ungrateful. Nonetheless, in Seneca's view, those who are intentionally ungrateful should not be accorded generosity:

> If you are imitating the gods, you say 'then bestow benefits also upon the ungrateful; for the sun rises upon the wicked, and the sea lies open to pirates'. This point raises the question whether a good man would bestow a benefit upon one who was ungrateful, knowing that he was ungrateful ... Understand that according to the system of the Stoics, there are two classes of ungrateful persons. One man is ungrateful because he is a fool ... Another man is ungrateful, and this is the common meaning of the term, because he has a natural tendency to this vice. To an ingrate of this first type ... a good man will give his benefit ... To the ingrate of the second type ... he will no more give a benefit than he will lend money to a spendthrift, or entrust a deposit to a man whom many have already found false.[55]

We will not linger on the theme of the reciprocation of parental favour. We simply note that Hierocles in his work, *On Duties*, observes that the measure of childrens' gratitude (εὐχαριστία) towards their parents is measured by their 'perpetual and unyielding eagerness to repay their

---

52 Pseudo-Demetrius, *Epistolary Types*, 21. II cent. B.C.–III cent. A.D.
53 Pseudo-Libanius, *Epistolary Styles*, 64. IV–VI A.D.
54 On the importance of the benefactor assessing the character of recipients prior to the conferral of benefits, see Harrison, *Paul's Language of Grace*, 70, 256 n. 170.
55 Seneca, *Ben.* 4.26.

beneficence (τὸ ἀμείβεσθαι τὰς εὐεργεσίας αὐτῶν)'.[56] The incentive given for the perpetuity of this obligation is seemingly the status that parents possessed as images of the gods.

Finally, Dio Chrysostom reveals the hidden pressure that arises when a favour promised by a benefactor is inadvertently forgotten. According to Dio, on such an occasion, the promised favour rapidly escalates into an obligation that demands payment:

> For there is nothing more weighty, no debt bearing higher interest, than a favour (χάριτος) promised. Moreover, this is the shameful and bitter kind of loan, when, as one might say, because of tardy payment the favour (χάριν) turns into an obligation, an obligation the settlement of which those who keep silent demand altogether more sternly than those who cry aloud. For nothing has such power to remind those who owe you such obligations as your having utterly forgotten them.[57]

How did the ethos of reciprocity affect the relationship between the gods and human beings? In a first-century B.C. decree in honour of Aristagoras we hear of the gods being placed under obligation to the benefactor. On acount of Aristagoras' cultic donations and piety as a priest of Apollo, he obtained 'double gratitude both from the gods and from those he benefited'. This idea of the gods reciprocating gratitude for human benefactions is entirely alien to the New Testament (e.g. Rom 11:35; 1 Cor 4:7), but it was ubiquitous in the ancient world:

> ... he honoured the city and the gods with festal gatherings to which all were invited and by sacred processions and by donations to the tribes, wishing to make this clear, that there is gratitude (χάρις) alike from gods and from men who receive benefits for those who conduct themselves in the life of the city with reverence and with noble purpose ...
>
> ... again, three years later, when the people ... were seeking a priest of Apollo, the Healer, men's private resources being under severe pressure, he made offer of himself and coming forward before the assembly he assumed the same crown, so obtaining double gratitude (χάριτας) for himself both from the gods and from those he benefited.[58]

The Emperor Hadrian envisages a similar exchange in an inscription from A.D. 125. In the inscription Hadrian presents a sacrificial offering—a recently killed she-bear—to the god Eros. By way of reciprocation for his cultic piety, Hadrian makes the request for favour or (possibly) sexual beauty of Eros:

> Child with the bow of Cyprus and the melodious voice, you who live in Thespiae on Helicon, near the flowery garden of Narcissus, grant me your favours. What Hadrian offers you, receive it as the first fruits of a she-bear which he has killed in striking it from the top of his horse. But you, in return (ἀντί), O Sage, breathe to him the grace (or 'beauty', χάριν) of Aphrodite Ourania.[59]

In another revealing inscription, the Emperor Nero announces his (short-lived) liberation of the

---

56 Hierocles, *On Duties*, 'How to Conduct Oneself Towards One's Parents', Stob. 3.52. On parental favour in the reciprocity system, see Harrison, *Paul's Language of Grace*, 340–42.

57 Dio Chrysostom, Or., 40.3-4. On the importance of this text for our understanding of the Jerusalem collection, see Harrison, *Paul's Language of Grace*, 312–14. The reverse side of the problem is seen when a beneficiary is overwhelmed by a benefactor's benefits. Ammonius (*P. Oxy. XLII.* 3057. I–II cent A.D.) pleads with his superior in the Egyptian bureaucracy to stop inundating him with kindnesses, because (in his words) 'I can't repay them (ἀμείψασθαι)'.

58 *SIG*³ 708. 100 B.C. Provenance: Istropolis.

59 J. Pouilloux, *Choix D'Inscriptions Grecques: Textes, Traductions et Notes* (Paris: Belles Lettres, 1960), §48. c. A.D. 125. Provenance: Thespies.

province of Greece in A.D. 67. His act requites the good will and piety of Greece towards himself. More importantly, it reciprocates the care of the Greek deities for the Emperor. As Nero pithily concludes:

> At present it is not out of pity (οὐ δι' ἔλεον) for you but out of good-will (δι' εὔνοιαν) that I bestow this benefaction, and I give it in exchange (ἀμείβομαι) to your gods, whose forethought on land and sea for me I have always experienced, because they granted me the opportunity of conferring such benefits.[60]

Significantly for our context, Nero claims that his beneficence was not motivated by 'pity' (or 'mercy', ἔλεος), but was a reciprocation of the 'good-will' (εὔνοιαν) of the Greeks. As we shall see, in the Jewish world-view of Jesus, the motivation for all beneficence is God's mercy.

By contrast, in a papyrus the socially inferior Hermaios admits that he cannot reciprocate his benefactor's generosity and leaves his requital with the gods. Here we see the vast gulf that exists between Nero, who had the social capital and largesse to reciprocate the gods, and the 'small' Hermaios, who has neither the status nor resources to do so:

> Hermaios greets the most esteemed Aelius Apollonius. Both in this and in all the rest, Lord, you supply to me the good will (εὔνοιαν) fitting for you and friendship (φιλίαν) and while I am small (μικρός) to know gratitude (χάριν) to you, the Gods will requite (ἀμείψονται) you.[61]

Finally, a funerary epigram (North Galatia: mid III cent. A.D.) speaks of parents faced with the fickleness of the gods who have snatched all their children from them through their premature death. The gods must be reciprocated, as per the reciprocity system. But how does one reciprocate such callous and uncaring gods? The answer is that one bitterly returns to them 'thankless thanks' (ἄχαρις χάρις):

> The fates have seen the place which is always just, and fixed the end of life as our portion. For they have snatched away the finest bloom of beloved youth and we shall no more arrive at the prime (?) of life. This tomb conceals first of all our virgin sister, called Olympias, and then to us, prematurely dead. Theseus was the eldest brother, and my name was Amemptos, a child, younger in age. His cheeks bloomed with a thin down and he was in the flower of youth, like the gods. Theseus died in the winter, then Amemptos in the fourth month, at the beginning of summer. Here may be seen the thankless thank offering (ἄχαρις χάρις) of their wretched parents, a libation on the tomb for their children who died before their wedding day. First virgin Olympias, then Theseus with the unflawed bloom on his cheeks, then a third end took away Amemptos. They lie here as a common family and the tomb has joined their remains together.[62]

2.2. Jewish Critiques of the Ancient Reciprocity System

What evidence is there for a critique of Graeco-Roman reciprocity in our sources? The rarity of such critiques of the Graeco-Roman benefaction system underlines how dominant reciprocity conventions were and their axiomatic status. In this instance, we will confine ourselves to two Jewish critiques of the reciprocity system as the appropriate backdrop to Jesus' own critique.[63]

---

60   *SIG*³ 814. Provenance: Acraephiae. A.D. 67.
61   *P. Brem.* 49. II cent. AD. For additional Jewish critiques, see nn.13 and 17 above.
62   S. Mitchell, *Regional Epigraphic Catalogues of Asia Minor: The Ankara District Inscriptions of North Galatia II* (Oxford: BAR, 1982), §392.
63   For Graeco-Roman critiques of reciprocity in the papyri, see Harrison, *Paul's Language of Grace*, 83-84.

First, Philo probes each side of the benefaction ritual, exposing (what he perceives to be) the mercenary nature of the relationship between benefactors and their beneficiaries:

> Look around you and you shall find that those who are said to bestow (χαρίζεσθαι) benefits sell rather than give (δωρουμένους), and those who seem to us to receive them (λαμβάνειν χάριτας) in truth buy. The givers are seeking praise (ἔπαινον) or honour (τιμήν) as their exchange (ἀμοιβήν) and look for the repayment (ἀντίδοσιν) of the benefit (χάριτος), and thus, under the specious name of gift (δωρεᾶς), they in real truth carry out a sale; for the seller's way is to take something for what he offers. The receivers of the gift (τὰς δωρεάς), too, study to make some return (ἀποδοῦναι), and do so (ἀποδιδόντες) as opportunity offers, and thus they act as buyers. For buyers know well that receiving and paying (ἀποδοῦναι) go hand in hand. But God is no salesman, hawking his goods in the market, but a free giver of all things, pouring forth fountains of free bounties (χαρίτων), and seeking no return (ἀμοιβῆς). For He has no needs Himself and no created being is able to repay His gift (ἀντιδοῦναι δωρεάν).[64]

In the view of Philo, benefaction is at heart a financial transaction. Benefactors 'sell' their benefits in exchange for praise and honour; conversely, the beneficiaries 'buy' their benefits, with gratitude and public honours to the benefactor the currency of trade. The Cardamylae inscription, discussed above, bears a strong resemblance to Philo's portrait of the benefaction system and represents best the view that Philo is caricaturing. Last, while Philo highlights the spontaneous generosity of God, his theology is Stoic rather than Jewish.

Finally, of particular interest is Ben-Sira's insightful exposé of the hostility implicit in benefaction rituals, engendered by the grudging hospitality of the benefactors, and by the ingratitude of their beneficiaries:

> The chief thing for life is water, and bread, and clothing, and a house to cover shame. Better is the life of a poor man in a mean cottage, than delicate fare in another man's house. Be it little or much, hold yourself contented, for it is a miserable life to go from house to house: for where you are a stranger, you dare not open your mouth. You shall entertain, and feast, and have no thanks (ἀχάριστια): moreover you shall hear bitter words: Come, stranger, and furnish a table, and feed me of that you have ready. Give place, stranger, to an honourable man; my brother comes to be lodged, and I have need of my house. These things are grievous to a man of understanding; the upbraiding of houseroom, and the reproaching of the lender.[65]

Ben-Sira's portrayal of the social humiliation implicit in the benefaction system stands in stark contrast to the positive inscriptional catalogues of honours that were rendered to benefactors in recompense of their munificence to their local communities. Clearly Jews other than Jesus were critical of the Graeco-Roman reciprocity system, whether it be the civic munificence of the Hellenistic city-state or the traditional household hospitality of the village.[66]

We turn now to Jesus' critique of the reciprocity system in Luke 6:31-36. Does this tradition originate with the historical Jesus or is it a case of Lucan redaction for his Gentile audience?

---

64 Philo, *Cher.*, 122-123.
65 Sir 29.21-28.
66 Note too the logion of Antigonos of Sokho (II. cent B.C.) who rejects any expectation of reciprocation of one's service: 'Be not like servants who serve the master for condition of receiving a reward, but be like servants who serve the master not on condition of receiving a reward'. As noted, see the rabbinic criticism of Roman benefactors (b Shabbat 33[b]; cf. 'Abodah Zarah 2[b]) in n. 17 above.

3. The Historical Jesus as Social Critic
3.1 The Relationship of Matthew 5:43-48 to Luke 6:27-36

Matthew 5:43-48	Luke 6:27-36
⁴³ You have heard that it was said, 'You shall love your neighbour and hate your enemy'.	
⁴⁴ But I say unto you, Love your enemies,	²⁷ But I say to you that hear, Love your enemies, do good (καλῶς ποιεῖτε) to those who hate you, ²⁸ bless those who curse you,
and pray for those who persecute you, ⁴⁵ so that you may be sons of your Father who is in heaven; for he makes his sun rise on the evil and on the good, and sends rain on the just and unjust.	pray for those who abuse you.
	²⁹ To him who strikes you on the cheek, offer the other also; and from him who takes away your coat do not withhold even your shirt. ³⁰ Give to every one who begs from you; and of him who takes away your goods do not ask them again. ³¹ And as you wish that men would do to you, do so to them.
⁴⁶ For if you love those who love you, what reward (τίνα μισθόν) have you?	³² If you love those who love you, what credit (χάρις) is that to you?
	For even sinners love those who love them. ³³ And if you do good to those who do good to you, what credit (χάρις) is that to you?
Do not even the tax-collectors do the same?	For even the sinners do the same.
⁴⁷ And if you salute only your brethren what more are you doing than others?	³⁴ And if you lend to those from whom you hope to receive, what credit (χάρις) is that to you?
Do not even the Gentiles do the same?	Even the sinners lend to sinners, to receive as much again. ³⁵ But love your enemies, and do good (ἀγαθοποιεῖτε) and lend, expecting nothing in return; and your reward (μισθός) will be great, and you *will be* sons of *the Most High*; for he is kind (χρηστός) to the ungrateful (τοὺς ἀχαρίστους) and selfish.
⁴⁸ You, therefore, must be perfect, as your heavenly Father is perfect.	³⁶ Be merciful, even as your Father is merciful.

Gos. Thom. 64

The servant came, he said to his master: 'Those whom you have invited to the dinner have excused themselves'. The master said to his servant: 'Go out to the roads, bring those whom you shall find, so that they may dine. Tradesmen and merchants [shall] not [enter] the places of my Father'.

Luke 14:12-14

[12] He said also to the man who had invited him, 'When you give a dinner or a banquet, do not invite your friends or your brothers or your kinsmen or rich neighbours, lest they also invite you in return (ἀντικαλέσωσίν σε), and you be repaid (ἀνταπόδομά σοι). [13] But when you give a feast, invite the poor, the maimed, the lame, the blind, [14] and you will be blessed, because they cannot repay you (ἀνταποδοῦναί σοι). You will be repaid (ἀνταποδοθήσεται) at the resurrection of the just'.

The fundamental issue is the degree to which Luke has adapted Jesus' teaching in 6:27-36 and 14:12-14 for his Hellenistic audience. Does the Lucan account—with its sharp rebuttal of reciprocity conventions—retain elements of the authentic teaching of Jesus? If so, how radical is Jesus' critique of reciprocity? Jesus' comments on reciprocity are found in the Q tradition common to Matthew and Luke. As noted, D. Lührmann has argued that the Sermon on the Mount and the Sermon on the Plain have significant parallels throughout and that the order of the subject matter is the same.[67] The parallelism between Matt 5: 44a/b, 46a/b, 48 and Luke 6:27, 28b, 32a, 33b, 36 underscores this feature. Notwithstanding the attempt of many scholars to dismiss the Matthean antitheses (Matt 5:21ff, 27ff, 33ff, 38ff, 43ff) as redactional creations,[68] the partial antithesis in Luke 6:27a confirms that Jesus did speak in a way that accentuated his authority over against the scriptural traditions of the Old Testament and the religious traditions of Second Temple Judaism.[69]

However, care must be taken with our pericope. D.A. Hagner observes that while there are common elements, the material is quite different in its order and wording.[70] First, as regards order, the motif of divine sonship, common to Matthew and Luke, is located differently in each pericope (Matt 5:45a; Luke 6:35b), whereas the Golden Rule occurs in different redactional contexts (Matt 7:21; Luke 6:31).

Second, as regards wording, there are also clear differences. A few examples will suffice. In Matthew 5:46, 47 the Jewish terminology of 'tax-collectors' (οἱ τελῶναι) and 'Gentiles' (οἱ ἐθνικοί) is rendered as 'sinners' (οἱ ἁμαρτωλοί) in Luke 6:32, 33, 34. Accordingly, there might be a temptation to view Matthew's account as closer to the teaching of the historical Jesus precisely because of its Jewishness. However, it is quite feasible that Matthew is heightening the Jewishness of Jesus for his own theological ends. Furthermore, although there are Hellenistic phraseology and themes

---

67 See Lührmann, 'Liebet eure Feinde'.
68 E.g. M.J. Suggs, 'The Antitheses as Redactional Products', in *Essays on the Love Command*, ed. L. Schottroff *et al.* (Philadelphia: Fortress Press, 1978), 93-107.
69 See J. Jeremias' defence (*New Testament: Theology Volume 1* [London: SCM Press, 1971], 250-55) of the authenticity of the Matthean antitheses. See, too, D. Daube's helpful discussion of the antitheses in their rabbinic context (*The New Testament and Rabbinic Judaism* [London: School of Oriental and African Studies, University of London, 1956], 55-66). Daube allows for the possibility that Jesus might have prophetically expressed his consciousness of supreme authority in the 'I say unto you' logion (*ibid.*, 58), but he unnecessarily plays down the force of Matthew's contrast in its rabbinic context (*ibid.*, 59ff; contra, Matt 28:20a; Mark 1:22, 27a). Contra, see Ranjar, *Be Merciful Like the Father*, 84.
70 D.A. Hagner, *Matthew 1-13* (Dallas: Word Books, 1993), 133. See also the helpful comments of R.A. Horsley, 'Ethics and Exegesis: "Love Your Enemies" and the Doctrine of Nonviolence', in *The Love of Enemy and Nonretaliation in the New Testament*, ed. W.M. Swartley (Louisville: Westminster/John Knox Press, 1992), 80-81.

in Luke 6:32-35 (ἀγοθοποιεῖν: vv. 33, 35; χάρις: vv. 32, 33, 34; ἀχαρίστους: v. 35) and the presence of reciprocity terminology in 14:12-14,[71] Luke retains his own Jewish emphases. One such example is Luke's emphasis on the mercy of God (Luke 6.36: οἰκτίρμων), in contrast to Matthew's perfection of God (Matt 5:48: τέλειος).[72] In my opinion, the Lucan paradigm coheres better with the concentration of the historical Jesus upon the mercy-code—over against the boundaries imposed by the Pharisees' extension of the temple holiness code to everyday life—throughout his ministry.[73]

In sum, we are probably dealing with two independent traditions, each deriving from Jesus, but with common elements of teaching underlying each.[74] We must therefore leave open the possibility that Luke did capture the authentic voice of Jesus in Luke 6:27-36. But what about the Lucan material on reciprocity (Luke 6:32-35; cf. 14:12-14) paralleled nowhere else in the Gospel tradition? Is this merely a case of Lucan redaction for his Gentile auditors in a later generation or do we have here an authentic critique of the reciprocity system delivered (substantially) by the historical Jesus?

3.2 Jesus' Critique of the Reciprocity System (Luke 6:32-36/14:12-14)

It is simplistic to dismiss the special Lucan material in 6:32-36 and 14:12-14 as theological invention. Referring to Luke 14:12-14, I. H. Marshall has astutely commented: 'the sentiments are those of 6:32-35, and while the thoughts would be congenial to Luke, there is no evidence that they are created by him or the early church'.[75] There are sound reasons for accepting Luke 6:32-35 and 14:12-14 as authentic Jesus tradition.

First, there were other first-century Jews such as Philo (*Cher.*, 122-123) and Josephus (*AJ* 6. 341-342) who were critical of elements of the Graeco-Roman reciprocity system. As noted, the writings of Ben Sira (Sir 29.21-28: c. 180 B.C.) exposed the tensions and humiliation accompanying reciprocity conventions in households. It begs the question: could not Jesus have mounted a similar critique as well? Such an astute observer as Jesus of contemporary ruler-benefactors (Luke 13:31-32; 22:25-27; Mark 12:16-17) would hardly have missed the reciprocity rituals supporting the power base of the Herodian Kings, the imperial rulers, and their prefects in Judaea.[76] Even in the case of the synagogues of Galilee and the treasury of the Jerusalem Temple, there were the benefactors who drew the stinging criticism of Jesus for a variety of reasons (Matt 6:2-4; 23:6; Mark 12:41-44). It should be no surprise that Jesus attacked the *do ut des* mentality ('I give so that that you may give') animating patronage in antiquity.

Second, there are elements of teaching in Luke 6:27-36 and 14:12-14 that are striking in both their Jewish and Graeco-Roman context. We have already observed how Jesus' emphasis on God's

---

71 Jesus' critique of reciprocity ideology in Luke 14:12-14 is underscored by the use of ἀντί compounds in vv. 12 and 14. A spread of reciprocity ideology, including ἀντί is employed in the Cardamylae inscription (*SEG* 11[948)]), discussed above. For discussion of the reciprocity terminology in that decree, see Harrison, *Paul's Language of Grace*, 51-52.
72 In defence of Luke's 'mercy' terminology, Ranjar (*Be Merciful Like the Father*, 96) cites T.W. Manson (*The Sayings of Jesus* [London: SCM Press, 1971], 55): 'in the Old Testament the epithet 'merciful' is given to God, hardly ever to man; and the epithet 'perfect' to man, never to God'.
73 E.g. Mark 1:41. See M.J. Borg, *Conflict, Holiness, and Politics in the Teachings of Jesus* (Lewiston/Queenston: Edwin Mellen Press, 1984).
74 By contrast, Ranjar (*Be Merciful Like the Father*, 112-14) argues that the Q-Sermon existed as one unit, with Luke and Matthew making their respective redactional changes to it, even if some of the sayings independently were circulating at a pre-Q stage. But, as noted above (n. 4), if the 'chaotic' theory of Q has credence, we are more likely dealing with independent traditions in this instance.
75 I.H. Marshall, *Commentary on Luke* (Grand Rapids: Eerdmans, 1978), 583.
76 In regard to Mark 12:17, Reed (*Archaeology and the Galilean Jesus*, 98) notes Jesus' wry observation that the coin would 'soon enough return to Caesar'.

mercy flew in the face of Nero's stated policy of only reciprocating the good will of his Greek subjects (*SIG*³ 814). Further, this mercy of God is unilateral and unconditioned. The God of Jesus, unlike the Greek deities, cannot be put under counter-obligation (*SIG*³ 708; J. Pouilloux, *Choix D'Inscriptions Grecques*, §48). Moreover, Jesus' command of unconditional beneficence towards the enemy—not simply the ungrateful—would certainly have earned the disapproval of people like Seneca (*Ben.*, 4.26). The postponement of reward till the eschaton and its democratisation would have puzzled the honour-driven city of Cardamylae and undermined the meritocracy associated with the reciprocity system more generally (*SEG* XI[948]). The admission of people with disabilities to the eschatological banquet (Luke 14:12-14)—who were marginalized by the priestly holiness system and who were unable to reciprocate favour precisely because of their disability—would have shocked the Qumran community. The Qumran covenanters, as the new Temple community, excluded people with disabilities from their fellowship as they awaited their eschatological vindication over the 'sons of darkness' on the Day of the Lord.[77]

Of particular interest is the way that the Gospel of Thomas 64 excludes tradesmen and merchants from the Parable of the Marriage Feast. This quasi 'Gnostic' Gospel excises the Lucan reference to the inclusion of people with disabilities at the eschatological marriage. The second century A.D. writer replaces the motif with an ascetic ideal that scorned the accumulation of personal wealth (*Gos. Thom.* 54; 110), symbolised in this context by the merchant.[78] This highlights how offensive Jesus' teaching in Luke 14:12-14 about the inclusive nature of the Kingdom community was to various groups.

Third, several features of Jesus' teaching elsewhere cohere with the sketch outlined above. Jesus reminds his disciples that in their healing ministries they were to demand no reciprocation at all because of God's unilateral beneficence towards themselves: 'You have received without paying, give without pay' (Matt 10.8). Jesus eschews the imposed demands of reciprocity. In Luke 7:1-10 the Jewish elders remind Jesus that a centurion benefactor (in the parlance of the inscriptions) was worthy of counter-favour because he had funded the construction of a synagogue. Significantly, Jesus resists the cultural pressure of reciprocation, healing the sick slave of the centurion only because of his master's remarkable faith. The independent logion of Jesus ('It is more blessed to give than to receive' [Acts 20:35]) is another instance of the up-ending of the reciprocity system.

Further, Jesus inverts the models of benefaction. Now an impoverished widow—not celebrated benefactors like Poseidippos (*SEG* XI[948])—images true generosity (Luke 21:1-4) and the disciples themselves are to be servant-benefactors (Luke 22:24-30). Although Jesus affirms a continuing care for parents, its motivation flows from the Torah and not from the Hellenistic benefaction system (Mark 7:9-13; cf. Hierocles, *On Duties*, 'How to Conduct Oneself Towards One's Parents', Stob. 3.52). Indeed, Jesus' hard sayings concerning the burial of fathers (Matt 8:21-22), division within the household (Matt 10:35-39; Luke 12:52-54), and the relativisation of family ties (Luke 11:27-28; Mark 3:21, 31-34) would have seemed to many a savage betrayal of family reciprocity ethics.[79]

Fourth, Jesus' emphasis on the politics of mercy (Luke 6:35) over the politics of holiness (Matt

---

77 1QM 7:3-9; 1QSa 2:3-10; 11QT 45:12-14; CD 15:15-18; 4QMMT 40-53; cf. 2 Sam 5:6-8 [Josephus, *AJ* 7:61]; *m. Bek.* 7:1; *b. Ber.* 58b; Josephus, *Ap.* 2.1-32. For further discussion, see A. Shemesh, '"The Holy Angels Are in Their Council": The Exclusion of Deformed Persons from Holy Places in Qumranic and Rabbinic Literature', *Dead Sea Discoveries* 4 (1997), 179-206.

78 A. Marjanen, 'Is Thomas a Gnostic Gospel', in *Thomas at the Crossroads. Essays on the Gospel of Thomas*, ed. R. Uro (Edinburgh: T&T Clark, 1998), 129. Note the comment of A.J. Hultgren (*The Parables of Jesus: A Commentary* [Grand Rapids: Eerdmans, 2000], 336): 'commerce is incompatible with the contemplative life required of the true Gnostic'.

79 On the eschatological urgency of mission subordinating household ties, see S.C. Barton, *Discipleship and Family Ties in Mark and Matthew* (Cambridge: Cambridge University Press, 1994). See also the discussion of Harrison, *Paul's Language of Grace*, 340-42.

5:48), while sitting comfortably within mainstream Judaism and the Old Testament covenantal tradition,[80] would not have been endorsed by the Qumran covenanters. The enemy, in their view, was to be accorded no mercy (*1QS* 2.5-8):

> Be cursed in all the works of our guilty wickedness,
> May God make you an object of terror by the hands of all the avengers of vengeance ...
> Be cursed, *without mercy*, according to the darkness of your works.
> Be damned in the place of everlasting fire.

Similarly, in the context of Graeco-Roman reciprocity conventions, mercy was not the primary motivation for beneficence. As noted, Nero had offered the Greeks 'good will' in liberating Hellas, not 'mercy', in repayment of the Greek gods' care for him on land and sea (*SIG*^{3} 814). D. Senior draws out the significance of Jesus' teaching here most effectively:

> The teaching is rooted in an experience of God as gracious, merciful and indiscriminately loving. This element, common to Matthew and Luke, was surely part of Jesus' own teaching: his boundary-breaking ministry to outcasts and sinners, his many parables about the mercy of God, and his interpretation of law with love and compassion as first principles all reflect Jesus' *own experience* of God as lavishly merciful.[81]

Fifth, this cross-cultural critique challenges first-century assumptions about who 'the enemy' actually is,[82] as defined by the operation of the reciprocity system.[83] As noted, Pseudo-Libanius defines the enemy thus: 'the ungrateful (ἀχάριστοι) forget noble men, and in addition ill-treat their benefactors as though they were enemies (ὡς ἐχθρούς). Jesus, as depicted by Luke, multiplies the phrases describing the enemy in Luke 6:27ff (vv. 27b: 'who hate you'; vv. 28a/28b: 'who curse you', 'who abuse you'; vv. 29a/29b, 30b: 'who strikes you', 'who takes away your coat', 'if anyone takes away your goods'),[84] charting thereby a progression of provocation and social domination that ranges from insult to injury and theft.[85] By contrast, the believer's 'love' is progressively amplified in vv. 29b, 30b, 35 (v. 29b: 'do not withhold even your shirt'; v. 30b: 'do not ask for them again';

---

80 E.g. TBenj. 4.1-5.4. Cited by P. Perkins, *Love Commands in the New Testament* (New York/Ramsey: Paulist Press, 1982), 18. Catchpole (*The Quest for Q*, 116) cites *Tg. Yer. I* Lev 22:28: 'As our Father is merciful in heaven, so be merciful on earth'. See also K. Stendahl, 'Hate, Non-retaliation, and Love: 1 QS 10.17-20 and Rom 12:19-21', *HTR* 54.4 (1962), 343-55; O.J.F. Seitz, 'Love Your Enemies: The Historical Setting of Matthew v.43f.; Luke vi.27f.', *NTS* 16 (1969-1970), 39-54.
81 D. Senior, 'Jesus' Most Scandalous Teaching', in *Biblical and Theological Reflections on the Challenge of Peace*, ed. J.T. Pawlikowski and D. Senior (Wilmington: Michael Glazier, 1984), 55-69, here 61. My emphasis.
82 For excellent discussions of the 'enemy' in ancient context, see L. Schottroff, 'Non Violence and the Love of One's Enemies', 9-39; W. Wink, 'Neither Passivity nor Violence: Jesus' Third Way (Matt. 5:38-42 par.)', in Swartley, *The Love of the Enemy*, 102-32. Note the perceptive comment of W. Klassen, 'The Authenticity of the Command: "Love Your Enemies"', in *Authenticating the Words of Jesus*, ed. B. Chilton and C.A. Evans (Leiden-Boston-Köln: Brill, 1999), 400: 'between the time Jesus spoke these words, and the Gospel editors transmitted them the definition of enemy changed; few definitions change as quickly'.
83 J.P. Meier (*A Marginal Jew: Rethinking the Historical Jesus. Volume IV: Law and Love* [New Haven and London: Yale University Press, 2009], 528-51) has powerfully shown that Jesus' 'Love your enemies' command is without real precedent in both the Old Testament, Second Temple Judaism, and the Graeco-Roman world.
84 Note the comment of J.R. Edwards (*The Gospel According to Luke* [Nottingham: Apollos, 2015], 198) regarding Luke 6:29b: 'the instruction to surrender not only your "coat" (Gk. *himation*, outer garment) but also your "shirt" (Gk: chiton, undergarment worn next to skin) is not to arm oneself in the face of evil and injustice, but to become naked in the face of it'. M. Wolter (*The Gospel According to Luke. Volume 1: Luke 1-9:50* [Waco: Baylor University Press, 2016], 279) adds the following qualification: 'This could, of course, also be a completely sensible survival strategy, but the rational of the exhortation certainly does not reside in this'.
85 Kirk, '"Love Your Enemies"', 681.

v. 35: 'love ... do good ... lend'), but without any reference as one might expect to the reciprocity system or its rewards ('expecting nothing in return').

The practical care towards the enemy enjoined by Jesus in this context finds a strong parallel in Proverbs 25:21-22 (cf. Rom 12:20): 'If your enemy is hungry, give him food to eat; if he is thirsty, give him water to drink' (v. 21).[86] Although the human motivation for this act is notoriously unclear in Proverbs 21:22b (is the beneficence extended to the enemy designed to exacerbate his resentment or elicit his repentance?),[87] the prospect of divine reward is nevertheless held out ('the Lord will reward you': Prov 25:22b). This is the case, too, in Luke 6:35 where Jesus says: 'your reward will be great, and you will be sons of the Most High'. But, in sharp contrast, Jesus expands unequivocally on the divine motivation undergirding beneficence towards the enemy. The believer is to act with the same impartial kindness (χρηστός) as the divine Benefactor does towards those who reject his beneficence (τοὺς ἀχαρίστους) and who respond in ways contrary to his will (τοὺς πονηρούς). According to Jesus, the paradigm for believers is God's covenantal mercy (Luke 6:36b: οἰκτίρμων [Rom 12:1]; cf. οἰκτίρμων: Ex 34:6; Joel 2:13; Jonah 4:2; Pss 86:15[LXX Ps 85:15]; 103:8[LXX 102:8]; 145:8 [LXX 144:8]).[88] It expresses 'the profligate generosity of the Father and his sons toward men who give nothing in return'.[89] Ultimately, it is the Father who undermines the reciprocity system by refusing to restrict in advance his beneficence to the grateful.

In sum, we are witnessing a highly original and wide-ranging theological critique of aspects of Graeco-Roman and Jewish reciprocity. It stands in marked contrast to the Stoic clichés of Philo (*Cher.*, 122-123) and the moralistic stance of Josephus (*AJ* 6. 341-342). We pay Luke too high a complement when we assign the entire tradition to his theological creativity. More likely, Luke has faithfully rendered Jesus' inversion of reciprocity rituals and has added several deft Hellenistic touches of his own.

Curiously, J.P. Meier has suggested that Jesus was disconcertingly silent on the social issues of his day.[90] I remain uneasy about this observation. In the case of Jesus' searing critique of reciprocity,[91] a central pillar of Graeco-Roman social ethics was pulled askew. The edifice would continue to crumble under the weight of history when Paul radically redefined beneficence and located its supreme expression in an impoverished benefactor (2 Cor 8:9; cf. Mark 12:41-44).[92]

Nor can we assert, as several scholars do, that Jesus intended a revitalization or transformation of *traditional* reciprocity ethics, either within Judean village life or as a social expression of the Kingdom of God. Rather, if Luke 6:31-36 and 14:12-14 are any indication, Jesus was supplanting the traditional reciprocity system with a radically new Kingdom community, stripped of any suggestion of hierarchy and meritocracy (Matt 23:5-10; Luke 22:24-27). It operated with divine mercy towards its enemies and honoured the marginalized by including them at the core of its

---

86 Noted by Wolter, *The Gospel According to Luke*, 278. The heavy ethical emphasis upon practical outcomes is underscored by Jesus' use of sixteen imperatives in Luke 6:27-38: eight imperatives in vv. 27-34, four in vv. 35-36, four in vv. 37-38 (A.A. Just, *Luke 1:1–9.50* [St. Louis: Concordia Publishing House, 1996], 291-92).
87 See W. Klassen, 'Coals of Fire: Sign of Repentance or Revenge?', *NTS* 9 (1963), 337-50.
88 Marshall, *Jesus, Patrons, and Benefactors*, 237.
89 P.S. Minear, *Commands of Christ* (Nashville-New York: Abingdon Press, 1972), 73. Note the telling comment of D. Constan, *Pity Transformed* (London: Duckworth, 2001), 124. 'Although the pagan Greek and Roman gods might feel pity on occasion, it was not their primary trait, and philosophers never endorsed it as such'.
90 J.P. Meier, *A Marginal Jew: Rethinking the Historical Jesus. Volume 2* (New York: Doubleday, 1994), 332. Meier omits any discussion of Luke 6:27-36. Similarly, H.J. Cadbury (*The Peril of Modernising Jesus* [London: Macmillan, 1937], 95) and R. Bultmann (*Jesus and the Word* [Gmn orig. 1926; New York: Scribner's, 1934], 103).
91 Wolter (*The Gospel According to Luke*, 282) speaks of 'the nullification of the principle of ethical reciprocity in vv. 32-34'.
92 See Harrison, *Paul's Language of Grace*, 250-68.

beneficence. Whatever vestiges of reciprocity remained, they have been profoundly transformed. This is emphasized by the Lucan threefold repetition of χάρις, the *leitmotiv* of the reciprocity system, in vv. 32a, 33a, and 34a. In each case, the inadequacy of the traditional reciprocity ritual is spotlighted by the reference to the ubiquity of its operation among 'sinners' (vv. 32b, 33b, 34b). Only by loving, doing good, and lending without expectation of return (v. 35) and by one's motivation being informed by divine mercy (v. 36) will a new understanding of χάρις emerge.[93]

But what about the reciprocity envisaged in the Golden Rule (Luke 6:31)?[94] How does this relate to Jesus' critique of the reciprocity system in vv. 32-36? For Jesus and many other Jews, the Golden Rule represented a popular formulation of the Levitical love command (Lev 19: 18b: 'You shall love your neighbour as yourself'),[95] an ethic that marked off Israel as God's holy people (Lev 19:2b: 'You shall be holy, for I the Lord your God am holy'). It is against the backdrop of the Levitical tradition that Jesus' authoritative introduction (Luke 6:27a: 'But I say to you' [ἀλλὰ ὑμῖν λέγω]) is probably to be understood.[96] Moreover, whereas in Second Temple Judaism the Golden Rule is largely negative

---

[93] By contrast, A. Kirk ('"Love Your Enemies"', 682) posits no new understanding of χάρις: 'The salient feature of vv. 32-34, however, is not repudiation of reciprocity behaviour and its animating principle, χάρις, but the turning on its head of the evaluative ancillary evaluative framework'. It is also interesting to speculate whether Jesus might have delivered his teaching occasionally in Greek (including Luke 6:27-36?), as S. Porter ('Jesus and the Use of Greek in Palestine', in Chilton and Evans, *Studying the Historical Jesus*, 123-54) has recently proposed. Did Jesus himself inaugurate the redefinition of χάρις that Paul later brought to fruition in his theology of the 'reign of grace'? While this proposal is initially attractive, its force is lessened when one remembers that the language of grace is especially prominent in the Lucan writings (ἀχάριστος: Luke 6:35; εὐχαριστέω: Luke 17:16; 18:11; 22:17, 19; εὐχαριστία: Acts 24:3; χάρις: Luke 1:30; 2:40, 52; 4:22; 6:32, 33, 34; 17:9; Acts 2:47; 4:33; 6:8; 7:10, 46; 11:23; 13:43; 14:3, 26; 15:11, 40; 18:27; 20:24, 32; 24:27; 25:3, 9; χαρίζομαι: Luke 7:21, 42, 43; Acts 8:14; 25:11, 16; 27:24; χαριτόω: Luke 1:28). Therefore, it is argued, this profuseness of Lukan usage points to the evangelist's adept literary accommodation to the dominant leitmotif of the Graeco-Roman benefaction system. However, the objection is not insurmountable. While it could be legitimately argued that χάρις represents Luke's redaction for the Matthean μισθός ('reward': Matt 5:12//Luke 6:23), Matthew's own use of μισθός could equally be redactional, being a favourite of the evangelist, used some 10 times in his Gospel (Ranjar, *Be Merciful Like the Father*, 86). More likely Luke's explosion of 'grace' language was occasioned by the impetus of Jesus' radical re-definition of the reciprocity system in terms of gift-giving without any expectation of recompense. Thus Jesus' rejection of reciprocity ethics through the paradigm of the unconditioned mercy of God towards his enemies is expanded upon throughout the Gospel of Luke in the evangelist's presentation of beneficence under the rubric of the operation of divine χάρις. In other words, we must not mistake in this instance the historical phenomenon of social innovation for mere literary dependence upon popular tropes or as an expression of the redactional activities of the evangelist.

[94] For discussions of the Golden Rule, see Dihle, *Die Goldene Regel*; Furnish, *The Love Command in the New Testament*; Schottroff, *Essays on the Love Commandment*; Piper, 'Love Your Enemies'; Perkins, *Love Commands in the New Testament*; W. Klassen, *Love of Enemies: The Way to Peace* (Philadelphia: Fortress, 1984); idem, 'The Authenticity of the Command'; D. Flusser, 'Jesus, His Ancestry, and the Commandment of Love', in *Jesus' Jewishness: Exploring the Place of Jesus in Early Judaism*, ed. J.H. Charlesworth (New York: Crossroad, 1991), 153-76; Swartley, *The Love of the Enemy*; G. Theissen, 'Nonviolence and Love of Our Enemies'; P.S. Alexander, 'Jesus and the Golden Rule', in *Hillel and Jesus: Comparisons of Two Major Religious Leaders*, ed. J.H. Charlesworth and L.L. Johns (Minneapolis: Fortress, 1997), 363-96; Meier, *A Marginal Jew Volume 4*, 551-57. Meier (*A Marginal Jew Volume 4*, 557) argues that the historical Jesus did not teach the Golden Rule, though he concedes that his case is not 'airtight'. But why wouldn't Jesus endorse such a commonplace in Judaism and the Graeco-Roman world more generally? The real question is *how the logion functions* in Luke 6:27-36. For example, F. Bovon (*Luke 1: A Commentary on the Gospel of Luke 1.1-9.50* [Fortress: Minneapolis, 2002], 241), expounding the Golden Rule in Luke 6:31, proposes that 'Christian ethics in Luke aim at a new form of reciprocity, with its roots in God'. This, however, is still too minimalist an interpretation. Rather, as L.T. Johnson (*The Gospel of Luke* [Collegeville: Michael Glazier/Liturgical Press, 1991], 112) argues, 'Luke has Jesus demand of his followers a standard for human relationships that involves a "going beyond" or "more" than the norm of reciprocity, of *do ut des*. The "golden rule" of "do as you want done" is not the ultimate norm here, but rather, "do as God would do"'.

[95] Bock, *Luke 1.1-9.50*; Johnson, *The Gospel of Luke*, 109; Just, *Luke 1:1-9:50*, 293.

[96] Note the comment of J.A. Fitzmyer (*The Gospel According to Luke I-IX* (New York: Doubleday, 1981), 639-40: 'It is useless to try to establish that the positive form used by Jesus in Matthew and Luke is actually superior to the negative; it all depends on *the context* in which the rule is set' (emphasis added).

in its orientation,[97] Jesus opts for the more positive rendering of the Golden Rule found in some quarters of Judaism (e.g. TNaph. 1; 2 En. 61.1). The reason why Jesus prefers the Golden Rule over the Levitical love command is because of its strong emphasis on 'doing' (Luke 6:31: ποῖωσιν, ποιεῖτε). In a bold move, Jesus expands the boundaries of beneficence from the 'neighbour' to the 'enemy' (Luke 6:27: καλῶς ποιεῖτε).[98] Further, by insisting that his disciples do good to the enemy (Luke 6:35: ἀγαθοποιεῖτε), Jesus destroys the *do ut des* expectation of the Graeco-Roman reciprocity system (6:33-34, 35 ['expecting nothing in return']).

Therefore, v. 31 looks back to vv. 27-30. In including the enemy within the boundaries of beneficence,[99] Jesus asserts his messianic understanding of the Kingdom community (Luke 6:27a; cf. 4:16-21; 7:18-23 [Isaiah 35:5-6; 52:7; 61:1-2; 11QMelchizedek 2.13-13-20; 4Q521]) over the restriction of the love command to covenantal members (Lev 19:18a, 18b).[100] Jesus also sets his messianic understanding against the negative expression of the love command in Second Temple Judaism. So far Jesus' critique is confined to the intra-mural debates of Judaism.

But v. 31 also looks forward to vv. 32-36. Here Jesus moves beyond the Torah-based controversies of his contemporaries to a cross-cultural critique of the ancient reciprocity system per se. There is nothing improbable about attributing this strategy to the historical Jesus. The reciprocity system reached from the imperial rulers to the Herods, embracing both the Sadducean and Pharisaic parties,[101] as much as the local benefactors in the villages and larger cities of Palestine. These networks of privilege and status defined in advance who the 'neighbour' was and who was worthy of beneficence. Furthermore, as noted, Philo, Ben-Sira, and later rabbinic traditions were critical of the Graeco-Roman benefaction system.[102] By contrast, Jesus' Kingdom community of the marginalized (Luke 14:13-14, 21-24), founded on divine mercy towards the enemy (6:36), experienced and embodied an overflow of divine grace (6:38) that would eventually challenge the social relations of the day (22:24-27). Jesus' critique of the reciprocity system represented an important building block in this new social vision.[103]

4. Conclusion

'Q' studies have flourished in the Third Quest for the historical Jesus. The possibility is sometimes overlooked that 'Q' might render independent historical traditions regarding Jesus' critique of social relations in the Jewish and Graeco-Roman world. We have argued that the 'Q' tradition of Luke 6:27-36 is a case in point.

---

97 Sources cited by Marshall, *Commentary on Luke*, 262. Contra, see Ranjar, *Be Merciful Like the Father*, 187: 'Luke presents the Golden Rule without the support of the Hebrew Scriptures'.
98 Green, *The Gospel of Luke*, 273.
99 Note the astute observation of D. Flusser regarding the mentality of the writers of the Dead Sea Scrolls ('A New Sensitivity in Judaism and the Christian Message', *HTR* 61 [1968], 107-27, here 121): 'The biblical command of mutual love is in the Scrolls restricted to the Sons of Light (1QS i.9-11) and is paralleled by the sectarian command of hatred towards the Sons of Darkness'.
100 On Jesus' messianic consciousness, see C.A. Evans, 'Jesus and the Messianic Texts from Qumran: A Preliminary Assessment of the Recently Published Materials', in *Idem, Jesus and His Contemporaries: Comparative Studies* (Leiden-New York-Köln, 1995), 83-154, esp. 118-24, 128-29.
101 For client-patron relationships in the high priesthood of Caiaphas, see H.K. Bond, *Caiaphas: Friend of Rome and Judge of Jesus?* (Louisville: Westminster John Knox Press, 2004), 43.
102 See above n.17 and §2.2 above.
103 Ranjar (*Be Merciful Like the Father*, 191) writes: '(Luke) also intends to overturn the popular notion of human reciprocity and, at the same time, to emphasize God's grace on those who go beyond the normal human practice of reciprocity'.

By the first century A.D., the reciprocity system shaped social relations in the eastern Mediterranean basin, flowing from the capital of the imperial rulers to the palaces of the Herods to the villages of Galilee. As important as reciprocity was for social stability, there were dissenting voices, including Philo and Ben Sira in a Jewish context, that were critical of the darker social realities behind the benefaction system. Luke 6:27-36 presents Jesus as one such figure.

Jesus emerges as one who critiques the reciprocity-based social relations of his day. According to the messianic perspective of Jesus, his eschatological community of the marginalised, at least as depicted in Luke 4:18-19 and 14:12-14, 21,[104] would extend beneficence to those in need without any expectation of return. We are witnessing the emergence of a new understanding of divine and human χάρις—pressed down, shaken together, running over (Luke 6:38)—that would up-end the ancient benefaction system and undermine our perception of those we treat as our 'enemy'.

---

[104] Luke, however, reveals elsewhere that there were also socially high-placed believers who belonged to Jesus' eschatological community (e.g. Luke 8:2-3, 27; Acts 6:7; 13:7, 12; 16:14; 17:33; 18:8).

Digging, Going Deep, Laying a Foundation

Luke 6:48, Ancient Building and Cultural Communication

CHRIS SPARK

In comparison to Matthew's version of the parable of the two builders (Matthew 7:24-27), Luke's rendition (Luke 6:47-49) is 'similar in content but almost as different in wording and in the way the story is constructed as it would be possible to be while relating the same teaching' (France 2007, 296). As for much other material shared only by the Gospels of Matthew and Luke ('Q' material), scholars have postulated many reasons for, and implications from, the differences between the two renditions. One striking difference which is often noted is the fact that Luke includes a short but vivid description of the building process of the first house, a description which Matthew completely lacks. In Luke 6:48, when speaking of a man who built a house, Jesus says:

> ἔσκαψεν καὶ ἐβάθυνεν καὶ ἔθηκεν θεμέλιον ἐπὶ τὴν πέτραν
> 'he dug and went deep and laid a foundation on the rock'[1]

It is most often assumed by commentators that Luke added this short narrative sequence to the story, and in a way that reflects Hellenistic building practice.[2] Usually it is claimed Luke did this in order to help his Greco-Roman readers relate to the story. A few scholars dispute this and say it fits well into Judean and Galilean building practice.[3] However, proffered evidence on both sides is usually light, if presented at all. This article seeks to consider how likely it is that Luke has added this sequence, by examining ancient building practice, both in the wider Greco-Roman world (as described by Vitruvius' standard architectural work), and in Jewish territories (as seen especially in archaeological finds from the Galilean area where Jesus spent much of his time). This exploration

---

1 All translations are mine unless otherwise noted. Matthew does have the words ἐπὶ τὴν πέτραν but lacks the rest of the phrase.
2 This majority view is noted by Bock (1994-1996, 1:621), and is put forward, for example, by Jeremias (1972, 26-27), Marshall (1978, 275, tentatively), Fitzmyer (1981-1985, 1:644, cf. 58) and Bovon (2002, 255 n. 67, cf. 9). Luz, though uncertain which version of the parable is more original, thinks Matthew's imagery is 'closer to the rural, Palestinian milieu' (2007, 385).
3 A notable example is Gundry (1994, 134). Davies and Allison (1988-1997, 1:721 n.47) and Bock (1994-1996, 1:621) consider the claim of intentional Hellenization here to be uncertain.

will potentially yield a better understanding of what Luke was trying to achieve, whether by addition or retention, through including this phrase.

Jeremias is typical of those who see Hellenizing in Luke's sequence when he says that 'in the translation into Greek' elements underwent '"translation" into terms of the Hellenistic environment', and this included 'the substitution of Hellenistic building technique' (1972, 26-27). In the footnote giving specifics, he notes with regards to Luke 6:47-48 'houses with cellars (not usual in Palestine)' (27, n. 9).[4] Luz similarly suggests that Luke's wider picture in the story is suggestive of 'a stone house over a cellar' in contrast to Matthew where 'the thought [...] is probably of mud houses' (2007, 385). Such a view is understandable, given Luke's language, that the builder not only 'dug' (ἔσκαψεν), but also that he 'went deep' (ἐβάθυνεν).

However, a number of questions can be raised about underlying assumptions. Firstly, is Luke's language actually speaking of a cellar? Could it not be simply digging deep for the laying of foundations? Secondly, if a cellar is envisaged here, then it remains to ask whether houses with cellars do indeed represent a particularly Greco-Roman style of building. Did such houses appear in the Jewish territories, and, if so, how common were they? But on the other hand, if a cellar is not necessarily in view, then was deep digging for foundations more of a Greco-Roman than a Jewish building practice?[5] In addition to these questions, the more 'standard' redaction-critical questions can also be asked, such as whether the language used here is particularly Lukan, and whether it therefore could be thought likely to have been added by him. These linguistic questions will be addressed first.

Linguistic factors

According to Bock, one linguistic factor within this sequence possibly points to a Judean/Galilean origin in early tradition—the repeated occurrence of καί (Bock 1994-1996, 1:621). This repetition is sometimes seen as reflecting Semitic use, hence therefore telling against a Lukan-Hellenistic generation of the sequence. Indeed, BDF (one of the sources Bock cites) does note Luke 6:48 as an example of '[p]arataxis instead of a supplementary or circumstantial participle' (§471.4), suggesting the participle βαθύνας would have been smoother than Luke's aorist finite verb (ἐβάθυνεν, which is connected with καί). Indeed, using a repeated καί, rather than a participle phrase, often reflects the Hebrew use of וְ (BDF §458). However this does not go far enough in helping decide whether or not Luke may have created this phrase, since Luke is not averse to Semitisms on the whole, especially when they reflect the style of the LXX (Wifstrand 2005, 30-36). In particular, Luke uses a repetition of καί in his unique ('L') material (Luke 15:8, where we might expect a participle phrase) and also retains the repeated καί in material he seems to have reworked considerably (18:32 [cf. Mark 10:33-34]).

---

4   Jeremias in this connection also mentions Luke 11:33, where he understands εἰς κρύπτην to refer to (not) putting a lamp into a cellar. Further, he notes 8:16 and 11:33 again as pointing to a house that has an entranceway for light to shine on those who enter, which he again says reflects Hellenistic building style. Many scholars agree (e.g. Fitzmyer 1981-85, 1:644, 719; Moxnes 1994, 380 n. 5; Flemming 2005, 251). Further still, in the parable of the two builders, Jeremias and others see other elements reflecting a perspective from outside Judea and Galilee, particularly the geography and phenomena of the river and flooding (Jeremias 1972, 27 n.11; Nolland 1989-1993, 1:310; Luz 2007, 385). Gundry questions the legitimacy of seeing Hellenization in Luke 6:47-49 in either the building description or that of geography and weather (1994, 134). All of this is noted to acknowledge that there is more to the question of Luke's Hellenization here than just the unique sequence in 6:48. But this article is dealing simply with this sequence, in order to contribute to the wider picture.

5   This seems to be what Nolland has in mind (1989-1993, 1:310).

Thus, while repeated καί may be Semitic in flavour, it is not out of keeping with Lukan style or preference, so it tells us very little about whether Luke created the sequence in 6:48 or not.

A potentially more fruitful linguistic investigation is that of the vocabulary used by Luke in this sequence. The sequence effectively consists of three verbal phrases. The first is based around the verb σκάπτω ('to dig'), which occurs only twice more in the New Testament, and on both occasions in parables from 'L' material (Luke 13:8; 16:3). In the LXX it occurs only in Isaiah 5:6 and its parallel, the Book of Odes 10:6, though Moulton and Milligan indicate that it occurs frequently in koine literature (1930, 576).[6] Given its New Testament occurrences are exclusively in Luke, it is not surprising that Denaux et al classify it as 'Lukan notable' (2009, 561). The second verb in the sequence, βαθύνω, referring to 'going deep', is a *hapax legomenon* in the New Testament, though it does appear three times in the LXX (Jer. 30:2, 25; Ps. 91:6), and a few times in Philo and Josephus.[7] It is difficult to deduce whether it is particularly Lukan given it is not used elsewhere by Luke or by other authors. The final phrase, ἔθηκεν θεμέλιον, is best considered as a unit. This is because, while τίθημι is a common word in Luke and in the wider New Testament, with θεμέλιος it occurs in the Gospels only here and once more in Luke 14:29 (yet another 'L' passage). Further, the only other place these words occur together in the New Testament is in 1 Corinthians 3:10-11, where they occur twice (they do not occur together in the LXX).[8] Again it is not surprising that Denaux et al consider it 'notable' (2009, 600).

So it would seem the language in the unique sequence in 6:48 is, on the whole, relatively 'Lukan', with σκάπτω being rare and having a tendency to occur in 'L' material, and ἔθηκεν θεμέλιον being Lukan amongst the Gospels, and again connected with 'L' material. This could indicate that Luke created this sequence, or equally that he shaped it in his own style, or again that it came from the same source as that of the other 'L' material.[9] A decision between these options may be impossible, and is certainly beyond the scope of this article.

With these linguistic observations in place, ancient building practices will now be considered, in order to see the contextual factors that may help illuminate Luke's building description.

Vitruvius and Greco-Roman building practice

Of the few surviving authorities on ancient architecture, 'none is as important as Vitruvius [...] whose *On Architecture* was penned under Augustus' patronage' (Richardson 2004, 9). This work seems likely to have been written before 27 B.C.E., and had become a standard work at least before the end of the first century C.E. (Granger 1931, 1: xiv-xv; cf. Johnson 2000, 125). Although the work was written in Latin rather than Greek, it nevertheless provides a good point of comparison as to whether the description of building in Luke 6:48 resonates with standard Greco-Roman practice.

Vitruvius outlines three important qualities in architecture: strength, utility and grace. He then vitally notes that '[a]ccount will be taken of *strength* when the foundations are carried down to the solid ground (*ad solidum depressio*), and when from each material there is a choice of supplies

---

6   The range of citations contained in the entry in LSJ similarly indicates that the term was commonly enough employed by Greek writers more generally (LSJ σκάπτω).
7   Philo: *Post.* 118; *Spec.* 2:172; 3:147; *Virt.* 158. Josephus: *B.J.* 1:405; 5:130, 512.
8   Very interestingly, this passage in 1 Corinthians speaks of Paul laying a foundation 'as a wise builder' that others are building on, and of that foundation being Jesus Christ. All of this is resonant with the themes in the parable of the two builders, and especially with Luke's specific emphasis on *the laying of good foundations*.
9   Davies and Allison consider the vocabulary in this part of Luke 6:48 to be 'typically Lukan' (1988-1997, 1:721).

without parsimony' (1.3.2 [Granger]). Such instructions about going deep to lay foundations on solid ground come up repeatedly throughout *On Architecture*. For instance, in speaking of the building of town walls and towers, he says: 'If such foundations can be found, they are to be dug down to the solid and in the solid' (1.5.1 [Granger]).[10] In a chapter on the foundations of temples, a very similar statement is made: 'Let the foundations of those works be dug from a solid site and to a solid base if it can be found' (3.4.1 [Granger]).[11] This repeated picture of carrying foundations deep down to solid ground clearly resonates with Luke's description in 6:48.

It might be objected that, apart from the general statement in 1.3.2 above, the examples cited are not for houses, which are the type of buildings in focus in Luke's sequence. However, in Vitruvius' section on how to ensure the stability and durability of houses (see 6.7.7), he notes that houses built level on the ground 'will no doubt last to a great age, if their foundations are laid in the manner which we have explained in the earlier books, with regard to city walls and theatres' (6.8.1 [Morgan]). Clearly again, this is to be considered standard practice. But as he continues directly, he reveals something else relevant to the present enquiry: 'But if underground rooms and vaults are intended, their foundations ought to be thicker than the walls which are to be constructed in the upper part of the house'. This plainly assumes it is not a *standard practice* to have cellars, and therefore also his previous statements about digging deep to lay foundations on solid ground are not primarily referring to the construction of buildings with cellars. Cellars were an option if desired, but if they were to be included, foundations remain vital for durability and strength.

From this brief engagement with Vitruvius, it seems that Luke's picture of the first builder's practice fits well with Greco-Roman building standards, and would likely sound familiar to Greco-Roman ears. A cellar need not be envisaged in Luke's words for this to be the case, and indeed Vitruvius' more general discussion of digging deep to lay foundations renders questionable the assumption that a cellar is envisaged—not that Jesus' words in Luke *could not* refer to a house with a cellar, but rather that the language Luke uses does not seem to *require* a cellar.

However another question still remains: is Luke's description of building shaped for Greco-Roman ears *in particular*—or would Jewish ears (including even those who heard Jesus originally) have recognised this picture just as well? This question can be approached through a consideration of Galilean archaeological finds.

Jewish building practice in Galilean towns

As noted earlier, a counter-claim is sometimes made to the idea that Luke 6:48 reflects Greco-Roman building practice, namely, that Jewish buildings sometimes have just the sort of architecture envisaged by Jesus' words in Luke. Gundry, who makes this counter-claim, points to a rabbinical reference to excavation in *Yal.* 1.766 (Num. 23.9; Gundry 1994, 134). Regarding cellars

---

10 This somewhat opaque sentence is clarified in Morgan's translation: 'Dig down to solid bottom, if it can be found, and lay them therein, going as deep as the magnitude of the proposed work seems to require'.

11 The similarity of this to the statement about walls, and therefore the likelihood that this was a standard expectation of Vitruvius, can be seen even more clearly when the Latin of the two phrases are placed next to each other (slightly extended from the sentence quoted in English above to show the fullness of the parallel):

   1.5.1 (on walls):
   si queat inveniri, ad solidum et in solido, quantum ex amplitudine operis pro ratione videatur

   3.4.1 (on temples):
   si queat inveniri, ad solidum et in solido, quantum ex amplitudine operis pro ratione videbitur

in particular, Keener notes in passing that they were 'not uncommon in Palestinian houses', even if 'used more often in Greek architecture' (1993, on Luke 6:46-49). Archaeological work carried out on sites in Galilee enables such claims to be assessed as to whether they to provide a Judean/Galilean counterpart to the picture drawn from Vitruvius.[12]

In the first section of his book *Building Jewish in the Roman East*, Peter Richardson presents findings from archaeological sites in Galilee, particularly from Khirbet Qana (about 13km north of Nazareth), Yodefat (about half way between the Sea of Galilee and the Mediterranean), and Gamla (a town in the Golan heights, east of the northern tip of the Sea of Galilee).[13] This region, of course, is generally speaking the area where Jesus grew up according to the Gospels, and also where both Matthew and Luke present him as delivering the parable of the two builders, as part of his Galilean ministry. So, at the very least, the houses that were in these regions were the kinds of dwellings that would be familiar to Jesus as Luke presents him and to those listening to Jesus as Luke presents them.[14] Additionally, according to Katherina Galor, the area of Galilee and Golan is '[m]ore thoroughly surveyed than other regions of Palestine' (2010, 424). This more thorough surveying presents us with some other data with which to compare Richardson's presentation. Even so, some caution is warranted as we deal with this evidence: 'Since houses were often occupied for centuries, their evidence is usually complex […and] data for the study of first-century houses is still somewhat sparse and not broadly available' (2004, 75).[15] Nevertheless, even with this caution heeded, on balance, the available material is both relevant and illuminating for this study.[16]

Firstly, Richardson demonstrates that, at a general level, there was a fair amount of Hellenistic influence on building in Galilee. For instance, the Greek style of Hippodamian planning seems to have influenced all three towns to a surprising degree, even if it is merely an influence, rather than a strict following of a Hippodamian design (Richardson 2004, 45, 57-58,c f. 61).[17] Corbo also notes Roman influence in Capernaum, another Galilean town of note for Jesus' ministry according to the Gospels, in that the pavements were made in a way that imitated the paving of Roman roads (1969, 39). Further, with a view to the wider Jewish territories (but specifically citing as examples

---

12 In addition to the evidence we are about to consider, Plummer notes the interesting testimony of Edward Robinson (Plummer 1901, 193). Robinson was in the region of Nazareth on Sunday 17th June, 1838, when he visited the new, not quite completed house of Abu Nâsir. He says of his host: 'In order to lay the foundations, he had dug down to the solid rock, as is usual throughout the country; here to the depth of thirty feet, and then built up arches'. (Robinson and Smith 2015, 338) While this is obviously centuries removed from Jesus' time and only distantly related to Luke's building description, it is interesting that the *need* to dig very deep to bedrock in order to lay foundations was present in the area where, according to the Gospels, Jesus grew up.

13 See Richardson 2004, 45-46, 55-56, 57-58. Khirbet Qana is the site usually preferred by scholars for the Cana of John's Gospel, reinforcing the connection of this area to Jesus (Richardson 2004, 55-56; Douglas 1996, 161; Keener 1993, on John 2:1). Yodefat is a town that Josephus attempted (and failed) to defend from Vespasian and Titus in A.D. 67, as seen in B.J. 3:145-349, where it is called Ἰωτάπατα.

14 Although Matthew (4:25) and Luke (6:17) both have people from various regions listening to Jesus during his Galilean ministry, it is still a *Galilean* ministry, so we would expect people from the Galilean region to be numerous amongst those listening to him.

15 Virgilio Corbo notes this sort of complexity in the particular case of a house in Capernaum, traditionally known as Peter's house, which was used over centuries and had a church built on its site (1969, 39).

16 Galor expresses considerable confidence in the outcomes of archaeological studies on domestic architecture: 'Based on the evidence available from the literary sources and the abundant archaeological material of late, we are able to reconstruct the physical appearance of ancient dwellings in Roman-Byzantine Palestine with a rather high degree of accuracy' (2010, 435). While Richardson's and Corbo's caution is wise when it comes to details, Galor's optimism about general accuracy of our understanding of domestic architecture seems reasonable.

17 Hippodamian planning is a Greek method of city design dating from the fifth century B.C.E., being 'a grid plan that divides the residential areas into symmetrical blocks separated by right-angle dissecting streets' (Ortiz 2000, 107; cf. Kelley 2016, n.p.).

the Galilean locales Sepphoris and Gamla), Galor notes that more Greco-Roman elements, '[c]olumns, decorative stucco revetments, mosaic floors, and fresco decorations', are found in both large cities and small towns, in places known to be exposed to international trade and those more isolated and culturally insulated (2010, 435). A general, sharp differentiation between Greco-Roman and Jewish building is therefore not to be claimed too easily.

A number of relevant connections to Luke's picture emerge from the more specific description of the remains of houses in the Galilean towns described by Richardson. First of all, some houses did have cellars. For instance, a photograph in the illustration section of Richardson's book shows terraced housing on the east side of Khirbet Qana, where the 'basement of the higher-level house has survived, with early Roman walls and Byzantine period flagstone floor and steps' (2004, caption of Plate 13). Galor also notes that cellars were one possibility for storerooms in Jewish dwellings (2010, 433). Further, rock cut foundations were not uncommon, even where there were not basements, as Richardson observed in Yodefat, in both terraced housing on the steep east slope and in less steep areas (77, 78, cf. Plate 6). Both the presence of cellars and the hard work of cutting foundations into rock give us a picture of careful building which, although not exactly the same as Luke 6:48, is similar enough to ensure that people from this area would have found it easy to relate to the picture Jesus was painting.

Yet the picture is still more complex. In Yodefat, Richardson notes most houses were of very simple construction, using mud in part, and often 'ground floors were equally simple, of beaten earth or roughly leveled exposed bedrock, and occasionally plaster or rough flagstone' (76-77). A similar picture emerges in Capernaum from Corbo's excavations, where almost all the habitations 'had a floor made of black basalt stones' and 'the stones do not rest on beds of lime but on earth' (1969, 39). This contrasts with the picture of deeply dug or worked foundations. But, again, on the other hand, there is notable variation. For example, an 'elite house' on a hilltop in Khirbet Qana, which seems to have come at least in part from early Roman times (Richardson 2004, 104), was presumably better built for it certainly had more lavish decorations and materials. Galor also notes that '[f]looring materials in ancient Palestine varied greatly', and that 'flooring was usually a clear reflection of the owner's economic means and the house's standard of construction' (2010, 432).

So in summary, there was considerable variation in Galilean building (as well as that in wider Jewish territories). This variation was both in terms of general building practice (including the presence of Hellenistic influence), and in terms of the presence and absence of cellars and deeper foundation work in different cases. The Galilean towns considered here, let alone those in the wider Jewish territories, did not simply have mud houses, and did not have a single standard type of building.

Answering questions about Jewish building, Greco-Roman building, and Luke

In the light of both Vitruvius and Galilean archaeology, what can be said to answer the questions asked earlier regarding Luke's building description?

Firstly, was a cellar necessarily envisaged? Vitruvius demonstrates that considerable foundation work, and the idea of digging deep, was standard Greco-Roman practice for building a strong house, whether or not a cellar was involved. Luke's language in saying the builder 'dug and went deep' (ἔσκαψεν καὶ ἐβάθυνεν) does not necessarily refer to a cellar, and Vitruvius' similar language (albeit in Latin) suggests that the assumption of a cellar is unnecessary. Further, there were indeed houses with cellars in Jewish territories, often built into rock, even in the towns of the Galilean area in which Jesus operated according to the Gospels. Secondly, as to whether cellars were a particularly non-Jewish feature, even if a cellar were envisaged here (as seems unlikely), a Jewish audience would be familiar with the idea of some strong houses having cellars. These may have been less common in the Jewish territories than in the wider Greco-Roman world, but Vitruvius does not give reason to think they were a standard feature of Greco-Roman building either.

When we ask the third question, whether deep digging for foundations was more of a Greco-Roman than a Jewish building practice, the answer can only be 'perhaps to a degree, but not entirely'. Vitruvius does emphasise foundations and their importance for strong building, and, being a standard work, this may mean that this was prominent in the Greco-Roman expectation of quality building. But at the same time, there is good evidence that well-built houses often had good foundations in Galilee, dug into rock, even if many houses were of simpler construction. When this fact is combined with the presence of Hellenistic influence on building even in rural Galilee, it seems clear that contrasting Jewish and Greco-Roman building practices must be done cautiously. A simple contrast of houses with cellars being Greco-Roman and those without being Jewish, or a statement that deeply dug foundations show a non-Jewish perspective, is not legitimate. Therefore conclusions about Luke creating this building description in order to relate to Greco-Roman hearers seem to be over reaching. From the evidence assembled here, it would be possible that he did create it, *or* that he reshaped a tradition he received from the early Christian community, which could go back to Jesus' own teaching in Judea and Galilee.[18]

Jesus' description of the building of the house in Luke 6:48 would have indeed sounded like houses with which Greco-Roman readers were familiar. But at the same time, the evidence allows the safe conclusion that Jewish hearers would also have recognised that he was describing a kind of very well built house known to their experience. If Luke did have Greco-Roman hearers especially in mind (as seems likely for his Gospel generally),[19] this description would have spoken to their understanding of building solid houses. However it would very likely have spoken to Jewish ears almost as clearly. In 6:48, Luke's Jesus speaks to the wider Mediterranean world, but he also speaks to people in his homeland.[20]

Bibliography

Barnett, Paul. 1999. *Jesus & the Rise of Early Christianity: a History of New Testament Times.* Downers Grove: IVP Academic.

Blass, Friedrich, Albert Debrunner and Robert W. Funk. 1961. *A Greek Grammar of the New Testament and other early Christian literature.* Translation and revision of the 9th-10th German ed., incorporating supplementary notes. Chicago: University of Chicago Press.

---

18 Alternatively, Luke could have included a statement that was already shaped by oral tradition—if so, it would probably be the same tradition source that shaped the other parts of the 'L' material that share similar language as noted earlier. Although this is a real possibility, it seems less likely than that the language reflects Luke's own style.

19 See Harnack 1907, 119 n.2; 126 n.1; Barnett 1999, 378; Bock 1994-1996, 1:14-15; Bruce 1988, 11-13; Caird 1963, 44; Fitzmyer 1981-85, 1:57-59.

20 Thanks are due to Professor Paul Trebilco of the University of Otago, and Dr Peter Bolt of the Sydney College of Divinity, for guidance and assistance with access to resources for this article.

Bock, Darrell L. 1994-1996. *Luke*. 2 vols. Baker Exegetical Commentary on the New Testament. Grand Rapids: Baker Academic.

Bovon, François. 2002. *Luke 1: a Commentary on the Gospel of Luke 1:1-9:50*. Edited by Helmut Koester. Translated by Christine M. Thomas. Hermeneia. Minneapolis: Fortress. Translation of *Evangelium Nach Lukas: 1;* EKK; Zurich: Benziger, 1989.

Bruce, F. F. 1988. *The Book of the Acts*. The New International Commentary on the New Testament. Revised Edition. Grand Rapids: Eerdmans.

Caird, George B. 1963. *The Gospel of St Luke*. The Pelican New Testament Commentaries. Middlesex: Penguin.

Corbo, Virgilio. 1969. *The House of St. Peter at Capharnaum: a Preliminary Report of the First Two Campaigns of Excavations, April 16-June 19, Sept. 12-Nov. 26, 1968*. Translated by Sylvester Saller. Jerusalem: Franciscan Printing Press.

Davies, W. D. and D. C. Allison. 1988-1997. *The Gospel According to St Matthew*. 3 vols. International Critical Commentary. Edinburgh: T. & T. Clark.

Denaux, Adelbert, Rita Corstjens and Hellen Mardaga. 2009. *The Vocabulary of Luke: An Alphabetical Presentation and a Survey of Characteristic and Noteworthy Words and Word Groups in Luke's Gospel*. Biblical Tools and Studies 10. Leuven: Peeters.

Douglas, J.D. 1996. 'Cana.' Page 161 in *New Bible Dictionary*. Edited by D. R. W., Wood and I. H. Marshall. Third ed. Downers Grove: IVP.

Fitzmyer, Joseph A. 1981-1985. *The Gospel According to Luke: Introduction, Translation and Notes*. 2 vols. Anchor Bible 28. New York: Doubleday.

Flemming, Dean. 2005. *Contextualization in the New Testament: Patterns for Theology and Mission*. Downers Grove: IVP.

France, R.T. 2007. *The Gospel of Matthew*. New International Commentary on the New Testament. Grand Rapids: Eerdmans.

Galor, Katherina. 2010. 'Domestic Architecture'. Pages 420-39 in *The Oxford Handbook of Jewish Daily Life in Roman Palestine*. Edited by Catherine Hezser. Oxford: Oxford University Press.

Granger, Frank. 1931. 'Introduction'. Pages ix-xxxi in Vitruvius, *On Architecture*. Translated by Frank Granger. 2 vols. Loeb Classical Library. Cambridge, MA: Harvard University Press.

Gundry, R.H. 1994. *Matthew: A Commentary on His Handbook for a Mixed Church Under Persecution*. 2nd ed. Grand Rapids: Eerdmans.

Harnack, Adolf von. 1907. *Luke, the Physician: the Author of the Third Gospel and the Acts of the Apostles*. Translated by J R Wilkinson. English ed. London: Williams & Norgate.

Jeremias, Joachim. 1972. *The Parables of Jesus*. Translated by S. H. Hooke. 3rd edition. London: SCM. Translation of *Die Gleichnisse Jesu*; fifth edition; Gottingen: Vandenhoeck and Ruprecht, 1970.

Johnson, Dianne B. 2000. 'Art and Architecture: Greco-Roman.' Pages 121-25 in *Dictionary of New Testament Background: A Compendium of Contemporary Biblical Scholarship*. Edited by Stanley E.

Porter and Craig A. Evans. Downers Grove: IVP.

Keener, Craig S. 1993. *The IVP Bible Background Commentary: New Testament*. Downers Grove: IVP.

Kelley, Justin L. 2016. 'Dor.' In *The Lexham Bible Dictionary*. Edited by J. D. Barry et al. (Electronic edition.) Bellingham: Lexham Press.

Liddell, H.G., and R. Scott. 1996. *A Greek-English Lexicon*. 9th ed. revised and augmented by Henry Stuart Jones, with the assistance of Roderick McKenzie. Supplement edited by P. G. W. Glare. Oxford: Clarendon.

Luz, Ulrich. 2007. *Matthew 1–7: a commentary on Matthew 1–7*. H. Koester, Ed. Revised ed. Minneapolis: Fortress Press.

Marshall, I. Howard. 1978. *The Gospel of Luke: A Commentary in the Greek Text*. New International Greek Testament Commentary. Exeter: Paternoster.

Moulton, James Hope, and George Milligan. 1930. *The Vocabulary of the Greek Testament: Illustrated from the Papyri and Other Non-Literary Sources*. Grand Rapids: Eerdmans.

Moxnes, Halvor. 1994. 'The Social Context of Luke's Community.' *Interpretation* 48/4: 379-89.

Nolland, John. 1989-1993. *Luke*. 3 vols. Word Biblical Commentary 35. Dallas: Word.

Ortiz, Stephen M. 2000. 'Archaeology of the Land of Israel.' Pages 100-111 in *Dictionary of New Testament Background: A Compendium of Contemporary Biblical Scholarship*. Edited by Stanley E. Porter and Craig A. Evans. Downers Grove: IVP.

Plummer, Alfred. 1910. *A Critical and Exegetical Commentary on the Gospel According to St. Luke*. Fourth ed. International Critical Commentary. Edinburgh: T. & T. Clark

Richardson, Peter. 2004. *Building Jewish in the Roman East*. Waco, TX: Baylor University Press.

Robinson, Edward, and Eli Smith. 2015 (1857). *Biblical Researches in Palestine and the Adjacent Regions, Volume 2*. Third ed. Cambridge: Cambridge University Press.

Vitruvius Pollio. 1914. *Vitruvius: The Ten Books on Architecture*. M.H. Morgan, Ed. Medford: Oxford University Press.

Vitruvius Pollio. 1931. *On Architecture*. Translated by Frank Granger. 2 vols. Loeb Classical Library. Cambridge, MA: Harvard University Press.

Wifstrand, Albert. 2005. 'Luke and the Septuagint'. Pages 28–45 in *Epochs and Styles: Selected Writings on the New Testament, Greek Language and Greek Culture in the Post-Classical Era*. Edited by Lars Rydbeck and Stanley E. Porter. Translated from the Swedish Originals by Denis Searby. Wissenschaftliche Untersuchungen zum Neuen Testament 179. Tübingen: Mohr Siebeck.

What Actually Happened on Resurrection Morning?
A Clear and Simple Account

PETER G. BOLT

1. Rationalism, Resurrection, and Robust Reading

To ask 'what actually happened on resurrection morning?' is an historical question.[1] It is a perfectly legitimate task for the narrative critic to explain the four resurrection narratives in terms of their literary art.[2] It is still a legitimate task for a redaction critic to identify how earlier sources were edited into a final form to suit the church of the editor's day.[3] But in view of centuries of historical skepticism and a resultant disillusionment about even the possibility of recovering the historical events behind the texts, it must be asserted that it remains a legitimate and essential task to pursue the question: what actually happened?

In order to answer historical questions, all available literary sources need to be considered, as well as contextual evidence such as topography and archaeological remains. The historian of the Gospels is well supplied with sources. Like Socrates, Jesus of Nazareth made such an impact on the people of his times that the problem is not too few, but too many sources of information about him. The four Gospels which were recognized from their first reception as authoritative remain at the core of any historical enquiry, each providing an account of Jesus which draws upon numerous eyewitness reports.[4] Given the importance of multiple attestation for the historian, comparing this material has been a staple of Gospels research for centuries.

However, alongside the privilege of multiple sources comes the challenge presented by their differing versions of the same events. Historical research is necessarily empirical, for the historian can only work with the records and remains that have survived, and negotiating such differences in the evidence is a normal and necessary part of any empirical historical analysis. Since the Gospels arise from the ordinary life of the first century, it is no surprise that comparing the good evidence for Jesus also yields points of

---

1   An earlier popular-level version of this article was published in *Southern Cross*, May 2012. It has been further developed in 2018 through presentations to the SCD Centre for Gospels Research and to the ANZATS conference in Brisbane, as well as being delivered as the Rev Han, Kyung-Jik Co-memorial Lecture, at Soongsil University, Seoul, South Korea.
2   E.g. Moloney, *The Resurrection of the Messiah*.
3   E.g. Bode, *The First Easter Morning*.

4   For a renewed interest in eyewitnesses, see Bauckham, *Jesus and the Eyewitnesses*.

difference between the sources.

Unfortunately, for centuries Gospels scholarship has been from without confronted by (e.g. Celsus; Porphyry), and from within labouring under a rationalistic approach which demands greater precision and uniformity from the Gospels texts than the complexities of ordinary life and conversation—in the present, let alone the past—can or do deliver. In 1983, reflecting upon this enduring tendency within the New Testament guild—and especially within his own Tübingen heritage—Martin Hengel noted that:

> The destructive skepticism, a particular feature of the modern world, which works in a predominantly analytical way, often ultimately ends up, not by furthering real historical understanding but by making it impossible.[5]

Over a decade later, he expressed his continued frustration with New Testament scholarship:

> There is a radical form of criticism which in the end must be said to be uncritical, because it wants neither really to understand the sources nor to interpret them, but basically destroys them in order to make room for its own fantastic constructions.[6]

At that same time, he spoke of:

> the spreading inability within our unhappy "New Testament scholarship" to study ancient sources and use them to argue historically […] In any case it is easier to keep hawking round scholastic clichés and old prejudices pseudo-critically and without closer examination, than to occupy oneself with the varied ancient sources which are often difficult to interpret and remote.[7]

As one of the Tübingen fathers of this 'uncritical criticism', D.F. Strauss not only illustrates the problem, but in large part his work had a significant role in ensuring the rationalistic approach became entrenched in Gospels research. He did not approach the accounts of the resurrection of Jesus from an empirical starting point, but from a rationalistic *a priori* analysis of 'the proposition: a dead man has returned to life'. Resolving the illogicality of that statement requires that the man was either not dead, or not subsequently alive.[8] The previous hopelessness of the disciples is sufficient to overturn the objection, as old as Celsus, that, being friends rather than enemies, the witnesses are not impartial.[9] But even if there might be grounds to be open to the possibility that this illogicality had somehow been overturned by historical reality, the differences in the resurrection narratives present an insurmountable problem.

> We might rest satisfied with the evangelical testimonies in favour of the resurrection were but these testimonies in the first place sufficiently precise, and in the second, in agreement with themselves and with each other […]
>
> [compared to the 'general and vague' reports in Paul] the more fully detailed narratives of the Gospels, in which the resurrection of Jesus appears as an objective fact, are, from the contradictions of which they are convicted, incapable of being used as evidence.[10]

However, rather than adopting such 'divide and conquer' methods—which unfortunately still live on, fed by the same skeptical rationalism—an empirical historical method listens carefully to the available sources, and works with the 'discrepancies' in the sources—which are entirely normal and true to ordinary life and

---

5 Hengel, *Between Jesus and Paul*, xiv.
6 Hengel & Schwemer, 'Preface', *Paul Between Damascus and Antioch*, ix.
7 Hengel & Schwemer, *Paul Between Damascus and Antioch*, 15; and again: 'Scholars should read more ancient texts and less hypercritical and scholastic secondary literature', p.11.

8 Strauss, *Life of Jesus*, 735–736.
9 Strauss, *Life of Jesus*, 738.
10 Strauss, *Life of Jesus*, 739.

communication— in order to arrive at a coherent account of what actually happened. Properly listening to the sources requires going beyond a mere 'bookish' comparison of the surface details of the texts to hear the voices of the eyewitnesses that may (or may not) lie behind them. A coherent account then sets both texts and eyewitnesses into the historical and social context of what was real life for them at the time. It also views the reports within the sequence of events that gave rise to them and also those which resulted from them, and within the network of relationships amongst themselves and others caught up in the same events. For the reports and the movement are mutually illuminating. A coherent historical account must also have plausibility, not when set against the rationalistic propositions of a later age of armchair critics, but when set against the historical realities which pertain to the original events, insofar as they can be known. When destructive rationalism is replaced with a robust empirical method, rather than differences too quickly becoming contradictions disqualifying the sources from providing any understanding of underlying events, careful exposition of each source in relation to the others may actually lead the historian to see how they dovetail to yield an even fuller perspective on those events than can be derived from any of them taken in isolation.[11]

Such empirical enquiry brings the historian to very different conclusions. For example, Hengel's robust historical method led him to the conclusion that:

> earliest Christianity [was] an intrinsically connected and in essentials quite amazingly coherent movement which developed out of the activity of Jesus and the "saving event" of his crucifixion and resurrection.[12]

Of the two parts of this 'saving event', even Strauss could see 'the precise and internally consistent attestation of [Jesus'] death', but various contradictions in the accounts caused him to 'be induced to doubt the reality of the resurrection'.[13] This article aims to show that, to the contrary, when read from a robust empirical perspective, the four accounts can be seen to dovetail nicely to yield a coherent account of the events of resurrection morning. Rather than reading them rationalistically, leading to despair about ever answering the historical question, it is possible to give a clear and simple account that is true to the sources, takes account of other relevant historical information, and thoroughly plausible in regard to the people involved at the time.[14]

Whereas detractors of the Christian message claim that the four accounts of Jesus' resurrection contain discrepancies that are irreconcilable and so fatal to the Gospels'

---

11 The normal and thoroughly legitimate historical quest for coherence through dovetailing sources should not be written off by using 'harmonisation' as a swear word. See, for example, Strauss, *Life of Jesus*, 710, who derogates 'the artifices of the harmonisers'.

12 Hengel, *Between Jesus and Paul*, xi.

13 Strauss, *Life of Jesus*, 739.

14 Because decisions need to be made about the evidence at almost every step, other accounts can also be given—as will be (partially) shown in the footnotes. But the possibility of alternative accounts does not negate the historical enterprise. The rationalistic drive for absolute certainty may be appropriate for an invented system like mathematics, but it founders on the complexities of ordinary life, both in the present and in the past. Given the nature of those complexities, the presence of alternative conclusions about the same historical evidence is completely predictable and generates the need for further discussion about which alternative best explains all the evidence. But such discussions do not operate from an assumption of incoherence, but are framed by a basic commitment to uncovering coherence. This article aims to show that (at least one) coherent account can be given of the accounts of Jesus' resurrection in the canonical Gospels.

authenticity and truth,[15] the extraordinary events of that amazing day can be told in a clear and simple account.

2. A Dawn Discovery

It was Sunday, the 5th April A.D. 33,[16] and the action began around dawn.

Interpreters have been troubled by the differences between the Gospels in reporting the time of day.[17] Did the women arrive 'early, while it was still dark' (πρωΐ σκοτίας ἔτι οὔσης, John 20:1); 'at deep dawn' (ὄρθρου βαθέως, Luke 24:1); 'early ... at the [day's] dawning' (Ὀψὲ ... τῇ ἐπιφωσκούσῃ, Matt. 28:10; cf. Luke 23:54); or 'very early ... when' —or even 'after'— 'the sun had risen' (λίαν πρωΐ ... ἀνατείλαντος τοῦ ἡλίου, Mark 16:1).

Because the women did not attend the grave at a point in time, but across a period, these differences can be explained by the phenomenology of dawn reflected in their slightly differing reports with which they informed the evangelists. In this regard, it is worth noting that astronomers distinguish three different 'dawns'. Prior to Astronomical Dawn, the sky is in absolute darkness and all heavenly bodies visible to the naked eye can be seen; during Nautical Dawn, most stars become visible to the naked eye, but artificial light is still necessary for outdoor activities; and after Civil Dawn only the brightest celestial objects can be seen with the naked eye and artificial light is no longer necessary.[18] In addition, astronomical calculations enable the time of the women's visit to the tomb to be given with some precision (see Table 1).[19]

Table 1: Twilight on Resurrection Morning

Date	Astronomical Dawn	Nautical Dawn	Civil Dawn	Sunrise
9 April A.D. 30	4:56	5:26	5:55	6:19
5 April A.D. 33	5:00	5:29	5:58	6:23

In terms of the participants in the events at that early hour, exactly three women were involved.

---

15 E.g. Strauss, *Life of Jesus*, 709–710, amongst other things, noticed differences in the number of women, the time of the visit, what the women saw on arrival at the tomb, what they see and learn at the tomb, the nature of their communication with the disciples, and whether or not other disciples visit the tomb.

16 Hoehner, *Chronological Aspects*, Ch. 5; Steinmann, *From Abraham to Paul*, Ch. 13. Although others have been suggested, the only real alternative would be 9 April A.D. 30.

17 E.g. Strauss, *Life of Jesus*, 709. However, the textual history shows that, well before Strauss, the early scribes were also worried about the timing. ἀνατείλαντος clearly has the support of the best and most ancient mss. However, while a competent Greek speaker would know that grammatically the aorist participle simply expresses attendant circumstances ('came to the tomb *while the sun was rising*'), it troubled those in the West, presumably because it was potentially past-referring. D has the present form ἀνατέλλοντος and several Old Latin texts (it^(c,d,n,q)) and authors (Tyconius, Augustine) followed that lead, and others omitted the entire expression (it^k according to UBS 5, but CNTTS associates this ms with the aorist participle). Even some later Greek mss inserted ἔτι 'still' (found in John 20:1, but in an entirely different expression), to make the sense of the aorist participle's attendant circumstances a little clearer (W Θ 1 017 034 038 041 565 1582* f1 Eusebius) ἔτι ἀνατ[ε]ίλαντος. Differing placement in the textual tradition may also indicate some discomfort with Luke's expression ὄρθρου βαθέως, which appears to conflict so strongly with Mark's.

18 www.timeanddate.com/astronomy/different-types-twilight.html.

19 Following Humphreys & Waddington, 'The Date of the Crucifixion', Table 1, the new moon fell on 22 March in A.D. 30, and 19 March in A.D. 33, giving the day of resurrection as 9 and 5 April respectively. Since these dates correspond with the phases of the moon in the years 2012 and 2007 (see www.timeanddate.com/moon/phases/israel/Jerusalem, for 2012 & 2007), these years have also been used to approximate data for sunrise for their first century counterparts (www.timeanddate.com/sun/israel/Jerusalem, for April 2012 and 2007).

1. Mary of Magdala was one of several women who had followed Jesus in Galilee, and who supported his mission financially (Luke 8:2-3; Mark 15:41a). Jesus had cast seven demons out of Mary Magdalene, and she stuck with him until the cross and his burial (Matt. 27:55, 61; Mark 15:40-41, 47; [16:9]; John 19:25).

2. The second woman, also named Mary, was the mother of James (the younger) and Joseph (Matt. 27:56; Mark 15:40; 16:1; Luke 24:10). John's Gospel also tells us that she was the wife of Cl[e]opas, and the sister-in-law of Jesus' own mother (John 19:25).[20] That is, the 'other Mary' (Matt. 27:61; 28:1) involved on this amazing day was Jesus' Aunty. According to sources outside the New Testament, Jesus' Uncle Cl[e]opas was the brother of Joseph, his earthly father.[21] In the afternoon of resurrection day, Cleopas famously met the risen Jesus on the road to Emmaus, but was prevented from recognising him at the time (Luke 24:18).[22] Their son Symeon became the leader of the Jerusalem church after James the Lord's brother was murdered in A.D. 62.[23] Some have suggested that this Mary may have been Matthew's chief witness of these final moments in the account of Jesus' life.[24] She also may be the Mary who later became part of Paul's missionary team in Rome (Rom. 16:6).[25]

3. The third woman on that amazing morning was Salome, the wife of Zebedee and the mother of two of Jesus' disciples, James and

---

20 For discussion, see Bauckham, 'Mary of Clopas', *Gospel Women*, Ch. 6; for 'sister in law', see p.209. Bauckham (pp. 209-210) does not identify John's Mary of Clopas with the Synoptic's Mary mother of James and Joseph, arguing that it would be more likely to have her named after her more famous son Symeon. Robinson, *Redating*, 106-107, solves this problem by suggesting a date for the Gospels prior to A.D. 62, when James was killed and Symeon took over.

21 Eusebius of Caesarea, quoting the 2nd century historian Hegesippus: *H.E.* 3.11; 3.32.6 Clopas 'an uncle of the Lord'; cf. 4.22.4; 3.32.3 Mary, the wife of Clopas, the father of Symeon. Epiphanius, *Panarion* 78.8-9, bishop's list, ?derived from Eusebius, *Chronicle*: 'Symeon, the son of James' uncle, with them—Symeon, the son of Cleopas the brother of Joseph'; 'Symeon was crucified under Trajan'.

22 The variation in spelling is of no consequence— Clopas (in John) being his semitic, and Cleopas (in Luke) (=Cleopatros) his Greek equivalent; see Bauckham, *Gospel Women*, 211; Letronne, 'Sur les noms grecs de Cléopas'.

23 James was put to death by the high priest Ananus, son of the Ananus who appears in the New Testament accounts as Annas (Luke 3:2; John 18:13, 24; Acts 4:6). Due to the resultant outcry, Ananus, despite having held office for only three months, was dismissed by Agrippa II (Josephus, *A.J.* 20.200-203; Eus. *H.E.* 2.23.21-24; Epiphanius, *Panarion* 78.8-9: 'James, who was martyred in Jerusalem by beating with a cudgel, [lived] until the time of Nero'). Bauckham, *Gospel Women*, 209-210. Pixner, *Paths of the Messiah*, Ch. 31.

24 Most famously, J.J. Griesbach, who suggested (quite sensibly in principle, even if not in detail), that the differences in the accounts reflected different eyewitnesses informing the four evangelists; see Orchard & Longstaff, *J.J. Griesbach*, 53. Strauss, *Life of Jesus*, 713, disputes his approach: 'We cannot but wonder at the tenacity with which, according to this [theory], each must have clung to the narrative which he had happened first to receive, since the resurrection of Jesus must have been the subject of all others on which there was the most lively interchange of narratives amongst his adherents, so that the ideas concerning the first tidings of the event must have found their level'. But surely this same reasoning ought to lead to the opposite conclusion. If the differences were maintained with such 'tenacity', after such 'lively interchange' over such a significant event, then surely those involved considered their narratives to dovetail with one another, rather than to oppose.

25 Bauckham, *Gospel Women*, 181: 'The Mary (Μαρία) of Romans 16:6 seems to be someone whose identity could be well known just through the use of this name. If she is a Jewish Christian with the Hebrew name Miriam, rather than a Gentile Christian with the Latin name Maria, then she too may have come from Jerusalem, and could be identified with Mary the Mother of James and Joses, whom the Synoptic evangelists evidently expect to be someone their readers will know by repute (Matt. 27:56, 61; 28:1; Mark 15:40, 47; 16:1; Luke 24:10)'. Bauckham does not identify this Mary with Mary wife of Clopas, see note 20 above. For the people listed in Romans 16 being part of Paul's missionary team, see Bolt, 'Untangling the Pauline Handshakes'.

John (Mark 15:40, cf. Matt. 27:55; Mark 16:1) —the woman who famously asked for her sons (whom Jesus called 'Boanerges, the sons of thunder', Mark 3:17) to occupy the highest positions in Jesus' coming kingdom (Matt. 20:20).[26] In partnership with the Bethsaida brothers Peter and Andrew, the Zebedee family had a fishing business on Lake Galilee, based at Capernaum (see Mark 1:16-20; Luke 5:10), but they also had a home in Jerusalem (John 19:27). There is some evidence that, before he became a disciple of Jesus, son John may have conducted the business at the Jerusalem end— that is, selling the fish—and this was probably how he became well-known to the High Priests (John 18:15-16).[27] In Jesus' last week, the Zebedee's Jerusalem home was used as a base of operations for at least some of his disciples within the city of Jerusalem (John 19:27).[28]

Even before first light, Mary (Jesus' friend) and Mary (Jesus' Aunty), and Salome (the mother of Jesus' friends) went to Jesus' grave to put some perfumes on the body (Mark 16:1; Luke 24:1).[29] They knew they were going to have trouble with the huge stone across the entrance, and they talked about this on the way (Mark 16:2-3). But, when they got there, they saw that the stone had already been rolled away (Mark 16:4; Luke 24:2; John 20:1).

At this point, Mary Magdalene ran off to tell the disciples (John 20:2)—assuming that someone had taken the corpse (see her later words, John 20:13). Probably in the southwestern corner of the city,[30] the house where they were assembled was not a great distance away— about 800m. On seeing the grave open, her immediate thought must have been, 'We better tell Peter and the others!', and they were close enough for her to do so.

After she left the grave, her two companions, Aunty Mary and Salome Zebedee, took the next step. They entered the tomb. They were astounded to find no body and an angel (Matt.28:5; Mark 16:5), or two (Luke 24:4—cf. John 20:12), sitting there, ready to explain what

---

26 See Bauckham, 'The Two Salomes and the *Secret Gospel of Mark*', *Gospel Women*, ch. 7. She is called Salome only in Mark 15:40, 16:1. Although Matthew and Luke do not name her, since she is called 'the mother of the sons of Zebedee' in Matt. 27:56, 'it is often thought that these two women are the same', with Origen (*In Matthaeum: Commentariorum Series*, 141) being the first to make the identification; Bauckham, *Gospel Women*, 235 and n.46, 246. Bauckham himself does not favour the identification.

27 Wenham, *Easter Enigma*, 39–42, 138–139. John may have spent much of his time in Jerusalem because: 1) he may himself have been a priest, as stated by Polycrates, the bishop of Ephesus (where John spent the last part of his life) (Euseb. *HE* 3.21, 5.24); and, 2) he may have looked after the family business through selling their fish in the city; for, according to a 14th century manuscript: 'In the *Gospel of the Nazareans* [=2nd century] the reason is given why John was known to the high priest. As he was the son of the poor fisherman Zebedee, he had often brought fish to the palace of the high priests Annas and Caiaphas'. Cf. Barnett, *Jesus & the Rise*, 311–312.

28 Wenham, *Easter Enigma*, 15–16, 47, suggests Peter stayed there while he was in Jerusalem. The other base of operations in Jerusalem was the home of Mary, Mother of John Mark (Acts 12:12). It is also clear from the Gospel accounts, that the Bethany home of Simon, Lazarus, Mary and Martha was also a centre of operations for Jesus and his friends; Cf. Wenham, *Easter Enigma*, 17, 47–48, 59–60.

29 There is no reason to believe that the women who had followed Jesus from Galilee knew anything about Joseph of Arimathea and Nicodemus, for these prominent Jerusalemites were only disciples of Jesus in secret at this stage (Matt. 27:57; John 19:38-39), even if they became acquainted with Jesus' more public disciples at a later stage. The women saw the two strangers, but did not see what they did to the body.

30 Epiphanius, *De mensurius et ponderibus* 14 and the Pilgrim from Bordeaux, both writing in the 4th century, knew of seven synagogues and a Christian congregation that were once on Mt Zion. The later Church in this area, depicted on the sixth century mosaic map at Madaba, was probably built on an older meeting place. Some interpret first century archaeological evidence in the area now known as 'The Tomb of David' to be of a Jewish Christian synagogue; See Pixner, *Paths of the Messiah*, ch. 18; O'Connor, 'The Cenacle'.

had happened.³¹ 'You seek Jesus of Nazareth, who was crucified? He is risen, see the place they laid him' (Matthew 28:5-6; Mark 16:6; Luke 24:3-6). The women bowed down to the ground, so overwhelmed were they with fear and perplexity (Luke 24:5).

The angel/s helped them to process what they had encountered, reminding them that Jesus had said this would happen when he taught them in Galilee (Luke 24:7). At the angels' words, the women remembered this previous teaching (Luke 24:8; cf. 9:22, 44; 18:31).³²

The angel/s also clearly and directly told the women to go to tell the disciples that they will see Jesus in Galilee (Matthew 28:7; Mark 16:7; Luke 24:6), another echo of Jesus' previous teaching (Matthew 26:32; Mark 14:28).

No doubt already deeply traumatized by watching Jesus so brutally crucified on Friday,³³ the two women now had to cope with an empty grave and heavenly visitors. Little wonder that, as Mark (16:8) reports, 'Trembling and bewildered, the women went out and fled from the tomb. They said nothing to anyone, because they were afraid'.³⁴

Since this introduces other people into the sequence of events, people that they *could have* told something to, presumably they have left the grave, which was just outside the walls, and entered back into the city. They plunged into the morning crowds that were beginning to set up their market stalls ready for the hubbub of ordinary commercial life, at the beginning of yet another very ordinary week. But they were so stunned and frightened, perplexed and trembling, that they passed through the crowds and said nothing to anyone, for they were so afraid.³⁵

But that silent state would not last for too long. It *could not* last too long. The angel had given them a command. They had a mission. They had to tell the disciples, to get them ready to go to Galilee to see Jesus! But how will *that* message go down??

3. More Women Gather

What happened next can be guessed at by a little clue in Luke's account. Jumping ahead in the sequence of events, when the women

---

31   Mark's 'young man' is described with sufficient clues to indicate that he was a heavenly messenger, such as his dress, the women's apprehension, and his message of divine revelation; Novakovic, *Resurrection*, 79.

A clearly supernatural presence, the angels were particularly troubling for Strauss, *Life of Jesus*, 716–718, 744, who declared them to be superfluous and an embellishment.

Whether there was one angel or two has proven troubling for many interpreters, concerned about 'contradictions' between the accounts; e.g. Strauss, *Life of Jesus*, 711. The variation could be due to Matthew and Mark's economy and focus in telling the story, but Matthew more usually adds rather than subtracts characters. If it goes back to the different reports given by the women (see note 24), the evangelists have preserved their sources. It is also worth noting that in the phenomenology of angelic appearances, sometimes there is fluidity between whether they are seen as singular or plural. Most famously, see the interplay in Genesis 18 between 'the Lord' (vv.1, 3, 10, 13), 'three men' (vv.2, 16, 22); and in Genesis 19 between 'the two angels' (vv.1, 15), and 'the men' (v.16). It may also be relevant that in his final vision, Daniel saw two angelic figures (12:5), but only one of them spoke (v.6).

32   Here, apparently, Luke reports the first half of the angel's comments recalling Jesus' teaching (24:7, 'The Son of Man must be betrayed into the hands of sinful men, be crucified, and rise on the third day'), and Matthew and Mark report the second half (Matt. 28:7 and Mark 16:7: 'He is going ahead of you to Galilee; you will see Him there').

33   The trauma of the occasion explains why John took Jesus' mother away from the cross (John 19:25–27), and why she is not at the empty tomb, having been relieved of her normal burial duties by her friends and a relative.

34   Novakovic, *Resurrection*, 81–82, echoing many, notes this as 'the greatest oddity of Mark's ending'. She recognises, however, that the silence could have been temporary.

35   Contrary to Novakovic, *Resurrection*, 82, the failure to speak the angel's command is also a failure to speak of the empty tomb, for the prospective meeting in Galilee is predicated on an empty tomb. The women's experience is unlike the other commands to silence in Mark, and, in fact, the discoveries at the empty tomb are what accounts for their fear.

eventually get to the disciples to tell them what happened, at the report-back their little band has expanded, and one of the additions who is named alongside Mary Magdalene and Mary wife of Cleopas is a woman called Joanna (Luke 24:10). Commentators have consistently confused the picture by assuming that, at this point in his account, Luke introduces these three women as the ones who had been at the empty tomb.

Admittedly, it is easy to be led in this direction by Luke's text. Like Mark and Matthew, he reports that a group of women were present at the crucifixion and burial of Jesus, and at the empty tomb. Unlike the other two Gospels, he leaves the women at the crucifixion and the burial unnamed, preferring to refer to them as the group who had come with Jesus from Galilee (23:49, 55), and when the narrative moves on to the empty tomb he still refuses to be specific about who was present, continuing to speak of this group in general, by way of plural verbs, from their activity at the tomb (24:1-8), through to their decision to report what they had seen to the other disciples (24:9). When Luke finally names three women (24:10), from the generality in the flow of the narrative thus far it is not only easy to be misled into thinking that these three were all at the tomb, it is, in fact, usual to be so.[36]

However, to be more precise, the flow of the narrative simply places these three amongst *that group of women who followed Jesus from Galilee*, without necessarily demanding that the same individual members of the group were present on every occasion, even if the group was represented at the crucifixion, burial, and then first outside and then inside the empty tomb.[37] There was, in fact, a greater differentiation in the underlying historical realities. When he finally names Mary Magdalene, Joanna, and Mary the mother of James (= wife of Cleopas), Luke is specifically talking of the women who were present *when the report* of the empty tomb *was delivered to the disciples* (24:10). It is a strange irony that interpreters often demand extreme precision from the resurrection chapters, and yet, at this point, they overlook Luke's precision and then charge him with introducing confusion! Luke's interest is clear: he does *not* say that these three women were at the tomb. What he says is that these three women, 'told this to the apostles'. The three women named, and the others with them mentioned in general (v.10), were the ones who were at the report-back. Following the lead of the other Gospels, it seems clear that Joanna did *not* go with the women at the grave early in the morning, but she *was* at their report-back to the larger body of disciples.[38] This then raises the question, where did *she* come from??

4. Who was Joanna?

Joanna is not a complete stranger to the Gospel of Luke, for Joanna was also amongst that circle of female followers of Jesus in Galilee, alongside Mary Magdalene (Luke 8:2-3), who supported Jesus and his disciples out of their own resources.[39] Since Luke also noted that

---

36 E.g. Strauss, *Life of Jesus*, 709; Plummer, *Luke*, 549; Marshall, *Luke*, 887; Bock, *Luke 9:51-24:53*, 885; Edwards, *Luke*, 707; Bauckham, *Gospel Women*, 235; Novakovic, *Resurrection*, 86; Barnett, *Jesus & the Rise*, 116, 267.

37 Wenham, *Easter Enigma*, 128, may well be correct that probably only Mary Cleopas was present at the crucifixion, burial, and empty tomb. The texts note all three at the crucifixion and outside the grave to see the stone rolled away; Salome is not specifically noted at the burial; and Mary Magdalene is not with the other two when they find the grave empty.

38 If Luke is to be identified with Lucius of Cyrene (cf. Acts 13:1), and if he was previously a resident in Jerusalem prior to moving to Antioch (cf. Acts 11:20), then he may have been present to hear the report back for himself.

39 See Bauckham, 'Joanna the Apostle', *Gospel Women*, ch. 5.

she was the wife of Chuza, the manager of the household of Herod Antipas, the Tetrarch of Galilee, she may well have been 'contributing the lion's share of [this] economic support'.[40] Given her mention in 8:2-3 and then again in 24:10, Joanna was almost certainly one of Luke's major sources, supplying first-hand evidence of Jesus' last journey to Jerusalem.[41] Since she was an insider to the household of Herod Antipas, her testimony probably also contributed to the special interest in Herod Antipas shown in Luke's Gospel (Luke 13:31; 23:7-12, 15; cf. Acts 4:27).[42]

But we can probably say even more about Joanna by paying careful attention to other New Testament evidence. Evidently, from her lack of description, Luke assumes his readers would know her well. When all the pieces of the puzzle are put together, it is likely that Joanna later formed part of Paul's mission team in Rome, operating with her Latin name Junia, and Chuza may also have still been at her side, operating under the Roman name Andronicus (Rom. 16:7).[43] From the way Paul describes them, he actually counted them as his relatives (τοὺς συγγενεῖς μου),[44] and since Chuza/Andronicus was a Nabatean, it would have been Joanna, a Jew, who was the one directly related to the 'Hebrew of Hebrews' Paul (Phil. 3:5). As a member of the earliest Jerusalem Christian congregation and then a close member of the circle around Paul, both as relative and co-worker, Joanna would have also travelled alongside of Luke for many years, even before she became a source for his writing enterprise.

And there may be even more that we can say about Joanna. In summer 1983, an ossuary turned up in the Jerusalem antiquities market, which was acquired the following year by the Department of Antiquities and Museums (No. 84-503). The inscription on the ossuary shows that it contained the bones of a woman by the name of Yehoḥanah (Joanna). It is also the first known ossuary to specifically denote someone high priest.[45] Its three lines of text articulate the family relationships of the deceased:

---

40 Bauckham, *Gospel Women*, 161.
41 Cf. Bauckham, *Gospel Women*, 112–113, noting an inclusio between 8:2-3 and 24:10. Commentaries regularly list Joanna as one of Luke's sources.
42 Wenham, *Easter Enigma*, 50. Although, on this point, it should be noted that the earliest Christian movement had other connections to the Herodian court, such as Manaean (Acts 13:1), who clearly operated in the same circles as Luke (cf. Bauckham, *Gospel Women*, 119)—especially if Luke was Lucius of Cyrene (cf. Acts 13:1); and presumably some of the Herodians (Mark 3:6; 12:13; Matt. 22:16). Barnett, *Jesus & the Rise*, 116, asks whether Manaen was led to Christ by Joanna, and suggests that, as one of Antipas' leading men, he may have been at the banquet for which John the Baptist was beheaded. It is interesting to speculate whether others associated with Herod who ended up in Jesus' circle were also at that banquet and the impact it may have had on them in regard to becoming Jesus' disciple. Besides Manaen, any of those listed by Barnett as connected to Antipas could have been there: Joanna & Chuza, the royal official and the centurion from Capernaum, or even Levi/Matthew.
43 'Prominent among the apostles' may therefore indicate she was associated with the earthly ministry of Jesus and with the women who reported the empty tomb; see further, Bauckham, 'Joanna the Apostle', 166–186. For the list of persons in Romans 16 being Paul's mission team in Rome, see Bolt, 'Untangling the Pauline Handshakes'. In this case, her association with Mary wife of Cleopas (v.6) actively continued, see note 25 above.
44 As recognised by the classic stream of English translation ('kinsmen': AV, RV, ASV, NASB, ESV; 'relatives': NRSV), rather than the more recent ('fellow Jews': NIV; 'fellow countrymen': HCSB; 'compatriots': NET). Acts mentions two of Paul's relatives resident in Jerusalem (Acts 23:16) and no less than six persons are included in this number in Romans 16 (Andronicus and Junia, v.7; Herodion, v.11; Lucius, Jason, and Sosipater, v.21). Rom. 9:1 can be read more specifically and therefore more poignantly of Paul's actual kin. Bauckham, *Gospel Women*, 170, prefers 'fellow Jews', even though he acknowledges this is an unusual use of the word, and that there are other Jews in the chapter who do not get this designation. On this chapter, see my 'Untangling the Pauline Handshakes'.
45 Barag & Flusser, 'The Ossuary of Yehoḥanah', 39 n.1, 41. It was reported as coming from the village of Ḥizma, 7 km NNE of Jerusalem. See also the discussion in Evans, *Jesus and the Ossuaries*, 104–112.

Yehoḥanah

Yehoḥanah the daughter of Yehoḥanan

Son of Theophilus the High Priest

Josephus provides some information about this high priest named Theophilus. Vitellius appointed him after Passover A.D. 37 to replace Jonathan, who had succeeded Caiaphas very briefly for a month or two.[46] Theophilus served as high priest for just over four years until Agrippa I removed him from office on his arrival as king of Judea in mid A.D. 41 (Josephus, *A.J.* 19.297 [19.6.2]).[47] He was high priest during the major crisis when Caligula moved to erect a statue of himself in the Jerusalem temple (Philo, *Leg.* 207–260, esp. 222ff; Josephus, *B.J.* 2.184–203; *A.J.* 18.261–288, esp. 273ff).[48]

Theophilus was one of the five sons of Annas to hold the priesthood, and with Caiaphas being a son-in-law of Annas (John 18:13), he was therefore a part of the dynasty that dominated the high-priesthood across the first century. This high priestly family is well known to the New Testament. Annas and Caiaphas (Caiaphas alone: Matt. 26:3, 57; John 11:49; 18:28; Caiaphas and Annas: Luke 3:2; John 18:13-14, 24; Acts 4:6), of course, are also best-known from the role they played in the destruction of Jesus, and Jonathan—Theophilus' brief predecessor— is mentioned once by name along with the other two (Acts 4:6).[49]

The narrative accounts in the book of Acts do not mention Theophilus, however, whether by name or title, and quickly pass over the years of his tenure. When the converted Paul arrived back in Jerusalem in A.D. 36 (Acts 9:26-27), Caiaphas and Pilate remained in office—circumstances which allowed for the possibility of their former henchman being killed (v.29). By Acts 12, Agrippa is present and persecuting (A.D. 42), which leaves Theophilus' period covered by the intervening chapters. These depict the scattered Jerusalem Church enjoying a time of peace (9:31), which permitted Peter to also engage in some significant ministry on the coastal plain (Acts 10-11). This fits with Gaechter's observation that Theophilus and his son Matthias (who held the office when the Jewish war broke out in A.D. 66, Josephus, *A.J.* 20.223), were the only two high priests of the Annas family, who did not preside over a persecution of the Jesus movement.[50] It is interesting to ask why not.

But, of course, Theophilus is the same name as the person to whom Luke addressed both the Acts and his former book about Jesus (Luke 1:1; Acts 1:1). Just like much Lukan scholarship has been content to leave the historical Joanna unidentified, there has often been little interest in discovering the historical Theophilus. But given that the inscription has these two names that are so significant for Luke, what if Luke's Theophilus was the ex-high priest (A.D. 37–41), and Luke's Joanna was the

---

46 Jonathan was probably installed between mid December A.D. 36 and mid-January A.D. 37, when Vitellius visited Jerusalem to dismiss Pilate; Smallwood, 'High Priests and Politics', 22; see also her 'Date of the Dismissal'. In A.D. 37, Nisan 15 fell on Thursday 19 March; Midrash.org/calendar.

47 Steinmann, *From Abraham to Paul*, 328, estimates his arrival in the summer of A.D. 41. It is generally agreed that Agrippa I removed Theophilus after he arrived to take control of Judea in A.D. 41, although Schwartz, *Agrippa I*, 11–14, argues for the dismissal in A.D. 38. VanderKam, *From Joshua to Caiaphas*, 440–443, refutes Schwartz's arguments.

48 Although, as noted by Smallwood, 'High Priests and Politics', 23, and accepted by VanderKam, *From Joshua to Caiaphas*, 440 n.118 and Horsley, 'High Priests', 38, the accounts do not show him taking any leadership in resisting the assault on his people.

49 John is clarified by Codex Bezae and the Old Latin: Jonathas. Alternatively, Hengel & Schwemer, *Paul Between Damascus and Antioch*, 250 n.1309, identify the Jonathan of Acts 4:6 with the Jonathan, son of Theophilus, recorded in the inscription under discussion— mistakenly citing Barag & Flusser in support.

50 Gaechter, 'Hatred', 33–34.

granddaughter of Luke's Theophilus?[51] This would also make Joanna, the follower of Jesus, the grand-niece of Caiaphas and the great-granddaughter of Annas, the men who had Jesus executed. In addition, given that Joanna/Junia was a relative of Paul (Rom. 16:7), it would also bring the apostle to the Gentiles into the family circles of the high priests responsible for the death of Jesus. Such family connections would provide further insight into his former career as the chief persecutor of the earliest Christian movement, and underline his sense of the magnitude of the grace of God displayed in his conversion (Gal. 1:13-16).

Thus this inscription raises the intriguing possibility that Luke draws upon the testimony of Joanna/Junia, to write his accounts of Jesus and the Jesus' movement, which he then addressed to Joanna's grandfather, in an attempt to give him certainty about the things he had heard about for years, through being a member of this prominent high priestly family which, in the interests of keeping peace with Rome (cf. John 11:47-53),[52] was forced to deal firstly with Jesus of Nazareth, and secondly with the movement that sprang up in the wake of his grave being found empty.[53]

However, leaving these intriguing suggestions unexplored in the present article,[54] we should return to Luke's account, where Joanna is given a role on resurrection morning.

5. The Mid-Morning Report-Back

We left the story with the two (older) women, Mary wife of Cleopas and Salome Zebedee leaving the tomb in terrified silence (according to Mark). What happened next?

When Herod Antipas came to Jerusalem, Chuza would have come too, to look after the domestic arrangements in Herod's Jerusalem lodgings. Herod and his household manager probably had apartments in the grand palace built by Herod the Great on the Western edge of Jerusalem, which was the Roman Governor's residence when in Jerusalem, and also the Praetorium where Jesus had been tried before Pilate—only 220 m from Golgotha.[55] The only other place that Herod Antipas could have stayed would be the old Hasmonean palace on the eastern edge of the upper city, and, if so,

---

51 Theodore Hase, 'IV. ad praecedentem de THEOPHILO', appears to have been the first to suggest that Luke wrote to Theophilus the high priest. Occasionally accepted, but mostly ignored by subsequent scholarship, the view has recently been advanced at more length by Anderson, *Who Are Joanna and Theophilus?*.

52 For the role in keeping peace with Rome, see Horsley, 'High Priests', 32, 35-37.

53 Theophilus also had a son, Matthias, who became High Priest (A.D. 65–67), and he was the last legitimate high priest before the Jewish war took them all out of a job. Careful attention to the accounts in the New Testament and Josephus indicates that the House of Annas relentlessly persecuted Jesus and the Jesus movement across decades. But it is also intriguing to note that there appears to be two exceptions to that persecuting trend: Theophilus, and his son Matthias. The relatives of Joanna. See Gaechter, 'The Hatred of the House of Annas'.

54 I explore these connections further in 'Untangling the Pauline Handshakes', 'Sadducean Opposition to Earliest Christianity', and a larger work on Luke's Gospel currently in progress.

55 Identifying Herod's lodgings is a calculated guess. Logically, this would be the best place for him to be, under the watchful eye of Pilate. This would also allow for the ease of the two men's interaction over Jesus that is evident in Luke 23. There are three options for the location of the Praetorium. The Antonia Fortress was never the residence of the Roman Prefects/Procurators, for it was simply a barrack for the soldiers keeping an eye on the temple. Some suggest the Praetorium was located more centrally, in the old Hasmonean palace, which Pilate used as an administrative building, even while living in Herod's palace along the western city wall; so Pixner, *Paths of the Messiah*, chs. 21 & 22. It is clear from a later date that the Roman governor occupied Herod's palace and conducted official proceedings there (Josephus, *B.J.* 2.297–308, esp. 301), and likely that this practice began with the earlier prefects; Barnett, *Jesus & the Rise*, 77, 144.

Chuza and Joanna would have also been there.[56] But either palace is just a five minutes leisurely stroll from the crucifixion site, and about one third of the way to where the disciples would have been.

So, since Joanna wasn't at the tomb but she was at the report back, reading between the lines: Trembling and frightened, saying nothing to anyone, Aunt Mary (wife of Cleopas), and Salome Zebedee, heading south to where their family and friends were, seem to have made a short call at Joanna's place, which was on the way. How better to settle down after their shock, than to download in the company of their female friends from Galilee, who had also followed Jesus and supported his ministry?

Being somewhat outside the immediate situation, Joanna no doubt provided some sanity and common sense. It was not as if she didn't know Jesus' power, for she and Mary Magdalene and Susannah had been healed and delivered of demons up in Galilee (8:2-3). And she had heard Jesus' teaching and, yes, she would have remembered along with her friends, that he *had* said something strange, that on the other side of his death, he would rise. But with all that background taken for granted, there was only one thing they had to do now. The angel had given them an instruction. They had to tell the disciples.

And so, as a result of their brief stopover (was it 15 minutes? half an hour? surely not more than an hour?), the women continued the ten minute walk south to the disciples. And, for moral and emotional support, Joanna also came with them.

When they arrived, they immediately linked up with Mary Magdalene again, who had previously rushed off to tell Peter and John what she had seen when they first arrived at the grave to discover the stone already rolled away (Luke 24:10). With Joanna standing by in support, the three eyewitnesses gave their combined testimony—although Luke only singles out Mary Magdalene and Mary wife of Cleopas, suggesting, perhaps, that Salome, the wife of Zebedee, had stood with the other two, but had not herself spoken. The report was simple: not only was the stone rolled away (what all of them, including Mary Magdalene saw), but the tomb was empty and the body gone and an angel was saying to meet Jesus in Galilee (as Aunt Mary could report, and as Salome Zebedee could presumably agree to).[57]

At first, the disciples responded predictably—with disbelief, for the women's words sounded like nonsense (Luke 24:11). But then, Peter started thinking. Shortly before this combined report-back, Mary Magdalene had slipped into the room and told him and John what she had seen (John 20:2). Now these two eminently respectable women, with Joanna in support, had added a further dimension to her story. Suddenly Peter knew just what he had to do. He jumped up, and raced off to the tomb, only about 800 m to the North, to check it out for himself (Luke 24:12a; John 20:3-5). John Zebedee was also privy to Mary Magdalene's initial report of events (John 20:2), and now, after hearing what his own mother had seen, he too leapt to his feet and ran after Peter.[58] Perhaps younger and fitter, or more eager to see what had happened, he actually outran the (as we imagine him) big lumbering fisherman, arrived at the tomb and found it open. He bent over and looked in, seeing only the strips of linen used to wrap Jesus' corpse,

---

56 So Wenham, *Easter Enigma*, 15, 39; Pixner, *Paths of the Messiah*, Chs. 21 &22.

57 Matthew's account presents the testimony of the women as a combined witness, with that deriving from Aunt Mary and Salome (Matt. 28:5-8) and that deriving from Mary Magdalene's later encounter (Matt. 28:9-10; John 20:11 18) being treated as coming from 'the women' *en bloc*. Matthew's source may have been Mary wife of Cleopas. See note 24 above.

58 There is a trace of this in the 'some' of Luke 24:24. Noted by Strauss, *Life of Jesus*, 711; Bauckham, *Gospel Women*, 222–223. Novakovic, *Resurrection*, 88, points out that the recapitulation of the visit in 24:24 corroborates 24:12, even though it is a 'Western non-interpolation'.

and he stopped there and he didn't go in (John 20:5). Puffing and blowing, then Peter arrived and rushed straight inside the tomb and saw not only the strips of linen, but also their arrangement (John 20:6-7; Luke 24:12b). The body of Jesus had gone. Following Peter's lead, John also entered the tomb and saw the body had gone, and he saw and believed (John 20:8), at last realizing what Jesus meant when he taught that the Scriptures said he must rise from the dead, something none of them had grasped by this stage (John 20:9). Both men then returned to where they were staying, amazed, and wondering to themselves about this most extraordinary set of events (John 20:10; Luke 24:12c).

At this point (John 20:11), we learn that Mary Magdalene had also run after the two men, back to the tomb. Peter and John were probably so caught up in themselves, that when they took off, they left Mary crying outside the grave. Despite all that had gone on that crazy morning, she still did not know for sure what had happened, and where Jesus' body had gone. She still thought someone had taken it.

As she wept, she bent down and looked inside, and saw two angels seated where the body had been (John 20:12-13). 'Why are you crying', they asked. And she said, 'they have taken my Lord away, and I don't know where they have put him'. But, at that point, she turned around and saw Jesus himself — although she didn't recognize him at first. Jesus asked her the same question as the angels: 'Woman, why are you crying? Who is it you are looking for?'. She is sure someone had taken the body. Thinking this man must be the gardener she asked, 'If you have carried him away, tell me where you have put him, and I will get him' (v.15). Then, to help her in her distress, Jesus simply said, 'Mary' (John 20:16), and she immediately recognized him and fell at the feet of the teacher who meant so much to her (Matt.28:9-10; John 20:16-17), and he told her to go back to the disciples and tell them. So Mary raced back to the disciples and told them she had seen the Lord (John 20:18), winning a place in history as the first to have done so.[59]

6. Epilogue: The Rest of the Day

The amazing events of that day didn't stop there. Later that afternoon, Cleopas, the husband of 'the other Mary' who found the tomb empty, Jesus' Uncle, was walking to Emmaus with another person.[60] Jesus also appeared to them, and spoke with them at length (Luke24:13-32). They raced back to Jerusalem, now in the evening, to find that Jesus had also appeared to Simon Peter sometime earlier in the day (Luke24:34). And when the whole crowd of them had gathered, Jesus then appeared to all of them together (Luke24:36-49; John 20:19-23).[61] And this amazing day had, at last, come to an end.

But that end was really only the beginning. Despite the enormous implications of these events, there is absolutely no trouble presenting a clear and consistent account of what happened on the morning of that amazing day. The trouble comes in remembering that, on that amazing day, the world changed forever.

---

59 Mark 16:9—not part of the original Gospel—also reports that Mary Magdalene was the first to see the risen Christ. Note that this is not the same as the first to believe (contra Strauss, *Life of Jesus*, 714–715), an honour John gives to the beloved disciple (John 20:8).
60 δύο ἐξ αὐτῶν indicates it was not one of the apostles (see v.33), but one of the disciples more generally; Plummer, *Luke*, 551. Amongst other conjectures, some have identified him as Luke. Mark 16:12-13 also contains an allusion to the Emmaus story.
61 Thomas was not present on this occasion (John 20:24-25), but his doubts were laid to rest eight days later (John 20:26-29).

Bibliography

Anderson, R.H. *Who are Johanna and Theophilus? The Irony of the Intended Audience of the Gospel of Luke* (Wallingford, PA: R.H. Anderson, 2011).

Barag, D., & D. Flusser, 'The Ossuary of Yehoḥanah Granddaughter of the High Priest Theophilus', *Israel Exploration Journal* 36.1/2 (1986), 39–44.

Barnett, P.W. *Jesus & the Rise of Early Christianity. A History of New Testament Times* (Downers Gr., IL: IVP, 1999).

Bauckham, R. *Gospel Women. Studies of the Named Women in the Gospels* (Grand Rapids & Cambridge: Eerdmans, 2002).

Bauckham, R. *Jesus and the Eyewitnesses* (Grand Rapids: Eerdmans, 2006, rev. 2017).

Bock, D.L. *Luke 9:51-24:53* (BECNT; Grand Rapids: Baker Academic, 1996).

Bode, E.L. *The First Easter Morning: The Gospel Accounts Of The Women's Visit To The Tomb Of Jesus* (Rome: Biblical Institute Press, 1970).

Bolt, P.G. 'Untangling the Pauline Handshakes. Who is Greeting Whom in Romans 16', in P.G. Bolt & J.R. Harrison (eds.), *Romans and the Legacy of St Paul: Social, Theological, and Pastoral Perspectives* (Macquarie Park, NSW: SCD Press, 2018 [forthcoming]).

Bolt, P.G. 'Sadducean Opposition to Earliest Christianity', in P.G. Bolt & J.R. Harrison (eds.), *The Impact of Jesus of Nazareth: Historical, Theological, and Pastoral Perspectives. Vol. 2: The Theological Impact of Jesus of Nazareth* (Macquarie Park, NSW: SCD Press, 2019 [forthcoming]).

Edwards, J.R. *The Gospel According to Luke* (PNTC; Grand Rapids: Eerdmans, 2015).

Evans, C.A. *Jesus and the Ossuaries* (Waco, TX: Baylor University Press, 2003).

Gaechter, P. 'The Hatred of the House of Annas', *Theological Studies* 8.1 (1947), 3–34.

Hase, T. 'IV. Theodori Hasaei ad praecedentem de THEOPHILO dissertationem sicilimentum', *Bibliotheca Historico-Philogico-Theologica* Class. 4, Fasc. 3 (1721), 506–530. https://babel.hathitrust.org/cgi/pt?id=ucm.5324360082.

Hengel, M., & A.M. Schwemer, *Paul Between Damascus and Antioch. The Unknown Years* (J. Bowden, trans.; London & Louisville: SCM & Westminster John Knox, 1997).

Hoehner, H.W. *Chronological Aspects of the Life of Christ* (Grand Rapids: Zondervan [Academie], 1977).

Horsley, R.A. 'High Priests and the Politics of Roman Palestine. A Contextual Analysis of the Evidence in Josephus', *JSJ* 17.1 (1986), 23–55.

Humphreys, C.J., & W.G. Waddington, 'The Date of the Crucifixion', *JSAS* 37 (1985), 2–10.

Letronne, M. 'Sur les noms grecs de Cléopas (ΚΛΕΟΦΑΣ et ΚΛΕΟΠΑΣ)', *Revue Archéologique*, 1.2 (1844–1845), 485–491.

Marshall, I.H. *The Gospel of Luke: A Commentary on the Greek Text* (NIGTC; Grand Rapids: Eerdmans, 1978).

Midrash.org Midrash.org/calendar

Moloney, F.J. *The Resurrection of the Messiah: A Narrative Commentary on the Resurrection Accounts in the Four Gospels* (New York : Paulist Press, 2013).

Novakovic, L. *Resurrection* (London: Bloomsbury T. & T. Clark, 2016).

O'Connor, J. M. 'The Cenacle', in R. Bauckham (ed.), *The Book of Acts in its First Century Setting*, vol. 4: *The Book of Acts in its Palestinian Setting* (Grand Rapids & Carlisle: Eerdmans & Paternoster, 1995), 303–321.

Orchard, B., & T.R.W. Longstaff, *J.J. Griesbach: Synoptic and Text-Critical Studies, 1776–1976* (Cambridge: Cambridge University Press, 1978).

Pixner, B. *Paths of the Messiah and Sites of the Early Church from Galilee to Jerusalem* (R. Riesner, ed.; K. Myrick, S. Randall, M. Randall, transls.; San Francisco: Ignatius, 2010 [German: 1991]).

Robinson, J.A.T. *Redating the New Testament* (London: SCM, 1976; Eugene, OR: Wipf & Stock, 2000).

Plummer, A. *The Gospel according to St Luke* (ICC; Edinburgh: T.&T. Clark, 1981 [1896]).

Schwartz, D.R. *Agrippa I: The Last King of Judea* (Tübingen: Mohr Siebeck, 1990).

Smallwood, E.M. 'High Priests and Politics in Roman Palestine', *JTS* 13.1 (1962), 14–34.

Smallwood, E.M. 'The Date of the Dismissal of Pontius Pilate from Judaea', *JJS* 5 (1954), 12–21.

Steinmann, A.E. *From Abraham to Paul. A Biblical Chronology* (St Louis: Concordia, 2011).

Strauss, D.F. *The Life of Jesus Critically Examined* (P.C. Hodgson, ed.; G. Eliot, transl.; Philadelphia: Fortress, 1972 [4th German: 1846; 2nd English: 1892]; Ramsey, NJ: Sigler, 1994).

Timeanddate.com www.timeanddate.com/astronomy/different-types-twilight.html.

www.timeanddate.com/sun/israel/Jerusalem.

www.timeanddate.com/moon/phases/israel/Jerusalem.

VanderKam, J.C. *From Joshua to Caiaphas: High Priests after the Exile* (Minneapolis & Assen: Fortress & Van Gorcum, 2004).

Wenham, J. *Easter Enigma. Are the Resurrection Accounts in Conflict?* (Carlisle: Paternoster, 1984, ²1992; Eugene, OR: Wipf & Stock, 2005).

A Jerusalemite Source for the List of Nations in Acts 2?

DAVID EVANS

Abstract

Numerous explanations have been offered regarding the origin, content, and significance of the list of nations in Acts 2. Most suggestions propose a source list that Luke has adopted, modified, or mimicked in some way. This article proposes that Luke prepared his list from records or remembrances from the Jerusalem church, who could identify the nationalities of those who made up the earliest post-pentecost Christian community. In support of this proposal, four lines of evidence are offered: the existence of Elamites and Medes in the first century CE; the Jerusalemite perspective evident in the strange inclusion of 'Judea'; the lack of Cilicians on the list, which reflects the oppositional relationship between the early Christians and the Cilician Jews; and the absence of mainland Greeks from the list, which may reflect the financial depression of the region in the first century CE.

1. Introduction

The Pentecost account in Acts 2 includes a language miracle in which the disciples 'began to speak in other tongues as the Spirit gave them utterance' (Acts 2:4). The sound they created drew a crowd which was made up of 'devout Jewish men from every nation under heaven' (2:5). The crowd were amazed that the disciples were speaking in the native languages of those in the crowd (2:6), and listed the nations from whence they came: 'Parthians and Medes and Elamites and residents of Mesopotamia, Judea and Cappadocia, Pontus and Asia, Phrygia and Pamphylia, Egypt and the parts of Libya belonging to Cyrene, and visitors from Rome, both Jews and proselytes, Cretans and Arabians' (2.9-11).

This list of nations has inspired some conjecture amongst scholars, who have offered numerous explanations of its origin and significance, and of the reasoning behind the nations and regions included in the list. Most suggestions that have been put forward (and will be discussed below), propose a source list that Luke has adopted, modified, or mimicked in some way to produce the Acts 2 list. Luke certainly did not invent the 'list of nations' format, so it is a worthwhile endeavour to consider how his use of the format reflects the purposes of other lists.

This does not mean, however, that he was dependent on an obscure list for his. It will be proposed in this paper that a more likely scenario is that Luke shaped his list from records or remembrances from members of the Jerusalem church that could identify the nationalities of its earliest members.[1]

After providing a brief analysis of the list and survey of scholarship on it, four lines of evidence will be argued in support of the proposition of a Jerusalemite source. Firstly, the inclusion of 'Elamites and Medes' doesn't necessarily point to an older source list because this terminology can be seen to be in use in Jerusalem in the first century CE. Secondly, the inclusion of 'Judea' in the list argues for a Jerusalemite perspective in the list. Thirdly, the lack of Cilicians on the list reflects the oppositional relationship between the early Christians and the Cilician Jews. And fourthly, the absence of mainland Greeks from the list possibly reflects the financial depression of the region in the first century CE.

2. Residents or Visitors?

The first question to consider is the nature of the crowd. Luke uses the participle κατοικοῦντες ('dwelling') twice in the passage. In verse 5 he informs the reader about Jews from every nation 'dwelling in Jerusalem' (ἐν Ἰερουσαλὴμ κατοικοῦντες Ἰουδαῖοι). Later, the crowd includes 'residents of Mesopotamia, Judea...' (οἱ κατοικοῦντες τὴν Μεσοποταμίαν, Ἰουδαίαν...; v.9). Scholars have taken different positions on whether κατοικοῦντες refers to Diaspora Jews visiting Jerusalem for Pentecost (and thus only short term residents),[2] or Diaspora Jews who had now settled in Jerusalem.[3] Schnabel takes a sensible line on this, observing that the context of the scene—the Pentecost festival (2:1)—makes it likely that the crowd would include pilgrims and long-term residents from Diaspora origins, and that the use of ἐπιδημοῦντες ('visitors', in contrast to κατοικοῦντες; v.10) suggests that at the very least those in the crowd from Rome were short-term visitors to the city.[4]

The missiological significance of this has been considered by many scholars. This event may have led to the early establishment of the Christian church among the Jewish Diaspora as these pilgrims returned to their locations of residence.[5] But the likelihood of pilgrims in the crowd also raises another issue. Were there any diaspora locations that, for one reason or another, would hinder their Jewish population from participating in pilgrimage to Jerusalem?

---

1 It is not my intention to discuss the mechanism by which Luke may have accessed these sources, but simply to assert that Luke using a Jerusalemite source potentially offers some explanation of some curious elements of this list.
2 Bruce, *Acts*, 43; McKechnie, 'Jewish Christianity', 134, n.1.
3 Haenchen, *Acts*, 168; Johnson, *Acts*, 43; Witherington, *Acts*, 135.
4 Schnabel, *Acts*, 116, 19. Cf. Kistemaker, *Exposition*, 80, 82, 85. David Gurevich has recently argued that the intensification of Jewish pilgrimage to Jerusalem in the Hasmonean, Herodian and Roman periods is reflected in the city's infrastructure by the presence of numerous large pools which stored water for ritual use during religious festivals, most notably the Passover and the Pentecost. Gurevich, 'Water Pools', 119-29.
5 Keener, *Acts*, 850; Schnabel, *Acts*, 119. Cf. Acts 28:15, where Paul is welcomed by 'brothers' in Rome. Paul's arrival in Rome is not the foundation of the church in the city.

3. Inclusions and Exclusions

Even though Acts 2:5 says that the residents in Jerusalem came from every nation under heaven,[6] Luke only includes fifteen nationalities or regions in the list. The nations and regions listed are known to have had sizable Jewish communities,[7] but it is not an exhaustive list of the Jewish Diaspora. Other areas that the reader may have expected to see on the list, owing to Luke's knowledge of the presence of Jewish communities in them, include Syria, Cilicia, Galatia, Pisidia, Lycaonia, Macedonia, Achaia and Cyprus.[8]

The list begins with three nations: the Parthians, Medes and Elamites. These three were nations of the eastern regions beyond the Roman Empire. The Parthians were an empire contemporary with, and often in conflict, with Rome, and Media and Elam continued as districts within it.[9] Diaspora communities had existed in these regions since the Assyrian and Babylonian exiles,[10] and these communities had ongoing contact with Judea.[11]

Following the first three, nine regions (Μεσοποταμίαν... Κυρήνην; Acts 2:9-10) are listed that all have well attested Jewish communities.[12] The inclusion of Judea, however, has proven troubling since even the earliest commentators on this passage because: 1) it breaks the geographical flow as it doesn't lie between Mesopotamia and Cappadocia; and 2) Judeans were unlikely to be shocked that Galileans were speaking their language.[13] In light of these difficulties Tertullian and Augustine substituted 'Judea' for 'Armenia'; Jerome preferred 'Syria'; and Chrysostom preferred 'India'.[14] Further exchanges are made by other scholars, but Metzger has argued that the textual support for 'Judea' is sufficient enough to affirm its place in the text.[15]

The list ends with another three nations: Romans, Cretans and Arabians. Disagreement arises over how to understand rightly οἱ ἐπιδημοῦντες Ῥωμαῖοι (2:10). Some argue that the phrase refers to Jews who normally live in the city of Rome who are currently visiting Jerusalem.[16] Others prefer to understand it as a reference to Roman citizens more generally.[17] Considering the Acts narrative's trajectory towards Rome, and the more geographically specific nature of the list, it is best to understand these Romans as Jews from the city of Rome.

'Cretans and Arabians' provide an unusual ending. While the structure of the phrase matches the rest of the pairs in the list, it is awkwardly tacked on after Ἰουδαῖοί τε καὶ προσήλυτοι, a phrase which seems to summarise the whole list.[18] Hengel suggests that Crete and Arabia are included

---

6 A statement Witherington describes as Luke's 'typical rhetorical hyperbole', the point of which is 'to emphasize the scope of the audience'. Witherington, *Acts*, 135.
7 Haenchen, *Acts*, 169; Witherington, *Acts*, 136.
8 Acts 6:5; 6:9; 11:19; 13–14; Acts 17:1, 10, 17; 21:39. Taylor, 'List', 410–11.
9 Pliny, *Nat. Hist.* 6.31
10 b.Sanh. 94a. The Babylonian schools of the Amoraic period (230–500CE) cite Shush and Shushtri in Elam as two cities to which the ten tribes were exiled.
11 Jos. *Ant.* 17.23–6; 18.312–313; Philo *Leg.* 216; cf. Cohen, 'Travel', 204–05.
12 The shift from ethnic identifiers (Parthians, Medes, Elamites) to regional designations (Mesopotamia) reflects similar lists in the contemporary literature.
13 Pervo, *Acts*, 67.
14 Metzger, *Textual Commentary*, 254.
15 Metzger, *Textual Commentary*, 254.
16 Bock, *Acts*, 104; Bruce, *Acts*, 57; Haenchen, *Acts*, 170; Kistemaker, *Acts*, 83; Schnabel, *Acts*, 119; Taylor, 'List', 416.
17 Witherington, *Acts*, 137; Barrett, *Acts*, 123.
18 Hengel, 'Ἰουδαία', 162; Haenchen, *Acts*, 171; Fitzmyer, *Acts*, 243.

because they represent Judea's immediate neighbours.[19] Witherington, on the other hand, takes them as representative of the islands and desert regions.[20] Schnabel says that the Cretans and Arabs can be explained by the table of nations in Genesis 10. The two nations 'are descendants of Mizraim (Egypt), who settled in the territories of Palestine…and Nabatea'.[21] Hengel's suggestion is the most likely. At the very least it can be said that there were Jewish Diaspora communities in these regions—so they are believable inclusions in the list—and as Judea's neighbours they bring the list to a neat close nearby the Pentecost event.

4. The Search for a Source List

As noted above, there are numerous regions which the reader of Acts may expect to see on this list. Taylor's suggestions cited above focus on the regions connected with Paul's later missionary endeavours. He identifies these because the apostle's usual practice of first going to the synagogue in any given city (Acts 17:2) reveals that Luke was aware of Jewish Diaspora communities in these regions. However, since the Acts 2 list includes some of the areas to which Paul goes, such as Pontus, Asia and Phrygia, but not others such as Cilicia, Galatia or Achaia, his missionary travels obviously did not shape Luke's list in this instance. Numerous explanations for the exclusions in the list have come by way of the many and varied suggestions of a source list upon which Luke depended.

Stefan Weinstock argued in a 1948 article that Luke's list corresponded to lists of geographical astrology, which outline the zodiac signs that dominate various geographical regions. Weinstock focuses on a fourth century CE list from Paulus Alexandrinus which includes the following nations and their relevant sign: Persia (Aries), Babylonia (Taurus), Cappadocia (Gemini), Armenia (Cancer), Asia (Leo), Greece and Ionia (Virgo), Libya and Cyrene (Libra), Italy (Scorpio), Cilicia and Crete (Sagittarius), Syria (Capricorn), Egypt (Aquarius), the Red Sea and India (Pisces).[22] Though some parallels are evident between this list and the one in Acts 2, Weinstock's theory is unconvincing for a number of reasons. Firstly, as Metzger correctly pointed out, 'when one seeks for precise equivalents between Acts and either one of Paulus's lists, the results are meagre enough. Of sixteen names of countries or peoples in Acts, only five are identical with those in Paulus'.[23] Secondly it is unlikely that Luke would have had any interest in the astrological nature of a list like Alexandrinus'. Finally, the simplicity of Alexandrinus' list is crucial for Weinstock's argument, but its significantly later date in comparison to Luke is problematic.[24] Weinstock accurately argues that the astrological tradition stretches back before the first century CE—so Luke could have accessed a similar source—but these earlier sources bear even less resemblance to the Acts 2 list. The astrological list in Vettius Valens' *Anthology* (2nd Century CE) is far more convoluted—Taurus, for instance, dominates regions as disparate as Babylon, Cyprus, Arabia, Carthage and Germany.[25]

---

19 Hengel, 'Ἰουδαία', 179. He understands 'Cretans' as a euphemism for those living on the coastal plain, descended from the Philistines. This seems difficult, when Cretans were well represented in Graeco-Roman literature as being amongst the island peoples (Appian, *Civil Wars* II.10.71).
20 Witherington, *Acts*, 136. Cf. Conzelmann who also suggests the possibility of 'Westerners and Easterners'. Conzelmann, *Acts*, 14.
21 Schnabel, *Acts*, 120.
22 Weinstock, 'Geographical Catalogue', 43. Cf. Gilbert, 'List', 501.
23 Metzger, 'Ancient Astrological Geography', 131.
24 Weinstock, 'Geographical Catalogue', 44.
25 Vett. Val. *Anth.* 1.2

Another set of suggestions argues for the list to have been sourced from an eastern, pre-Roman source. Justin Taylor argues that Luke based his list off the 'official lists of places and people subject to the Persian (Achaemenid) Empire'.[26] His particular focus is on the 'preamble (§6) of the famous inscription... made by Darius I (reigned 522–486 B.C.) on a cliff-face at Behistun on the ancient road from Babylon to central Asia, about 518'.[27] The list includes Persia, Elam, Babylon, Assyrians, Arabia, Egypt, those who are at/in the sea, Sardis, Ionians, Media, Armenia, Cappadocia, and Parthia.[28] In Taylor's opinion, Luke's use of this list explains a number of the 'gaps' in the Acts 2 list: Syria in the 6th Century BCE was part of Babylon, not Persia; Cilicia was an ally, not a subject; Cyprus is not mentioned in any lists; and Greece was not in the Persian empire.[29] Pervo makes a similar suggestion to Taylor. He speculates that if the list originated in Seleucid-era Antioch, Syria would be understandably absent as the homeland, and Greece would be absent because it was outside of Seleucid control.[30] These suggestions do not, however, offer any explanation of the inclusion of Rome and Crete, and both Taylor and Pervo acknowledge as much.[31] The question remains that if Luke was happy to remove names from the list and add in new ones, why would he not include the regions that we might expect, such as Greece or Cilicia which both feature in the Acts narrative and were known to have Jewish communities?[32]

A further group of scholars suggest that the list is based off Jewish lists, including the Table of Nations in Genesis 10, Philo's list in *Legatio ad Gaium* 281–282, or Josephus' in *Antiquities* 1.122–147.[33] These theories face similar issues to those already discussed. The Table of Nations and the list in Acts 2 do not correlate closely, and a comparison with Philo and Josephus' lists of the extent of the Jewish Diaspora serves only to highlight the Diaspora centres that Luke was aware of and yet did not include in his list.[34]

Another possible explanation, suggested by Gary Gilbert, is that Luke was countering lists that described the extent of Roman Imperial domination. These lists were 'a means to persuade' and 'identified and secured the territorial dimensions of the Roman empire and impressed upon anyone who encountered them Rome's overwhelming power and universal authority'.[35] Luke, in mimicking this propagandist style, presents a counter-claim to this universal authority, and presents 'God's *oikoumenē*, which includes not only the provinces of the Roman empire but also Parthia and other lands beyond Rome's control'.[36] Gilbert does not, however, offer any sort of explanation as to why regions such as Achaia, Macedonia or Cilicia are not included. This is particularly surprising since they do appear on Roman lists that Gilbert cites,[37] and (at least in the case of Achaia and Macedonia) the Acts narrative emphasises the expansion of Christianity into these areas, the socially disruptive nature of Christianity within them, and the authority of God over them.[38]

---

26 Taylor, 'List', 412.
27 Taylor, 'List', 412–13.
28 Taylor, 'List', 413.
29 Taylor, 'List', 417.
30 Pervo, *Acts*, 68, n.81.
31 Taylor, 'List', 416; Pervo, *Acts*, 68.
32 Cilicia: the Cilician synagogue in Jerusalem (Acts 6:9); Paul's origins in and ministry in Cilicia (Acts 21:39; 22:3). Greece/Macedonia: Paul's second journey (Acts 16–18).
33 Keener, *Acts*, 840–44; Barrett, *Acts*, 122.
34 Gilbert, 'List', 502.
35 Gilbert, 'List', 518.
36 Gilbert, 'List', 528.
37 Gilbert, 'List', 513–14.
38 Acts 16:6–10; 16:26; 17:6–7; 18:9–10.

The arguments outlined above clearly demonstrate that lists of nations were utilized by many ancient writers to demonstrate the expansive influence of their empire or culture or describe the organisation of the world in light of a certain factor (such as the Table of Nations or geographical astrology). None of them, however, provides a convincing source for Luke's list. At best, it can be said that Luke contributes another example of a list of nations that we can compare to the others, but we are unlikely to find a list from which Luke clearly copied.

5. A Jerusalemite Perspective

Although the discovery of a list that Luke copied down is unlikely, it is reasonable to consider that Luke developed his list based on an early Christian source. Metzger noted an idea suggested by Bo Reicke, that, 'Luke may have been influenced in his choice of countries… by following a list kept by leaders of the church in Antioch of lands to which Christian mission had been sent prior to about the year A.D. 50'.[39] This suggestion seems unlikely, if only for the reason that the list omits Cilicia, within which Paul had conducted missionary activity by the mid-40s CE at the latest (Acts 15:41).[40] A better option is that Luke was dependent on a source from Jerusalem that was aware from which nations the first converts from the Pentecost event came—those who received the word, were baptized, and were 'added' to the disciples (Acts 2:41). Rather than borrowing an older list, Luke could have constructed this one from recollections or written sources from the Jerusalem Church.[41] This understanding of the list is supported by: 1) The presence of 'Medes and Elamites' in the first century CE; 2) the Jerusalem based perspective of the list evidenced by the presence of 'Judea'; 3) the lack of inclusion of Cilicia on the Pentecost list even though Luke knew that Cilicians were *in Jerusalem* at this time; and 4) the possibility that the economic situation in Achaia was sufficiently depressive for it to be unlikely that many Jews would make the pilgrimage to Jerusalem at this time.

5.1 Medes and Elamites

The first three nationalities included in Luke's list, 'Parthians, Medes and Elamites', have led some commentators to look for a significantly earlier source list. Richard Pervo labelled the three as 'an obscure and archaic trio not otherwise encountered'.[42] Hans Conzelmann asserted that Luke is dependent on a list which 'reflects the political situation of an earlier time', noting that the Medes had 'long since disappeared from history', and that the 'Elamites were…known from the literature' (and thus not from living history).[43] His characterisation of these two regions is not quite accurate. While they were no longer the empires they once were, Elam and Media were by no means lost in the sands of time. For example, Elymais is referenced by Pliny the Elder in his first-century text *Natural History* (6.31). D.A. Potts notes that 'Elymais' was simply the Hellenised form of 'Elam'; he establishes their increasing 'assertiveness' throughout the first centuries BCE and CE; and notes

---

39 Metzger, 'Ancient Astrological Geography', 132.
40 Eastman, 'Paul', 52, provides a comparison of six scholars' opinions of the dating of Paul's time in Cilicia, all of which range between the mid-30s to the mid-40s CE. Cf. Barnett, *Paul*, 86
41 As reflected in his claim to eyewitness testimony in Luke 1:1-4.
42 Pervo, *Acts*, 66.
43 Conzelmann, *Acts*, 14.

the ongoing presence of Elamites even up to the Islamic period.[44] This warns against dismissing 'Elam' as an archaic term without a first-century referent.

'Medes' also does not necessarily point to an a more ancient source. A Rabbi Elazar of Media is mentioned in the Babylonian Talmud (b. Meg. 1:35), and there was a 'Nahum the Mede' who was a judge of civil law in Jerusalem at the time of the fall of Jerusalem in 70 CE.[45] While these two Jewish 'Medians' may not establish a strong picture of Jews in first-century Jerusalem who identified as 'Medians', their existence should cause hesitation about assuming that the reference to Medians in Acts 2 points to an older source list. This evidence of first-century 'Medes and Elamites' opens up the possibility that Luke's list reflects the self-identification of Jews from the Median or Elamite regions who still referred to themselves with such identifiers.

5.2 The Jerusalemite Perspective Regarding 'Judea'

Martin Hengel has argued that 'Judea' should be understood as 'Greater Judea', including Syria, reflecting 'a Jewish contemporary linguistic context, behind which... may well stand expectations concerning the extensiveness of Eretz Israel in the messianic future'.[46] His suggestion offers a solution to the geographical issue noted earlier, since Syria sits between Mesopotamia and Cappadocia, and it rightly raises the possibility of the influence of a Jewish perspective on the list. However, it seems unlikely that Luke, who displays an awareness of Roman provincial divisions elsewhere (e.g. Acts 15:41–16:10), would somewhat randomly label Syria as 'Judea'.[47]

It is more likely that it is a Jerusalemite perspective that influences the inclusion of Judea. It can be seen in the Acts narrative that, when the narrative is set in Jerusalem, Jerusalem and Judea are perceived as separate regions. In Acts 1:8, when Jesus (in Jerusalem) commissions his disciples, he declares, 'You will be my witnesses in Jerusalem, in all Judea and Samaria, and to the ends of the earth'. When persecution under Saul's leadership erupts (Acts 8:1), again the divisions of space are Jerusalem, where the church began, and 'the regions of Judea and Samaria' into which they fled. Similarly, when Paul describes his earliest preaching ministry, he says that he preached 'to those in Damascus, then in Jerusalem and throughout the countryside of Judea, and also to the Gentiles' (Acts 26:20).[48]

A similar idea is seen in Philo's list of nations (*Leg. Ad. Gaium* 281–282), where Agrippa declares Jerusalem to be his 'father city' (ἐμὴ μέν ἐστι πατρίς) because he lives there, and describes it as the 'mother city', or metropolis (μητρόπολις), of Judea *and* other nations by way of all of its 'colonies' (τὰς ἀποικίας) spread among them.[49] There is a nuanced difference in relationship between the city those who live in it, to those who do not and yet view it as their 'mother city'.

The Jerusalemite perspective differentiates the city from its regional surrounds. In the context of regular pilgrimages to Jerusalem for major Jewish festivals, it is understandable that the

---

44 Potts, *Archaeology of Elam*, 7, 392, 404.
45 Neusner, *Rabbinic Traditions*, 413.
46 Hengel, 'Ἰουδαία', 179.
47 Dismissing Hengel's argument here raises the question of the absence of Syria from the Acts 2 list. The narrative of the expansion of the Christian message to Antioch in Acts 11:19-30 may suggest that Syrian Jews did not make up a significant group in the Jerusalem church. I suggest this cautiously, however, since one of the deacons appointed in Acts 6 is 'Nicolaus, a proselyte of Antioch'.
48 Elsewhere in Acts, 'Judea' seems to include, or refer to, Jerusalem. In these examples the perspective is from outside of Jerusalem. For example, in response to the message of a prophet from Jerusalem, Christians in Antioch send relief to the brothers in Judea (Acts 11:27-29); and the Roman Jews tell Paul that they had not received any letters 'from Judea' about him (Acts 28:21).
49 Leonhardt-Balzer, 'Diaspora Jewish Attitudes', 48.

resident population of the city would recognise the influx of visitors, whether they were from Judea or further abroad. The inclusion of Judea in the list, then, fits with the suggestion that Luke has accessed a source connected with the Jerusalem church.

5.3 Cilicians in Jerusalem

It is noteworthy that Luke does not include Jews from Cilicia in the list since he knows of their presence in Jerusalem at this time (Acts 6:9). Material evidence suggests a large Jewish population in Cilicia that was engaged in trade along the Palestinian coast.[50] If Luke had simply selected examples of Diaspora communities that were of a reasonable size and had some broader influence, surely the Cilicians would have provided an appealing option.

It is interesting to note, however, the characterisation of the Cilician Jews in the early stages of Acts. In these early stages, Cilician Jews are presented as opponents. The Cilician synagogue is included among those who disputed (συνζητοῦντες; 6:9) with Stephen and orchestrated his trial (6:11-13).

The lists at 2:9-11 and 6:9 overlap significantly except for the mention of the Cilicians. The Cyrenians, Alexandrians and Asians all find counterparts in the Acts 2 list, but the Cilicians are only in the later list. For example, some Cyrenian Jews were amongst the Pentecost crowd and presumably converted (Acts 2:10; 11:20), but there were also Cyrenians that were antagonistic to the Christians (6:9). In the case of the Cilicians, they are only listed as antagonistic (6:9). Considering this antagonism of the Cilician synagogue (and its chief exemplar, Saul), a possibility may be that no Cilicians were converted at Pentecost. If Luke drew upon eyewitness accounts from members of the Jerusalem church, they may well have remembered the Cilicians at that time as opponents of the church.

This picture of Cilician Jews is developed in the character of Saul, later revealed to be from Tarsus in Cilicia (9:11; 21:39), who is introduced as approving of Stephen's execution and being a major participant in the persecution of the church (7:58; 8:1-3). The vivid description of Saul in verse 3 includes the only occurrence of λυμαίνομαι (ἐλυμαίνετο; 'ravaged') in the New Testament. The term had been used in Greco-Roman literature to describe the destruction of a region by war[51] or wild animals.[52] Its application to Saul's actions characterises them with a particularly horrible type of violence.

To develop the picture further, Mark Wilson suggests that the 'Hellenists' that Paul disputed (συνεζήτει) with in Acts 9:29, after his conversion, are the same group as those who disputed (συνζητοῦντες; 6:9) with Stephen. Wilson says that the link between the two is strengthened by the fact that these are the only occurrences of the verb συζητέω in Acts,[53] but it could be added that the debate with Stephen occurs in the context of him being identified as a Hellenist (9:1,3,5). These Hellenists in Acts 9 tried to kill Paul, but the 'brothers... sent him off to Tarsus' (9:30). If these Hellenists include the Cilician Jews, the characterisation of fanatical opposition to the Church is strengthened by their violent rejection of one who was formerly one of their own number.

These passages in Acts present the Hellenistic Jews of Jerusalem as particularly oppositional to the early Christians, particularly those who had once been a part of their group before converting to Christianity. The Cilicians seem to be particularly noteworthy for their antagonism because

---

50   Fairchild, 'Jewish Communities', 209–10; Hengel & Schwemer, *Paul between Damascus and Antioch*, 161.
51   Appian *Rom. Hist* 4.11; 10.4.22
52   Euphorion *Poet. Frag.* 32, 82.
53   Mark Wilson, 'Cilicia', 17, n.7.

they are not included among those at Pentecost and the first recorded Cilician conversion is Saul's miraculous encounter with Jesus on the Damascus road. This suggests that Luke did not leave Cilicians off the list of those present at the Pentecost event because there were none in the city, but because they were remembered as antagonists against the church rather than those who joined the church at that early stage.

5.4 Achaian Depression

Martin Hengel asserted that no pilgrims from Greece were mentioned because the Jewish communities there were of less significance than those included in the list. He says, 'The Diaspora in Thracia, Macedonia, and Achaia are left out here because they are of less significance, while the Roman Jews had to be named due to their status as citizens of a metropolis',[54] and, 'in Jerusalem… the returnees from Babylon, Asia Minor, Egypt, Cyrenaica, and Rome possessed the greatest influence'.[55] He does not, however, provide any justification for his argument.

While it may be the case that the Jewish community in Greece was less significant, it has already been seen that 'significance' has not been a crucial factor in the selection of places mentioned in the list. It could be argued that literarily speaking, Greece would have been just the place that Luke may have wanted to include on his list. Josephus used the example of Athens and Sparta numerous times in his arguments, suggesting that these types of places were influential enough in the minds of his readers to use them as evidence.[56] If Luke was writing to a predominantly Gentile audience, it seems likely that he also would use Greece for this advantage.

There is, though, evidence that suggests that the diminished state of Greece in the first century could have led to lower mobility of the population. This may provide some explanation of the lack of Greek Jews in Jerusalem at this time.

Though the image of a wealthy and decadent Corinth is axiomatic in New Testament scholarship, the Roman colony was not necessarily representative of the rest of the Greek Peninsula in the first century CE. Indeed, within Corinth itself the distribution of wealth was not evenly shared amongst the inhabitants. Some estimates suggest that only 1% of the population was 'wealthy', while the vast majority existed on a subsistence or near-subsistence level.[57] Ancient reports on Athens in the first centuries BCE and CE, for example, describe the city as destitute. Cicero says that the 'present enfeebled and shattered renown of Greece' is only sustained by the *former* reputation of Athens.[58] Horace describes the city as 'vacuas Athenas'.[59] Pausanias similarly recounts how after being sacked by Sulla in 86 BCE, the city was 'sorely afflicted…but she flourished again when Hadrian was emperor'.[60] The 'affliction' of Athens, then, lasted from the early first century BCE through to the early second century CE.[61] James H. Oliver has observed that the experience of Sparta in the same period was even less promising than that of Athens.[62]

54　Hengel, 'Ἰουδαία', 179.
55　Hengel, 'Ἰουδαία', 179.
56　Josephus *Ag. Ap.* 2.130, 2.262–269.
57　Nash, *1 Corinthians*, 19–20. Cf. Morris, 'City as Foil', 147.
58　Cicero, *Flac.* 62.
59　Horace, *Ep.* II.2.81.
60　Pausanias, *Descr. Gr.* 1.20.6–7.
61　Shear, 'Athens', 370, comments, regarding the demolition of a residential and business district of Athens under Augustus, that 'it is an accurate measure of the city's depressed economic conditions that much of this neighbourhood seems afterwards to have lain vacant and unoccupied for a full century before any construction was undertaken'.
62　Oliver, 'Roman Emperors', 415–17.

If the experience of Athens is more representative of the rest of Greece than that of Corinth, it is understandable that the Jewish communities were not as likely to have been able to afford the travel to Jerusalem. M. Stern says that 'the diminished position of Greece during the imperial period is reflected in the history of the Jews in that country, who do not seem to have had any major impact of the Jewish world of those times'.[63]

Inscriptional evidence for the presence of Athenians in Judea in the first century CE is non-existent. There is an Ἀθήναιος mentioned in a burial inscription in Marisa, dated to the second or first centuries BCE,[64] but, as well as being too early, this is a personal name rather than an indicator of the individual's city of origin.[65] Instances of Ἀθηναῖος in eastern regions tend to date from the fourth and third centuries BCE, in the period of Greek domination in the region.[66]

In Athens, Jewish inscriptions from the first century CE indicate that the community was cosmopolitan, including Jews from eastern cities such as Antioch,[67] Jerusalem,[68] and possibly Marisa.[69] This could either suggest that the reciprocal travel between Athens and Judea, envisioned by the Athenians when they gave honours to Hyrcanus in the first century BCE,[70] continued into the first century CE. On the other hand, it may suggest that while people were still drawn to Athens as an intellectual centre, there were no, or fewer, instances of Jews established in Athens relocating to Judea. In relation to this point, it is noteworthy that Achaians and Macedonians are not included on the list of Hellenistic Jews in Jerusalem in Acts 9:29.

The depressed state of Greece and the sparsity of evidence of Greeks in Judea in the first century CE suggest that an historical reality lies behind Luke's non-inclusion of Jews from Greece in his Pentecost list. It is possible that few, or no, Jews from the Greek peninsula made the journey to Jerusalem in this period because of their fragile financial situation. While this economic disadvantage may have caused the Jews of the Greek peninsula to have a less significant impact on the broader Jewish world, their significance is not necessarily the cause of Luke's non-inclusion of them in his list. It is possible, rather, that their absence is an instance of Luke's historical precision[71]—there were no Greeks mentioned because there were no Greeks present, and since they were not present, Luke's source did not report them.

6. Conclusion

It has been argued above that the various scholarly suggestions for Luke's source for the Acts 2 list fail to explain convincingly the nations and regions included in and excluded from the list. An alternative proposal was made, that Luke depended on records or remembrances from the Jerusalem church. This proposal is supported by the reference to Medes and Elamites, the strange

---

63 Stern, 'Jewish Diaspora', 157–58.
64 *SEG* 34.1497. Oren & Rappaport, 'Necropolis', 147, 51.
65 In this case, Ἀθήναιος is a theophoric name, whereas Ἀθηναῖος is the ethnic indicator. *SEG* 39.316; Martin, ''Ἀθηναιοι'.
66 *SEG* 27.973; 35.1477.
67 IG II² 8231, 8232.
68 IG II² 8934.
69 IG II² 9285. Stern admits that the 'Theodorus' of this inscription only 'may' have been Jewish. Stern, 'Jewish Diaspora', 158.
70 Jos. *Ant.* XIV.151–152.
71 Forbes, 'Acts', 28–35, has recently discussed the occurrences of surprising historical and contextual precision in the Acts narrative. Like the one identified in this paper, those mentioned by Forbes are not necessarily central to the development of the story.

inclusion of 'Judea' in the list, the absence of Cilicians from the list, and absence of Jews from the Greek peninsula which reflected the restrictive nature of the economic situation in Greece at this time. The implication of this proposal is that Luke's list is not a simply a theological statement, nor an arbitrarily edited citation of list from some other literary source, but a construction that is based in the historical reality of the earliest Jerusalem church and accords with Luke's claim of accessing eyewitness sources (Luke 1:1-4).

The conclusions reached by this paper open some further lines of enquiry. Firstly, more investigation into Cilician Judaism is warranted to clarify further any characteristic traits of that group of Diaspora Jews and what influenced them. Secondly, the argument that Jews from the Greek peninsula were absent from Pentecost suggests that the Greek cities may not have had an early Christian presence like that which some scholars have proposed for cities such as Rome, that did have representatives at Pentecost. Following on from this, the lack of Jews from Greece at Pentecost may relate to the emphasis Luke places on Paul's movement from Troas over to Macedonia and Greece in Acts 16.

7. List of References
7.1 Ancient Sources

Appian. *Roman History, Volume I*. Edited and translated by Brian McGing. Loeb Classical Library 2. Cambridge, MA: Harvard University Press, 1912.

Appian. *Roman History, Volume II*. Edited and translated by Brian McGing. Loeb Classical Library 3. Cambridge, MA: Harvard University Press, 1912.

Euphorion. 'Poetic Fragments'. In *Hellenistic Collection: Philitas. Alexander of Aetolia. Hermesianax. Euphorion. Parthenius*. Edited and translated by J. L. Lightfoot. Loeb Classical Library 508. Cambridge, MA: Harvard University Press, 2010.

Herodotus. *The Persian Wars, Volume III: Books 5–7*. Translated by A. D. Godley. Loeb Classical Library 119. Cambridge, MA: Harvard University Press, 1922.

Josephus, Flavius. *Against Apion*. Translated by John M.G. Barclay. Leiden: Brill, 2013.

Josephus. *Jewish Antiquities, Volume IV: Books 9–11*. Translated by Ralph Marcus. Loeb Classical Library 326. Cambridge, MA: Harvard University Press, 1937.

Josephus. *Jewish Antiquities, Volume VI: Books 14–15*. Translated by Ralph Marcus, Allen Wikgren. Loeb Classical Library 489. Cambridge, MA: Harvard University Press, 1943.

Pliny. *Natural History, Volume II. Books 3–7*. Translated by H. Rackham. Loeb Classical Library 352. Cambridge, MA: Harvard University Press, 1942.

Vettius Valens. *Anthologies*. Posted online by Mark T. Riley. California State University. www.csus.edu/indiv/r/rileymt/vettius%20valens%20entire.pdf

7.2 Modern Sources

Barnett, Paul — *Paul: Missionary of Jesus*. Grand Rapids: Eerdmans, 2008.

Barrett, C.K. — *The Acts of the Apostles*, vol. 1 (Edinburgh: T. & T. Clark, 1994).

Bock, Darrell L. — *Acts* (Grand Rapids: Baker, 2007).

Bruce, F.F. — *The Book of the Acts* (NICNT; Grand Rapids: Eerdmans, 1988).

Cohen, Getzel M. — 'Travel between Palestine and Mesopotamia During the Hellenistic and Roman Periods: A Preliminary Study', in Markham J. Geller (ed.), *The Archaeology and Material Culture of the Babylonian Talmud* (Leiden: Brill, 2015), 186–224.

Conzelmann, Hans — *Acts of the Apostles*, Hermeneia (Philadelphia: Fortress, 1987).

Eastman, David L. — 'Paul: An Outline of His Life', in Mark Harding & Alanna Nobbs (eds.), *All Things to All Cultures: Paul among Jews, Greeks, and Romans* (Grand Rapids: Eerdmans, 2013), 34–56.

Fairchild, Mark R. — 'The Jewish Communities in Eastern Rough Cilicia', *Journal of Ancient Judaism* 5.2 (2014), 204–16.

Fitzmyer, Joseph A. — *The Acts of the Apostles: A New Translation with Introduction and Commentary* (New York: Doubleday, 1998).

Forbes, Christopher — 'The Acts of the Apostles as a Source for Studying Early Christianity', in Mark Harding & Alanna Nobbs (eds), *Into All the World: Emergent Christianity in Its Jewish and Greco-Roman Context* (Grand Rapids: Eerdmans, 2017), 5–36.

Gilbert, Gary — 'The List of Nations in Acts 2: Roman Propaganda and the Lukan Response', *JBL* 121.3 (2002), 497–529.

Gurevich, David — 'The Water Pools and the Pilgrimage to Jerusalem in the Late Second Temple Period', *Palestine Exploration Quarterly* 149.2 (2017), 103–34.

Haenchen, Ernst — *The Acts of the Apostles* (Oxford: Blackwell, 1971).

Hengel, Martin — 'Ἰουδαία in the Geographical List of Acts 2:9–11 and Syria as "Greater Judea"', *BBR* 10.2 (2000), 161–80.

Hengel, Martin, & Anna Maria Schwemer — *Paul between Damascus and Antioch: The Unknown Years* (Louisville: Westminster John Knox Press, 1997).

Johnson, Luke Timothy — *The Acts of the Apostles* (Collegeville: The Liturgical Press, 1992).

Keener, Craig S. — *Acts: An Exegetical Commentary. Volume 1: Introduction and 1:1–2:47* (Grand Rapids: Baker, 2012).

Kistemaker, Simon J. — *Exposition of the Acts of the Apostles* (Grand Rapids: Baker, 1990.

Leonhardt-Balzer, Jutta	'Diaspora Jewish Attitudes to Metropoleis: Philo and Paul on Balanced Personalities, Split Loyalties, Jerusalem, and Rome', in Steve Walton, Paul R. Trebilco, and David W.J. Gill (eds.), *The Urban World and the First Christians* (Grand Rapids: Eerdmans, 2017), 86–98.
Martin, Alain	''Aθηναιοι Et 'Aθηναιοι En Égypte Gréco-Romaine', *Ancient Society* 20 (1989), 169–84.
McKechnie, Paul	'Jewish Christianity to AD 100', in Mark Harding & Alanna Nobbs (eds.), *Into All the World: Emergent Christianity in Its Jewish and Greco-Roman Context* (Grand Rapids: Eerdmans, 2017), 134–57.
Metzger, Bruce M.	'Ancient Astrological Geography and Acts 2:9–11', in *Apostolic History and the Gospel: Biblical and Historical Essays Presented to F.F. Bruce on His 60th Birthday*, ed. W. Ward Gasque and Ralph P. Martin (Exeter: Paternoster, 1970), 123-133.
Metzger, Bruce M.	*A Textual Commentary of the Greek New Testament*, 2nd ed. (Stuttgart: Deutsche Bibelgesellschaft, 2000).
Morris, Helen	'The City as Foil (Not Friend nor Foe): Conformity and Subversion in 1 Corinthians 12:12–31', in Steve Walton, Paul R. Trebilco, and David W.J. Gill (eds.), *The Urban World and the First Christians* (Grand Rapids: Eerdmans, 2017), 141–59.
Nash, Robert Scott	*1 Corinthians* (SHBC; Macon: Smith & Helwys, 2009).
Neusner, Jacob.	*The Rabbinic Traditions About the Pharisees before 70, Part 1 the Masters* (Eugene: Wipf & Stock, 1971).
Oliver, James H.	'Roman Emperors and Athens', *Historia* 30.4 (1981), 412–23.
Oren, Eliezer D., & Uriel Rappaport	'The Necropolis of Maresha—Beth Govrin', *Israel Exploration Journal* 34.2 (1984), 114–53.
Pervo, Richard I.	*Acts: A Commentary* (Hermeneia; Minneapolis: Fortress Press, 2009).
Potts, D.T.	*The Archaeology of Elam: Formation and Transformation of an Ancient Iranian State*, 2nd ed. (Cambridge: Cambridge University Press, 2015).
Schnabel, Eckhard J.	*Acts* (Grand Rapids: Zondervan, 2012).
Shear, T. Leslie	'Athens: From City-State to Provincial Town', *Hesperia* 50.4 (1981), 356–77.
Stern, M.	'The Jewish Diaspora', in S. Safrai, et al (eds.), *The Jewish People in the First Century: Historical Geography, Political History, Social, Cultural, and Religious Life and Institutions* (Assen: Van Gorcum & Co., 1974), 117–83.
Taylor, Justin	'The List of the Nations in Acts 2:9-11', *Revue Biblique* 106, no. 3 (1999), 408–20.
Weinstock, Stefan	'The Geographical Catalogue in Acts 2:9-11', *JRS* 38 (1948), 43–46.

Wilson, Mark.	'Cilicia: The First Christian Churches in Anatolia', *Tyndale Bulletin* 54, no. 1 (2003), 15–30.
Witherington, Ben, III	*The Acts of the Apostles: A Socio-Rhetorical Commentary* (Grand Rapids: Eerdmans, 1998).

Book reviews

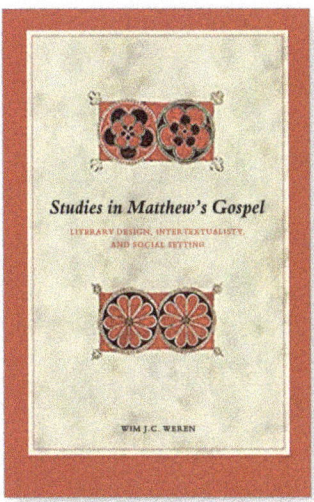

Wim J.C. Weren, *Studies in Matthew's Gospel: Literary Design, Intertextuality and Social Setting* (Biblical Interpretation Series 130; Leiden: Brill, 2014). xii+345 pp.

The eminent Catholic scholar Wim Weren was Professor of Biblical Studies (New Testament) at the University of Tilburg from 1984 to 2011. *Studies in Matthew's Gospel* is a collection of his published scholarship on Matthew over this period, much of it revised or abridged, with the studies grouped together into three parts according to theme.

The first part deals with literary design or, to use Weren's alternative title, 'intra-textuality'—dealing with relations within the text. The most significant chapter here is a study of Matthew's macrostructure (first published in 2006), proposing a multi-layered approach to the shape of the Gospel. At the first level, the structure is very coarse indeed, with a central section running from 4:18–25:46 and dealing with 'Jesus' ministry'. At the next level down, this central section is divided into two parts according to geography (away from Jerusalem, and then towards and in Jerusalem), separated by a 'hinge' section at Caesarea Philippi (16:13–28). Further levels in the scheme break down similarly, often into two parts separated by a 'hinge'.

The other studies in this part of the book take a broadly 'literary' approach to a number of subjects: children in Matthew (who function to represent both the vulnerable and humble disciple), to secret knowledge, and to life beyond death (which, Weren argues, is real and bodily).

In the second and longest part of the book, Weren turns to intertextuality. The first few of these studies are concerned with Old Testament quotations or allusions in Matthew. The main insights here come from a careful consideration of connections not just to the Septuagint but also to the Hebrew Scriptures, and from thinking through the meaning of texts in their original contexts (that is, rightly not just assuming Matthew has ignored these contexts). Weren considers the women in Matthew's genealogy, the foundational quotations from Isaiah in 1:23 and 4:15–16; and then (across two studies) the multiple texts connected to Jesus' teaching on divorce, and his entry into Jerusalem. The final three studies in this part also draw on related texts (that is, not connected directly to Matthew by quotation or allusion). For example, when examining the allusions to Isaiah 5:1–7 in Matthew 21:33–46 (the Parable of the Tenants), Weren also considers Mark 12, the Targum Jonathan and 4Q500. In a study on Matthew's view of the resurrection, he uses 4 Ezra as a point of comparison. The final study is a straightforward comparative study of the concept of community across Matthew, James and the Didache.

The third part of the book is perhaps the least satisfactory, dealing with the historical setting and origin of Matthew's Gospel. There is a study arguing for a three-stage evolution of the 'Matthean communities', with each stage rather crudely linked to a number of particular proof-texts across the Gospel. This is perhaps an improvement on the very static conceptions of the 'Matthean communities' in some scholarship, but the argument lacks any serious discussion of the function of Gospel (and its sources) for its original readers and hearers. Another study attempts to reconstruct the Q text of the Parable of the Guests (22:1–14), and then attempts to draw conclusions from the differences between this reconstructed text and the text of Matthew. The arguments in this part seemed speculative and verging on the circular, and perhaps tell us more about the state of biblical scholarship in the late twentieth century than they do about the Gospel of Matthew in the first.

> a careful and meticulous scholar at work

That said, the overriding impression one gets from working through these studies (especially those in parts one and two) is of a careful and meticulous scholar at work. The writing is at all times clear and understated. There is evidence throughout of a vast and thorough knowledge of Matthean scholarship. Most of all, there is almost always a very close attention to detail.

The results from this careful and sometimes lengthy analysis are occasionally interesting but often less than spectacular. The study of life after death in chapter four concludes that 'bodily aspects play a part in Matthew's imagining of Jesus' renewed life beyond death' (page 87). At this, and at the conclusion of other studies, I was left thinking 'Surely that was obvious?'. The study of connections between the Parable of the Tenants and Isaiah 5 in chapter 10 concludes that there are indeed connections between these (and other) texts. At this, and at the conclusion of other studies, I was left thinking 'And so...?'.

In other words, there is a neglect across these studies of the big picture of Matthew's Gospel, and the larger themes and questions of function and purpose. The implicit assumption seems to be that if we find it hard to draw firm conclusions on very narrow and particular issues and questions in Matthew, even after the most careful analysis, then how can we possibly begin to address these bigger issues? But this may well be a mistake. By focussing too narrowly, we exclude relevant contextual and narrative data, and impede our ability to draw conclusions.

The exception to this neglect of the bigger picture is the first study, on the macrostructure of the Gospel. Here the problems are different—if anything *too little* attention to detail. It would make more sense, I would have thought, to work first on the microstructure of the Gospel—where the patterns are clearer—and then work up to the macrostructure (rather than the other way round).

Nevertheless, *Studies in Matthew's Gospel* is a hugely helpful collection; and I would say, an essential read for Matthew scholars. There is not a page without something interesting or stimulating to dwell on.

Ben Cooper
Fulwood Bible Training, Sheffield, UK

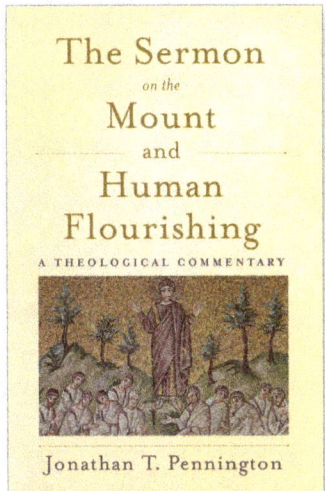

Jonathan T. Pennington, *The Sermon on the Mount and Human Flourishing: A Theological Commentary.* Grand Rapids: Baker Academic, 2017. 325 pp. $29.99

The book's main thesis, as its title makes clear, is "the Sermon on the Mount is Christianity's answer to the greatest metaphysical question that humanity has always faced—How can we experience true human flourishing? What is happiness, blessedness, *shalom*, and how does one obtain and sustain it?" (p. 14)

Pennington argues that the Sermon's answer to the human-flourishing question is that "true human flourishing is only available through communion with the Father God through his revealed Son, Jesus, as we are empowered by the Holy Spirit" (p.14). In this answer, Jesus provides "a Christocentric, flourishing-oriented, kingdom-awaiting, eschatological wisdom exhortation that situates the disciples into God's community or kingdom" (p.15). This flourishing through wholeness will only be experienced fully in the eschaton, when God finally establishes his reign upon the earth. "As followers of Jesus' journey through their lives, they will experience suffering in this world, which in God's providence is in fact a means to true flourishing even now" (p. 15).

The author describes his book as a historical, literary, and theological exposition of the Sermon on the Mount, in which he invites his reader to read the Sermon in "the dual context of Jewish wisdom literature and the Greco-Roman virtue tradition, both of which are concerned with the great theological and existential question of human flourishing" (p. 1). The assumption is that Jesus is the fulfilment and incarnation of both: he is the complete and virtuous human and the true philosopher king (pp. 15, 36).

After a brief history of interpretation of the Sermon, Pennington uses, in part one, Umberto Eco's notion of the cultural encyclopedia and the Model Reader to locate the Sermon in the complex context of Jewish wisdom literature with its emphasis on the restoration of *shalom* in the eschaton and the Graeco-Roman Aristotelian *eudemonistic* tradition, with its emphasis on human flourishing (pp. 35-38).

In the middle three chapters of part one, Pennington is probably at his best. He introduces two major contributions related to the Greek words: *makarios* and *teleios*. With respect to the first, *makarios*, he observes that all languages, European and non-European, beside English, make a clear distinction that he thinks the bible itself makes, between a blessing that is something God gives to people versus a description that someone else makes of a state of flourishing or *macarism* (p. 50).

When discussing the second, *teleios*, and how it should be translated in English, Pennington makes another careful distinction. He helpfully notices that the hypocrisy in Matthew (typically in the lives of the Pharisees and Scribes) is about doubleness of actions and the inner person or heart, not words and actions (Matt 15:8, cf. Isa 29:13, and Matt 23: 25-28) (p. 92). Hence, he suggested the word 'whole' or 'complete,' or even 'virtuous' instead of 'perfect' in Matthew 5:48, the verse that is central to the structure of the Sermon (p. 70). Pennington calls this reading a *"cardiographic reading of teleios"*. Jesus's consistent emphasis throughout is that whole-person righteousness (from the heart, or the inner person) is what real righteousness, godliness (godlikeness), and holiness look like (p. 82).

In chapter four, Pennington examines, very briefly, seven key terms: righteousness, hypocrisy, heart, gentiles/pagans, "the Father in Heaven", the Kingdom of God/Heaven, and reward, recompense and treasure. Chapter five provides a structure to read the Sermon. The author's conviction is that appreciating Matthew's literary skills is key to its proper understanding (pp. 105-106).

The second part of the book is a brief commentary on the Sermon (pp. 135-286—roughly half of the book), which reflects Pennington's conviction that the proper orientation toward the Sermon along with the appreciation of Matthew's literary skills are key to the proper understanding of the Sermon (and the whole of Matthew). Pennington's threefold approach in the commentary is quite clear: he examines the Old Testament context (most often, Isaianic), in order to identify how it helps the reader understand the Sermon, and finally how this understanding makes sense of the whole Gospel.

The Book's final part is given to theological reflection. Here Pennington shares six theses as the result of his long research in the history of interpretations of the Sermon and his interest in the philosophy of ethics and practical theology. His theological conviction is that the Greek philosophical system, which emphasized virtue leading to human flourishing, is not an enemy of Judaism and Christianity, because the story of the bible is about human flourishing as well. As believers are invited to live their lives wisely, in a way similar to what is found in Psalm one, they orient themselves towards God and experience flourishing as they enjoy *shalom*.

However, in agreement with N.T. Wright, Pennington clarifies that this flourishing is not mere individual, but communal, in which believers are called to be a royal priesthood and to generate justice and beauty (p. 297). His sixth thesis, drawing on Wolterstorff, notes that *Shaloming* the earth is core to the way in which God works in the world in which he spreads his Kingdom (p. 305).

Pennington's understanding of hypocrisy in Matthew as about doubleness of actions and the inner person or heart, not words and actions, is not without difficulty, especially considering the overlap between the Pharisees and Scribes' evil inner character and their evil deeds as well. Pennington himself notices that the Pharisees and Scribes could be the prime example of false prophets described in Matthew 7:22 (how they could cast out demons in Jesus' name is not explained by Pennington!) (p. 277), yet later he mentions that they were not surprised to be rejected by Jesus who describes them as workers of lawlessness (Matt 7:23) (p. 279). Could it be the case that their emphasis on the external purity was a deliberate attempt to hide both their evil heart and the hidden evil side of their double life, particularly when the reader sees how they consciously spread a false story to deny Jesus's resurrection at the end of the Gospel (Matt 28:11-15)?

Overall, Pennington's work is stimulating and challenging, especially his thoughtful engagement with the Reformed tradition to argue for a moral view of the bible, in which virtue and grace are compatible, not contrary (pp. 299-305).

Even for those not convinced of his final conclusions (e.g. his translation of the beatitudes in terms of flourishing), Pennington's work will prove to be a genuine contribution to the proper understanding of the Sermon's, and Matthew's, theology, and a foundation for discussing wider issues related to soteriology, discipleship, philosophy of ethics, and practical theology. In his own words, the Sermon on the Mount has a revealing litmus test function for different views (p. 39). I highly recommend this book for Matthean students as well as serious lay readers.

George Bishai
Alexandria School of Theology, Egypt
and Moore College, Sydney

Bradley T. Johnson, *The Form and Function of Mark 1:1-15: A Multi-Disciplinary Approach to the Markan Prologue* (Eugene, Or: Pickwick Publications, 2017). 173 pages.

The opening verses of Mark's Gospel are no strangers to scholarly attention. Debate continues over the text, extent, designation, structure, syntax, intertextual relationships and significance of Mark's opening section. In *The Form and Function of Mark 1:1-15*, the publication of his 2015 PhD, Johnson enters this discussion, aiming to determine the 'closing boundary' and purpose of Mark's opening unit.

In chapter 1 Johnson surveys recent research in Markan studies and in particular works dealing with Mark's opening materials (to 2014). This survey is structured around different methodological approaches and touches on works of redaction criticism, oral and performance criticism, composition criticism, narrative criticism, genre criticism, and rhetorical criticism. Johnson notes that the proliferation of interpretative approaches to Mark has only widened the range of suggestions regarding the form and function of Mark's opening.

Chapter 2 focuses on the formal integrity of Mark 1:1-15. Johnson highlights a constellation of syntactic and literary features that support the overall coherence of Mark 1:1-15 and contribute to its structure and function. Mark 1:1 is identified as a heading or *incipit* for the prologue. The citation in 1:2-3 is understood as distinct from 1:1 and subordinate to the description of John's appearance in 1:4. The parallelism between the accounts of John and Jesus and the inversion of focus from John to Jesus in 1:4-15 are emphasised. Perhaps most noteworthy in this material is Johnson's illustration of 'aural reading' from voice recognition software, and his argument that Μετὰ δὲ in Mk 1:14 marks a moment of climactic conjunction rather than disjunction.

The focus in chapter 3 shifts from the text itself to the world behind the text. Johnson explores the context within which Mark operated through an examination of the aural nature and rhetoric of Mark's world. After a brief introduction to Greco-Roman rhetoric, Johnson identifies the use of *ekphrasis* and *synkrisis* in Mark 1:1-15, and argues that Mark's opening functions as an *exordium* in which Mark establishes the credibility of his main character Jesus.

Importantly, Johnson concludes that while Mark demonstrates at least basic facility with Greco-Roman rhetoric, he also makes use of non-enthymatic, inartificial proofs (more characteristic of Jewish rhetoric).

In chapter 4 Johnson examines the form and function of prologues in antiquity through a survey of ten 'representative' examples of ancient Greco-Roman Βίοι. He concludes that Mark's opening fits the pattern of an expository

> **Mark demonstrates at least basic facility with Greco-Roman rhetoric**

prologue although with one significant difference—Mark includes no information on his central character's lineage or family origin. Johnson argues that Mark intends his opening to function as an expository prologue but utilises a different means to establish the significance of Jesus. (Of course the absence of this key feature could also be seen to undermine the identification of Mark's opening as an expository prologue).

Finally, in chapter 5 Johnson revisits a number of questions raised throughout his study and focuses on the function of Mark's opening. He concludes that Mark 1:1-15 is a coherent, formal unit that functions as an expository prologue to legitimate Jesus as the Anointed Son of God through a range of rhetorical devices suited to a mixed audience. For Jewish readers, Mark relies on the inartificial proofs of Scripture, the testimony of witnesses and the evidence of signs; for Gentile readers, Mark relies upon conventional Greco-Roman rhetorical devices including *ekphrasis* and *synkrisis*.

Johnson's work clearly demonstrates the importance of Mark's opening and its impact on the reading of Mark's Gospel as a whole. His argument is carefully developed and he addresses many of the significant questions surrounding the beginning of Mark's Gospel.

Johnson provides an example of Bauer and Trainas' Inductive Bible Study in action and his interaction with various methodological approaches, and in particular Greco-Roman rhetoric, serves to illustrate their potential value for reading Mark.

While no work can be truly exhaustive, there are some perhaps surprising omissions in the book. First, Johnson makes no reference to the works of Morna Hooker, Richard Dillon, or Augustine Musopole on the beginning of Mark. Second, although irony is identified in chapter 3 as a rhetorical device found in Mark, no sustained attention is given to the contribution of the prologue to the development of dramatic irony.

Despite these omissions, Johnson's book covers some important terrain for students of Mark. While it will not close the debate on Mark's opening, Johnson's contribution remains a helpful addition to it.

Peter Ryan
Moore College

Armin D. Baum, Detlef Häusser, Emmanuel L. Rehfeld (eds.), *Der jüdische Messias Jesus und sein jüdischer Apostel Paulus*, WUNT II.425 (Tübingen: Mohr Siebeck, 2016). viii + 417 pp., paperback. ISBN 978-3-16-153872-8, 94 Euro

The essays included in this volume have their origin in a conference held in June 2015 in Tübingen to honour the 65th birthday of Rainer Riesner. The essays are devoted to two emphases in Riesner's research and which he endeavoured to combine in his publications: the Jewish Messiah Jesus and his Jewish apostle Paul ("In seinen Arbeiten zu den synoptischen Evangelien betont er den jüdischen Hintergrund der Jesusüberlieferung, und ebenso sieht er in der alttestamentlich-jüdischen Tradition und namentlich in der Jesusüberlieferung einen Wurzelgrund der Botschaft des Apostels Paulus", v).

Part one offers four essays on the Jewish Messiah Jesus of Nazareth:

In his essay "Zu 'den Werken des Gesalbten' (Matt 11:2-6 par) vor dem Hintergrund der alttestamentlichen und frühjüdischen Traditionsgeschichte" (9-47), Thomas Pola notes that according to late Old Testament and early Jewish traditions the Messiah is expected to do certain works. He is to achieve the restitution of Israel, the construction of an eschatological temple, and eschatological atonement. In comparison to this expectation, the "works of the Messiah" listed in Matthew 11:5 par. are incomplete because v. 2-6 demonstrate the fulfilment of Isaiah 34f; 61:1-3 and a tradition close to 4Q521. According to Matthew 11:2-6 par., the new era expected by the Old Testament and early Jewish apocalyptic has begun without any preceding universal judgment. However, in Isaiah 7:1-17, the impetus of the expectation of an ideal Davidic ruler influences the specific definition of "faith" that shapes Messianic expectations in Isaiah 7:9 as well as in subsequent Old Testament and Early Jewish traditions.

Roland Deines' essay on the relationship between Jesus and the messianic expectations of his time ("Der Messiasanspruch Jesu im Kontext frühjüdischer Messiaserwartungen", 49–106) contends that the New Testament writings must be understood as *early Jewish writings*. Their common conviction is that Jesus of Nazareth was Israel's promised Messiah, sent by God to save his people. As such the New Testament writings can be seen as "parallel" readings of the Old Testament tradition alongside other early Jewish messianic traditions. By discussing various historical messianic realisations from Zerubbabel to Bar Kokhba, Deines shows an expectation that messianic claimants relate scriptural promises to themselves. Such "self-referential Scriptural exegesis" is among the tasks of a Messiah. Several messianic figures of the Second Temple Period are portrayed as teaching. Against this backdrop, Jesus' detailed and repeated recourse to Scripture should be seen as part of his messianic self-presentation. Jesus' knowledge can be traced back to his family ("Jesus und die davidisch-messianischen Traditionen seiner Familie", 95-100), which should be understood—in analogy to other contemporary messianic groups—as a Davidic clan anticipating the promised Nezer ("branch", Isa 11:1) who educated their children in a family-specific ("sectarian") reading of the tradition.

Emmanuel L. Rehfeld ("Der Christus Israels zwischen Golgatha und Galiläa: Beobachtungen zum Verhältnis von vorösterlicher Jesusbotschaft und nachösterlichem „Christus-Kerygma" in der Darstellung der Synoptiker", 107–136) starts with the acknowledgement that the Synoptic Gospels present the account of Jesus' life and ministry before Easter in the light of their post-Easter view of Christ. That perspective explains some internal tensions that are apparent in the Gospels' portrayals of Jesus: They reflect the conflict-laden process of substitution of the old with the new covenant. This process encompasses the Christ-event as a whole—both the pre-Easter ministry of Jesus (although in a proleptic and symbolic way) and his passion and resurrection. Hence, the Synoptic Gospels present the earthly Jesus on his way to the fulfilment of his own mission, which becomes intelligible only in light Jesus' death and resurrection. Therefore the so-called "kerygma" cannot be separated from the basic story of its fulfilment. With their combination of pre- and post-Easter-perspectives, the Synoptic Gospels make a substantial contribution to theology and preaching.

> **Jesus' family... [was] a Davidic clan anticipating the promised Nezer**

In "Zwischen Abschreibeverhältnis und frühjüdischer Gedächtniskultur McIvers experimentalpsychologische Kriterien zur Identifizierung eines Abschreibeverhältnisses zwischen den synoptischen Evangelien" (137-172), Armin D. Baum describes how in a number of experiments with prose texts that were designed to be analogous to the synoptic problem, Robert McIver and Marie Carroll have demonstrated that students are not able to remember unbroken sequences of more than 15 words in exactly the same order as in the source texts. In the Synoptic Gospels, McIver and Carroll found nine parallel prose passages with a sequence of exactly the same 16 or more words (up to a maximum of 31 words). They concluded that copying almost certainly occurred in these synoptic parallels. However, Baum argues that McIver and Carroll did not take into account the empirically demonstrable retention rates of people with a trained memory. As research from experimental psychology and into oral cultures reveals, such people can generate text reproductions of up to 36 words that are exactly the same as in the original. From the insights of experimental psychology even the longest exact word-for-word parallels in the Synoptic Gospels can be explained on the basis of memorisation. According to Baum, there are no examples of synoptic parallels that could not have been produced by human memory and must therefore be the result of copying. Some of the synoptic parallels with long sequences of exactly the same words can and should be explained as the result of memorisation.

The essays in *part two* ("The Jewish Apostle of Jesus: Paul of Tarsus") are: Volker Gäckle, "Dimensionen des Heils: Die βασιλεία τοῦ θεοῦ in der Verkündigung Jesu und in den Briefen des Apostels Paulus" (175-225); Joel R. White, "Führt der Messias sein Volk aus dem Exil? Eine kritische Auseinandersetzung mit N. T. Wrights These eines impliziten Metanarrativs hinter dem paulinischen Evangelium" (227-242); Hanna Rucks, "Paulus als Jude(n) lesen: Zur Auslegung von Römer 9-11 unter jesusgläubigen Juden" (243–264); Guido Baltes, "'Freiheit vom Gesetz'—eine paulinische Formel? Paulus zwischen jüdischem Gesetz und christlicher Freiheit" (265-314); Detlef Häußer, "Die Verkündigung des jüdischen Messias in der paganen Welt: Der Beitrag der Gemeinde in Philippi zur Mission des Apostels Paulus" (315-339); Alexander Weiß, "Paulus und die *coloniae*: Warum der Apostel nicht der einzige römische Bürger unter den frühen Christen war" (341–356) und Michael Theobald, "Alt und Neu: Innovative Begriffsbildungen in den Pastoralbriefen als Indiz ihres pseudepigraphen Charakters" (357-380). The volume closes with indexes of references, authors, names and subjects.

Christoph Stenschke
Biblisch-Theologische Akademie Wiedenest and Department of Biblical and Ancient Studies
University of South Africa
P O Box 392, Pretoria, 0003
Republic of South Africa
E-mail: Stenschke@wiedenest.de

Rhonda Burnette-Bletsch (ed.).
The Bible in Motion: A Handbook of the Bible and Its Reception in Film Part I + II, Handbooks of the Bible and Its Reception (HBR) 2 (Berlin, Boston: De Gruyter, 2016), published in two volumes: xviii + xvi + 921 pp., hardback. ISBN 978-1-61451-561-6 (identical ISBN). 239 Euro (for both volumes), e-book available (ISBN 978-1-61451-326-1).

These two volumes are dedicated to the cinematic afterlives of biblical characters and their appropriate study. The volumes present essays on biblical themes and various interpretive lenses, explore a wide range of film genres (from *film noir* to anime), introduce different film directors who have been drawn to biblical characters and themes and include voices from the margin.

The two volumes of this Handbook appear in a supplementary series to the *Encyclopedia of the Bible and Its Reception* (2009ff). As this Encyclopedia includes full coverage of the reception of biblical material in films, it is appropriate that a major handbook would address in detail the issues involved in and typical for this reception of biblical material.

In her introductory essay, "General Introduction: The Bible and Its Cinematic Reception" (I:1–14), Rhonda Burnette-Bletsch observes that the:

> open-ended conversation between text and reader can escape the limiting confines of confessional and academic communities and spill out into the broader culture, as illustrated by the pervasive presence of biblical tropes and images in literature and the visual arts. (2).

Burnette-Bletch argues that as part of the Bible's ongoing reception history, an overtly biblical film should not be evaluated based on its so-called "fidelity" to source material. "While fidelity may be a stated goal for some biblical films, all cinematic translations of the Bible are in fact interpretations". "Biblical" films should rather be understood as we would any other act of inner- or post-biblical interpretation, that is "as historically and culturally situated attempts to preserve and contemporize older traditions for new audiences" (2f). The relationship of Bible and film is best understood when both Bible and film are treated as equal partners in conversation. Films must be taken seriously on their own terms; they should not simply be mined for biblical references. One should also avoid heavy-handed, reductionist approaches that uncritically impose biblical interpretations without allowing films to speak with their own voice. "Even when a film's use of biblical material can be persuasively established, this intertextual connection cannot be imagined to exhaust the film's potential field of meaning. The Bible is but one of many syncretistic literary and cultural influences on cinema, all of which operate simultaneously" (3). In addition, both filmmakers and film-viewers should be recognised as active participants in the interpretive process. This means that establishing the meaning(s) of a film is not the sole domain of the filmmaker. According to Burnette-Bletch, there is a twofold process of interpretation that takes place when "(1) historically and culturally situated filmmakers appropriate biblical texts during a film's production and (2) equally situated film-viewers perceive (or fail to perceive) this connection during the film's reception. ... Like the readers of a text, film-viewers are not passive recipients of meanings encoded in a filmic 'text' but actively participate in the construction of a film's meaning" (3). Therefore, biblical reception occurs, in the broadest possible sense, whenever a situated reader/viewer notes what they perceive to be a significant connection between the Bible and a given film. Such interpretations must prove persuasive to others and promote a genuine and mutually beneficial conversation between Bible and film.

In the remainder of her essay, Burnette-Bletch discusses the wide range of cinematic receptions of the Bible from celebratory, transposed, genre-determined, hagiographic and secondary adaptations to the Bible as a book or cultural icon, from citations, quotations and paraphrase, paradigms, allusions and echoes to various analogues (3–10).

Part one is devoted to biblical characters and their stories in the Hebrew Bible. Each chapter moves from direct biblical adaptations to the appropriation of these characters and their stories in mainstream cinema. It contains: Theresa Sanders, "In the Beginning: Adam and Eve in Film" (17–34); Anton Karl Kozlovic, "Noah and the Flood: A Cinematic Deluge" (35–50); Peter T. Chattaway, "It's All in the Family: The Patriarchs of Genesis in Film" (51–64); Jennifer L. Koosed, "The Cinematic Moses" (65–82); J. Cheryl Exum; "Samson and Delilah in Film" (83–100); Matthew Page, "There Might Be Giants: King David on the Big (and Small) Screen" (101–117) and Carl S. Ehrlich, "Esther in Film" (119–136).

Part two offers a survey of biblical adaption and appropriation of different film genres and styles. The essays are as follows: David J. Shepherd, "Scripture on Silent Film" (139–159); Robert Ellis, "*Film Noir* and the Bible" (161–174); Adele Reinhartz, "The Bible Epic" (175–192); Robert Paul Seesengood, "Western Text(s): The Bible and the Movies of the Wild, Wild West" (193–207); Robert Paul Seesengood, "Mysteries of the Bible (Documentary) Revealed: The Bible in Popular Non-Fiction and Documentary Film" (209–221); Mary Ann Beavis, "From Skepticism to Piety: The Bible and Horror Films" (223–235); Frauke Uhlenbruch, "'Moses' DVD Collection': The Bible and Science Fiction Film" (237–251); Terry Lindvall and Chris Lindvall, "The Word Made Gag: Biblical Reception in Film Comedy" (253–266), R. Christopher Heard, "Drawing (on) the Text: Biblical Reception in Animated Films" (267–283) and Fumi Ogura and N. Frances Hioki, "Anime and the Bible" (285–295).

Part three examines how overarching biblical themes appear in films, that is, their "distinctive filmic afterlives" (12). It contains the following essays: Rhonda Burnette-Bletsch, "God at the Movies" (299–326); P. Malone, "Satan in Cinema" (327–339); Gaye Williams Ortiz, "Creation and Origins in Film" (341–354); Reinhold Zwick, "The Book of Job in the Movies: On Cinema's Exploration of Theodicy and the Hiddenness of God" (355–377); Matthew S. Rindge, "Lament in Film and Film as Lament" (379–390); Sandie Gravett, "What Lies Beyond? Biblical Images of Death and Afterlife in Film" (391–403) and Tina Pippin, "This Is the End: Apocalyptic Moments in Cinema" (405–415).

Volume II of this *Handbook* offers in *part four* a similar survey of New Testament characters and stories (419–531). In "Jesus and the Gospels at the Movies" (419–444), W. Barnes Tatum first describes the problems of the cinematic Jesus ("Jesus' transformation into a film star involves a particular set of complications", 419). There is the artistic, literary, historical and theological dimension. Cinematic interpretations of Jesus appear in filmed passion plays, in Jesus films based on the four Gospels, in films based on a single Gospel, in adaptions of modern novels, in adaptions of stage musicals and in films which tell stories in which characters, events, or details recall Jesus and his story. After a brief survey of a Jesus film based on the Quran, Tatum concludes:

> Since the first Jesus films in the last decade of the nineteenth Century, the tradition of Jesus on film has been approached in the literature in several ways. A common approach has been to consider the Jesus films discussed chronologically. Our approach has been to formulate a typology based on the sources of the screenplays of the films. This typological survey of Jesus films has identified and broadened the range of ways Jesus and the gospel story have been cinematically received and portrayed globally in the modern and post-modern worlds (442).

Catherine O'Brien examines "Women in the Cinematic Gospels" (449–462). She observes that from the earliest days of cinema, nameless women of the Gospel accounts have featured in New Testament screenplays to illustrate the transformative influence of Jesus (449). Some films have played on parallel lives between Mary and Mary Magdalene, others focus on the first female disciples. It becomes clear that attempts "to transpose the lives of the women of the Gospels to the screen—particularly in the case of Mary and Magdalene—reveal the difficulties of marrying theology with artistic inspiration, especially when gender issues are added to the mix" (459).

> **Nameless women of the Gospel accounts have featured ... to illustrate the transformative influence of Jesus**

In "Judas as Portrayed in Film" (463–482), Carol A. Hebron seeks to illumine the theological implications of the various depictions of Judas. Hebron identifies a "theology of rejection" of Judas. This consists of a rejection of Jesus as Messiah (Judas' bargaining with the chief priests, Judas' position at the table and body language, Judas' exit from the Last Supper), the dismissal of Judas at the institution of the Eucharist (Judas identified as the betrayer and expelled, the disciples' rejection of Judas), Judas' rejection of partaking of the bread and wine and the rejection of Judaism when Judas is perceived symbolically as the representative of Judaism as a whole. After a transitory stage in the 1950s, more recent interpretations indicate a "theology of acceptance" of Judas (acceptance of Jesus as Messiah, acceptance of Judas as betrayer and sinner and of his presence at the institution of the Eucharist, suggestions that Judas was acting out of his predestined role, suggestions that Judas was forgiven and the acceptance of Jewish religious and cultural traditions). According to Hebron, the reasons for changes in portrayals of Judas in post-Holocaust films were sympathy/guilt for the Holocaust, filmmakers' fear of accusations of antisemitism, a heightened sensitivity towards Judaism, and an improved critical understanding of the scriptures (479).

Clayton N. Jefford scrutinises the portrayal of "Jews and Judaism in New Testament Films" (483–495). Starting with a reminder of the brief history of cinema itself and the historic Westward orientation "that assumes audiences enculturated with English language and American and European values" (483), Jefford proposes that one can best:

> consider the role of New Testament Judaism in cinema from the angle of three related considerations: choice of New Testament texts; influence of screenwriter and director; and, circumstances of production. Rooted in contemporary history and perspectives, these elements typically guide decisions about how biblical Jews are depicted. They offer standards by which Jewish imagery and awareness are shaped, reflecting the values of an industry that necessarily seeks a large viewing audience

and worthy profit margin (483).

According to Jefford, "ultimately a century of Jesus epics offers more accurately a reflection of contemporary prejudices about Judaism than any actual concern for ancient Jewish perspectives" (493). Rather than learning something about ancient Judaism from the cinematic portrayal of New Testament texts, one understands how those who produce cinematic portrayals envision the faith and desires of their viewing audiences.

Richard Walsh writes on "Paul and the Early Church in Film" (497–515); Meghan Alexander Beddingfield contributes "Mythic Relevance of Revelation in Film" (517–531).

Part five consists of a survey of film directors who have drawn on biblical material (535–774). Noteworthy is the chapter by Samuel D. Giere (pp. 721–728) on Mark Donford-May's film *Son of Man* (2006). The *final part* brings together "voices from the margins" (777–866). This includes Adele Reinhartz', "Judaism and Antisemitism in Bible Movies" (777–791; why would this be a voice "from the margin"? How does this essay relate to Jefford's treatment of Jews and Judaism in New Testament films?) and the analysis of South African scholar Jeremy Punt, "Imperialism in New Testament Films" (853–866). Punt observes that the nexus between imperialism and New Testament films plays out in many different ways, namely, "in the relationship between imperialism, Jesus-followers and Romans; in satirical approaches to imperialism in New Testament films; and in the nexus of imperialism, messianism, and violence" (858). He argues that imperialism is an enduring aspect in New Testament films as many popular films explore the link between religion and hierarchies of control. "Films about Jesus and the early church stereotypically depict the oppressor-oppressed as stark binary. ... Messianism plays itself out within a context of imperialism, but a complex range of factors seems to determine the direction and nature of the violence involved" (864).

The volume closes with a detailed film index (853–898), Scripture index (899–908) and subject index which includes names (909–921).

The 56 chapters in this *Handbook* offer an excellent survey of the Bible and its reception in film. They introduce, discuss and apply the current methodological approaches and analyse a plethora of examples in different depth. The volumes are an invaluable point of departure and sure guide for all who want to enter and contribute to this fascinating field of the reception of the Bible. A one-volume study edition would be much welcome. For a selection of major films in this area see also Adele Reinhartz, *Bible and Cinema: Fifty Key Films* (London, New York: Routledge, 2013).

Christoph Stenschke
Biblisch-Theologische Akademie Wiedenest
and Department of Biblical and Ancient Studies
University of South Africa
P O Box 392, Pretoria, 0003
Republic of South Africa
E-mail: Stenschke@wiedenest.de

Samuel Byrskog, Tom Holmén, Matti Kankaanniemi (eds.), *The Identity of Jesus: Nordic Voices*. WUNT II.373 (Tübingen: Mohr Siebeck, 2014). X + 250 pp., paperback. ISBN 978-3-16-152204-8. 74 Euro

The present collection of essays had its origin in the first *Nordic Symposium on the Historical Jesus* in October 2010 in Turku/Åbo, Finland. The editors note in the foreword (vii–) that:

> Since the very days of the so-called Old Quest of the 19th Century, the search for the historical Jesus has been tackling the question of Jesus' identity. More becoming revealed about the context of Jesus, methods and axioms of the search being introduced, elaborated, refined and replaced, it is necessary every now and then to return to the question. Understandably, too, the concept of identity is an inseparable part of any attempt to profile a figure of the past (vii).

The editors observe that in historical sciences, which is the most comfortable and natural locus of the search for the historical Jesus, the term "identity" has been understood from a social psychological perspective. This emphasis is owed to the essentially relational and contextual nature of the concept. Therefore, in studying the identity of Jesus, it is necessary to approach this enigmatic historical figure from more than one perspective. This is what these essays attempt to do. The foreword provides a short summary of the following essays (except for Adna and Holmén).

Kari Syreeni ("The Identity of the Jesus Scholar Diverging Preunderstandings in Recent Jesus Research", 1–16), analyses the paradigms used in the different quests of Jesus. Special attention is given to the dichotomies often used by scholars in categorising the branch of New Testament scholarship.

Per Bilde contributes "Approaching the Issue of the Originality of Jesus" (17–37). Bilde argues that the features that make a person "original" or "exceptional" are probably imperative in identity formation. He concludes: "In comparison with other eschatological prophets of his day, Jesus seemed to be original, for example, in his announcement of the imminence of the kingdom of God, in his activity as a healer and miracle worker, and in his rather unique relationship with the Mosaic Law" (viii).

In the essay "Jesus the Son of Joseph: Reflections of Father-Son Relationship in the Ministry of Jesus" (38–57), Matti Kankaanniemi notes that the recent renaissance of the psychological studies of Jesus has produced different pictures of him. In particular, Jesus' childhood has been understood as an important factor in his identity formation. This is followed by two analyses of the paternal relationship of Jesus and Joseph. In view of the exegetical data and empirical developmental psychological research, Kankaanniemi argues that it is probable that John W. Miller—contra Andries van Aarde—"is correct in maintaining that Jesus had a warm and loving relationship with his father Joseph. Later, his socio-emotional skills as well as the inclusive and accepting attitude towards the marginalised and stigmatised can be seen as a result and manifestation of this" (viii).

Tobias Hägerland asks "A Prophet like Elijah or according to Isaiah? Rethinking the Identity of Jesus" (70–86). As identity is defined with the help of existing categories and significant figures in the context where a religious person operates, we must search for the most important points of identification for Jesus in the Scriptures. Hägerland concludes that while there are numerous similarities between the ministry of Jesus and Elijah (possibly consciously constructed by Jesus), "it was the anointed prophet in Isaiah 61 that in particular inspired the primary role-taking by Jesus. The charismatic experience of the Spirit and success as a healer led Jesus to consider the possibility that he might be the prophetic Messiah. This apparently led him to act out the other tasks of the anointed one" (viii).

In his essay, "Jesus as Preacher of the Kingdom of God" (87–98), the late Hans Kvalbein († 19. 12. 2013) argues that the identity of Jesus was strongly tied to the kingdom of God as the centre of Jesus' activities as teacher and prophet. Kvalbein emphasises the counter-cultural behaviour of Jesus as a preacher of the kingdom of God. According to Kvalbein, the table fellowship of Jesus with sinners should be understood as an "acted parable". The ethos of these meals lived on in the early Christian Eucharistic praxis.

Samuel Byrskog ("The Didactic Identity and Authority of Jesus—Reconsidered", 99–109) emphasises the "didactic" identity of Jesus. It included not only a verbal aspect but also visual teaching. Therefore, examination of Jesus' didactic identity in separation from his mighty acts is a misleading and biased scholarly practice. According to Byrskog, the role of Jesus as a teacher very likely includes more than meets the eye in the first reading. Readers must therefore evaluate other role categories.

Renate Banschbach Eggen ("Understanding the Identity of Jesus on the Basis of His Parables", 110–126), suggests that these figurative narratives as an important part of Jesus' teaching activity grant access to the voice of Jesus. However, the use of the parables as sources for the historical Jesus is complicated.

In "Revelation, Interpretation, Tradition Jesus, Authority and Halakic Development" (127–160), Thomas Kazen argues that the scholarly understanding of Jesus' identity can profit from detailed study of Rabbinic and Qumranic hermeneutical practices. This approach could illuminate the complicated question of the characteristics of the *halakhah* Jesus taught and its subsequent development in the tradition process. Kazen's emphasis on the conflict stories over *halakha* is an important contribution to the topic, since "the identity of a person is closely connected with the intergroup conflicts he or she participates in, either passively or—as in Jesus' and his followers' case—actively" (ix).

> **The identity of Jesus was strongly tied to the kingdom of God**

In the essay "The Role of Jerusalem in the Mission of Jesus" (161–180), Jostein Adna begins with Jesus' journeys from Galilee to Jerusalem. Then he examines Jesus' eschatological message about the coming of the kingdom of God, the significance and role of Jerusalem/Zion in apocalyptic-eschatological expectations (Zion traditions in the Old Testament and in early Judaism) and Jesus' final journey to Jerusalem as the climax of his eschatological mission (Jerusalem as the "city of the great king", the temple saying(s) of Jesus, the temple act, Jesus' violent death and the Zion traditions). In closing, Adna summarises the lasting impact and effect of Jesus' orientation towards Jerusalem. While there is no room within post-Easter Christian theology and eschatological expectation for a new physical temple on Mount Zion (179), such a profound theological transformation did not lead to a rejection of the Zion traditions. Adna concludes that the validity and importance of the Zion traditions for the historical Jesus are still recognisable in the material collected in the Synoptic Gospels. "Further, the choice of Jerusalem as the site of the primitive community in spite of the fact that this city had let down their Lord and delivered him to a shameful death on the cross, and that it was the most dangerous place to stay because the powerful enemies of Jesus were still present, shows that Jerusalem obviously continued to be significant" (179). Thus: "Jerusalem played a crucial role for Jesus' identity, not only by chance, but also in principle, grounded in the character of his messianic-eschatological mission to proclaim and accomplish the kingdom of God" (180).

Tom Holmén ("Caught in the Act: Jesus Starts the New Temple—A Continuum Study of Jesus as the Founder of the *Ecclesia*", 181–231) examines the sayings of Jesus which regard the temple or its equivalents from the viewpoint of its stones (Mark 13:1-2; Matt 16:18). Holmén studies how the Old Testament and second temple Jewish background of this particular imagery (stones of the temple) can illuminate those sayings and their significance in understanding the historical Jesus. Using the continuum approach or perspective to the historical Jesus (for a detailed description see T. Holmén (ed.), *Jesus in Continuum*, WUNT 289; Tübingen: Mohr Siebeck, 2012), Holmén also addresses the Christian ecclesia-temple stone texts. He surveys the theology and practice of stones of the Jewish temple, the stones of the Christian *ecclesia*-temple and the potential continuum. This has important implications for New Testament ecclesiology:

> Eventually, the sole builder of the ecclesia-temple became its sole foundation. I believe a key factor in this development was the Christological stone tradition, i.e., the tradition where the stone imagery is used to promote Christology. ... Just as Jesus the proclaimer of the kingdom became the proclaimed, Jesus the founder of the *ecclesia* became the founded, viz. its foundation. He became a layer in the foundation but our study suggests that he considered himself the layer of the foundation (230).

The volume closes with indexes of ancient literature (233–243), modern authors (244–248) and subjects (249–250).

The editors conclude that:

> it is evident that different "Jesuses" may be reconstructed on the basis of the presentations of the volume at hand. Some might want to highlight the contradictions in order to plead for the pessimistic assertion that the whole scholarship dealing with the "historical Jesus" is but a chaotic mess, a play-ground for subjective depictions and wishful thinking. Nevertheless, others could focus on the points of agreement between the different "Jesuses" and come to a conclusion that is quite the opposite or at least one that affords some credit and credibility to this branch of research (ix–x).

It might be asked what the notion of "Nordic" in the title stands for. The essays are "Nordic" insofar as they originate in Scandinavia. The designation is not meant to indicate a particular emphasis or approach such as the designation "nordisch" had in German research of the 1930s and early 1940s when the adjective meant "influenced by national-socialist ideology" and in clear differentiation from a Jewish Jesus (for a survey see S. Heschel, *The Aryan Jesus: Christian Theologians and the Bible in Nazi Germany* (Princeton: Princeton UP, 2008).

Christoph Stenschke
Forum Wiedenest, Bergneustadt, Germany
and Department of New Testament and Early Christian Studies
University of South Africa
PO Box 392, Pretoria, 0003,
Republic of South Africa
E-mail: Stenschke@wiedenest.de

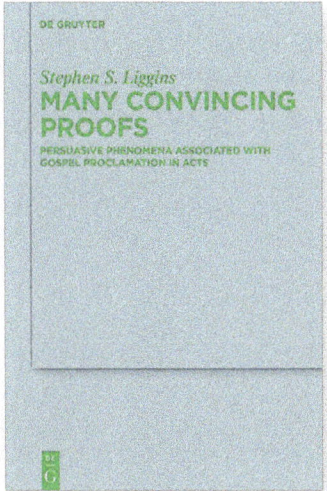

Stephen S. Liggins, *Many Convincing Proofs: Persuasive Phenomena Associated with Gospel Proclamation in Acts*. BZNW 221 (Berlin, Boston: De Gruyter, 2016). Xvi + 317 pp., hardbound. ISBN 978-3-11-045970. 130 Euro

Many readers of Acts will experience its reports of the tremendous success of the early Christian proclamation as a mixture of wistful nostalgia and scepticism. What, according to Acts, made this proclamation so convincing? In this monograph, based on a doctoral dissertation at the University of Sydney (2015), Australian scholar Stephen Liggins does not analyse the content of the apostolic message in great detail (which has been done over and over), but focuses on the "persuasive phenomena" associated with its proclamation and their intended impact on the early audiences of Acts. Persuasive phenomena are defined as "those phenomena associated with the communication of the gospel message in Acts that exerted persuasive force on the evangelistic audiences described within the text of Acts and encouraged them to make the desired response to the message" (1). These phenomena had persuasive force by suggesting divine authority and authentification or by appealing, in some way, to the audiences described in the narrative (7).

After a survey of the topic and the approach taken, Liggins briefly summarises in chapter one the evangelistic proclamation as presented in Acts (4–7) and describes four key persuasive phenomena: the use of and appeal to Jewish Scriptures in association with evangelistic ministry, the presence of witnessed supernatural events in association with evangelistic ministry, the appealing nature of the Christian community in association with evangelistic ministry as presented in the narrative, and skilful interaction with Greco-Roman culture (7–12). The latter involves the use of Greco-Roman sources of authority or concepts which would be appreciated in a Greco-Roman influenced context (12). Less prominent persuasive phenomena are:

> assertions by the evangelist of his good character (2:15-21); assertions by the evangelist of his truthfulness (26:25-26); adoption of an appealing manner of addressing the evangelistic audience (e. g., 22:29; 3:17; 7:2; 13:26. 38: 22:1: 23:1, 6; 26:2-3; 28:17); the presentation of the evangelist's personal conversion testimony (22:3-21; 26:4-23); the use of humour (2:15): and the use of evocative or emotional language (e.g., 2:40) (13).

The following aspects associated with evangelistic proclamation are aspects that facilitate ease of communication, rather than phenomena that exert persuasive force; therefore they have not been included (13): the adoption of an understandable language; the use of the spoken rather than written medium; and the conduct of evangelistic ministry in locations familiar to the evangelistic audiences described in the text, for instance, the temple in Jerusalem. With regard to methodology, Liggins rightly emphasises the need to take note of the narrative influence and socio-historical influence in interpreting Acts (14–26).

Chapter two discusses the early audiences and their perception of Acts (27–43, the early audience perspective, the composition of early audiences, the genre and credibility of Acts when it comes to its many speeches and references to the supernatural). This is followed in chapter three by an excellent survey of Jewish and Greco-Roman persuasive religious communication (44–108). In early Jewish sources, persuasive phenomena associated with Jewish proselytizing and conversion to Judaism include, among others, the Jewish Scriptures, human physical coercion (use or threat), Greco-Roman cultural interaction, the good character of Jews, the nature and attractiveness of the Jewish community, and witnessed supernatural events. In Greco-Roman sources on persuasive phenomena associated with Greco-Roman proselytising and adoption of Greco-Roman religions, Liggins identifies the following phenomena in persuasive communication: witnessed supernatural events, human physical coercion (use or threat), visual/concrete phenomena, Greco-Roman cultural interaction and rhetoric, oracles and community.

Against this backdrop, in chapters four and five Liggins examines the persuasive phenomena associated with evangelistic ministry in Acts 1–12 (109–164) and in Acts 13–28 (165–210). In both parts of Acts, the prominent four key persuasive phenomena of the Jewish Scriptures, witnessed supernatural events, the Christian community and Greco-Roman cultural interaction appear clearly. There is a complete absence of the use of threat of human coercion in association with evangelistic proclamation.

This is followed in chapter six by an analysis of the impact of these phenomena upon the early audiences of Acts ("Part 1: Phenomena, Contexts and Influence", 211–234), that is "considering how Luke's presentation of these phenomena would have resonated with the repertoire of those early audiences of Acts" (211). The aim is to:

> determine what the early audiences would have: identified and appreciated regarding the persuasive phenomena present and absent ...; observed regarding the varying contexts in which the key persuasive phenomena were presented ...; and gauged regarding the way in which the key persuasive phenomena would have influenced the evangelistic audiences described in the text (211).

Regarding the identified persuasive phenomena, Liggins concludes that:

> given their repertoire, the early audiences of Acts would have been able to identify and appreciate the four key persuasive phenomena present in the narrative ... and the one prominent persuasive phenomenon that was absent—the use (or threat) of human physical coercion ...

> Early audiences would also have been able to knowledgably observe the varying contexts in which the persuasive phenomena were presented ... They had the capacity to appreciate, for example, that: Paul's use of the Jewish Scriptures was more interactive than Peter's; the explicit use of Jewish Scriptures was particularly prominent in and appropriate for evangelistic ministry to people of a Jewish background; there was a minor emphasis on witnessed supernatural events in the Greco-Roman context; and the use of non-rhetorical Greco-Roman sources of authority was exclusively seen in Greco-Roman contexts (234).

In addition, the early audiences would have been able to appreciate how these persuasive phenomena would have influenced the various evangelistic audiences. These phenomena would have exerted a strong persuasive force on people of both Jewish and Greco-Roman backgrounds. This also applies to influence of the absence of the use (or threat) of human physical coercion on Jewish and Greco-Roman evangelistic audiences.

Chapter seven ("Impact on early audiences of Acts Part II: The Ongoing Mission", 235–251) analyses the impact of the description of persuasive phenomena in the ongoing mission of the audience. Would the early audiences of Acts have believed that they had a role to play in ongoing evangelistic proclamation and mission, and if so, in what way? Liggins argues that the force of the presentation of evangelistic proclamation in Acts would have encouraged the early audiences to take responsibility for the continuance of this proclamation and mission (239, "early audiences would have believed that evangelistic proclamation and mission needed to continue and that they had a role to play", 250). Those who accepted this calling would have looked to Acts for guidance regarding the extent to which, and the manner in which, persuasive phenomena should be associated with their evangelistic proclamation and mission in this regard (240). According to Liggins:

> Early audiences would have expected that all of the key persuasive phenomena could be appropriately and usefully associated with their evangelistic proclamation. This did not mean that they had to be so associated. Early audiences may have noted that there was selective modelling with respect to evangelistic ministry within the Acts narrative. They may also have noted that there was no specific textual mandate that any of the persuasive phenomena had to be associated with such evangelistic proclamation. However, for those persuasive phenomena whose implementation was within the control of the evangelist (i.e., the use of Jewish Scriptures, reference to the witnessed resurrection of Jesus, the association with Christian community, and the use of Greco-Roman cultural interaction) there was good reason to consider and, as appropriate, to employ such phenomena (250).

Regarding persuasive phenomena that would have required divine intervention or assistance (such as witnessed supernatural events—incidentally associated and deliberately performed), there would have been a varied expectation as to whether they were likely to be associated with their evangelistic proclamation. While there were good precedents for early audiences to employ persuasive phenomena in their evangelistic proclamation, these phenomena would be seen as subservient to the communication of the gospel (250f).

In addition, these phenomena:

> encouraged a voluntary response to the gospel message based on its perceived truth or appeal, rather than a forced response as would have been the case with the use (or threat) of human physical coercion. The persuasive phenomena associated with evangelistic proclamation in Acts sought to persuade the mind rather than coerce compliance (251).

Liggins observes that the key persuasive phenomena are all connected in some way to the gospel message itself: the gospel is grounded in the Jewish Scriptures; it contains witnessed supernatural events (i.e., the miraculous ministry and resurrection of Jesus); it leads to Christian community (as people believe and are included into the people of God); and focuses on Jesus (who employs rhetorical practices Himself). Thus, there is continuity between the evangelistic proclamation and the associated key persuasive phenomena (251).

Chapter 8 summarises the findings of the study (252–258), followed by tables on gospel components in the speeches of Acts (speaker, audience, location, the person and work of Jesus, response, consequences), bibliography and indexes of ancient texts and modern authors.

In this inspiring and fresh study, Liggins combines several important issues in current research on Acts (significance of the Old Testament, miracles, interaction with the cultural context). Due to the comprehensive scope of the inquiry, at times the critical interaction with existing research could have been more nuanced. The attractiveness of the essential contents of the Christian proclamation (such as the chance of receiving divine forgiveness or the gift of the Holy Spirit) should have received more attention for attaining an overall picture of the attractiveness of the apostolic ministry. Liggins' distinction, "they form part of the gospel message—they are not associated with it" (p. 13), fails to convince. Liggins offers important contributions to appreciating the rhetoric and purpose of Acts; its portrayal of Peter and Paul; the early Christian proclamation of the gospel; regarding the persuasive forces of religious speech and phenomena in antiquity (more general) and—last but not least—regarding early Christian mission and the mission and message of the church today.

Christoph Stenschke
Biblisch-Theologische Akademie Wiedenest
and Department of Biblical and Ancient Studies
University of South Africa
P O Box 392, Pretoria, 0003
Republic of South Africa
E-mail: Stenschke@wiedenest.de

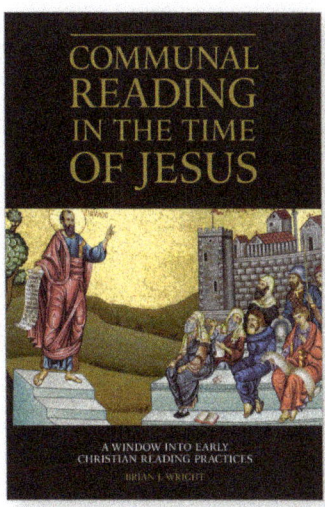

Brian J. Wright, *Communal Reading in the Time of Jesus: A Window into Early Christian Reading Practices.* Minneapolis, MN: Fortress Pr, 2017. xvii–xxvi + 293 pp. $39.00 USD. ISBN-10: 1506432506

In *Communal Reading in the Time of Jesus*, Wright argues communal reading was widespread and functioned as another control category of the Jesus traditions.

Wright is an adjunct professor at Palm Beach Atlantic University and New Orleans Baptist Theological Seminary. This is Wright's first book, though he has written several articles and one chapter in an edited volume (for a listing see: https://ridley.academia.edu/BrianJWright). This book is a published version of his PhD dissertation: "Communal reading events in the first century of the common era."

Communal Reading in the Time of Jesus asks "who was reading what in the first century and where? Why this matters? How were traditions passed along, what role did texts play? Who had access to this? What controlled the textual transmission and influenced its stability?" (www.youtube.com/watch?v=i8CJHu6SAUY).

Chapter 1 proposes *communal* reading as a new control category. Wright defines a control as "a tendency to preserve the integrity of a tradition's propositional content, even while acknowledging that variation was inevitable, and local contingencies could shape the preservationist tendency itself" (p. 4). Wright states that it is outside his scope, but that "future research should compare this type of control with others" (p. 4 n.13). But given that Wright claims this is a new category perhaps this should have been investigated a little more, especially since (see M. Metts review, Bulletin for Biblical Research) there is some overlap in how Wright describes communal reading as a control, with performance criticism as a control.

In chapter 2, Wright defines a communal reading event as "one in which two or more persons are involved" and it "can be public or private, but not individualistic" (p. 12). This chapter also states that Wright is primarily examining literary evidence, not epigraphical nor archaeological. Chapter 3 argues that the economic and political factors provided stability, and travel and mobility would have favored "the unhindered spread of communal reading events" (p. 37). Chapter 4 examines the social context and argues that "virtually all literature during this time period was composed to be read communally" (p. 59). That communal reading crossed social boundaries and took place in many different settings. Furthermore "the early Christian movement largely inherited the book culture, reading communities, and literary practices of Judaism, even if early Christian communities modified or transformed them in diverse ways" (p. 60).

To demonstrate that communal reading was a common part of the culture at large, chapter 5 surveys the following Greek and Roman authors: Epictetus, Strabo, Valerius Maximus, Chariton, Ovid, Martial, Persius, Dio Chrysostom, Statius, Quintus Curtius Rufus, Quintilian, Seneca the Elder, Celsus, Petronius, Seneca the Younger; and Jewish Sources: 4 Maccabees, Philo, Pseudo-Philo, Josephus, 4 Ezra. Various readers of texts are identified including "clerks, emperors, students, young boys, politicians, scribes, fathers, lectors, magistrates, plagiarists, old men, and young women" (p. 114) and audiences were varied including "emperors, children, men, women, slaves, students, plebs, assemblies, soldiers, Roman officials, invited guests, and crowds" (p. 114). Further "[t]hese events occurred in big cities like Rome, as well as faraway places of exile such as Tomis. According to these selected authors, people heard readings while standing, sitting, running, bathing, eating, dining, and swimming" (p. 114).

> **Confirmed the widespread nature of communal reading events**

Chapter 6 surveys the New Testament and found ample evidence for communal reading events in Christian circles. They were found in widespread locations including "Rome, Corinth, Achaia, Philippi, Thessalonica, Crete, Galatia, Ephesus, Colossae, Laodicea, Capernaum, Nazareth, Jerusalem, Galilee, Damascus, Cyprus, Pisidian Antioch, Iconium, Derbe, Lystra, Berea, Athens, Miletus, Smyrna, Pergamum, Thyatira, Sardis, and Philadelphia" (p. 201). Further there was a "broad range of venues, participants, and cultures also confirmed the widespread nature of communal reading events. There were public communal reading events (Acts 17 in Athens) and private communal reading events (Acts 5:42 in Jerusalem). They could be small (Acts 8), as well as large (John 6:59). There were formal settings, such as synagogues (Matt 4:23). There were informal venues, such as open-air marketplaces (Acts 17:17). There were also numerous places just about everywhere in between, such as private homes (Luke 1:40), the Bema (Acts 18:12-3), Paul's apartment (Acts 28:23), Solomon's colonnade (Acts 3:11), the temple courts (Mark 12:25), the Hall of Tyrannus (Acts 19:9), temple of the Lord (Luke 1:9), holy places (Luke 1:21-22), the ἐκκλησία (Acts 11:26), and public assemblies (Acts 19:30-31). Social inferiors were often portrayed as participating in them (John 6:31; Acts 8:27); this shows how communal reading events also crossed class boundaries (p. 205). The Pastorals, which Wright takes as authentic along with the other disputed Pauline letters, were intended for communal reading.

On the whole, Wright does a good job at surveying the vast relevant literature allowing his readers to assess the evidence and make their own decisions. However, a greater intrusion of his expertise would have been of great benefit to his readers, especially on those matters where his reexamination of the evidence led to a change of his own mind. Although the argument is strong, there is the occasional overstatement, such as when, with reference to Luke 5:14, Wright argues that "Jesus automatically assumes an unidentified leper knows what Moses commanded" (p. 135), and Wright uses the case of the leper to argue that communal reading was more widespread. While Luke 5:14 does require that somewhere down the line someone read what "Moses commanded", it seems more likely this illustrates the oral nature of the culture rather than its reading habits. It also seems unlikely that Jesus was literally reading scripture on the road to Emmaus (Luke 24:32, p. 133-134). With Jesus' parable of the rich man, Wright argues that Luke 16:29 indicates the brothers could attend a communal reading event to hear Moses and the Prophets (p. 135). While that might be true, it seems the point of the text is to highlight that one should obey the Scriptures, not that there is access to communal readings of them. In regard to Acts 19:19-20 and the burning of magic books, Wright suggests Christian written texts increased (p. 150). While this might be a long term result, it seems less likely this is the intent of the passage which points to the growth of the Lord's message in general, not specifically to that message in written texts. While it may be true, in regard to Rom 2:13, that the Gentiles lack communal reading of the law (p. 153), it seems more likely that Paul's point is that they lack the Law altogether, not communal readings of it in particular. With reference to Philemon 19, Wright argues that Paul is stating that he is writing with his own hand, indicating the letter was intended to be read communally as "this would be a moot point if only addressed to one person who could see the change in handwriting" (p. 183). But even if only one person were reading it, they may not have known who wrote the letter, or if the handwriting only changed here the individual would still be unaware of the reason. Paul by writing himself emphasizes his personal promise and commitment. Despite these various quibbles about various weaker examples, on the whole Wright's argument seems credible.

Wright's contribution that widespread communal reading widespread functioned as a control category seems likely, but to what extent requires further study. He also suggests that "the prevalence of communal reading events raises important new questions regarding the formation of the Jesus tradition, the contours of book culture in early Christianity, and factors shaping the transmission of the text of the New Testament" (p. 209). Certainly the epistles were generally intended for communal reading. However, it seems a little more complicated in regard to the Gospels. Communal reading no doubt affected the transmission of the Gospels, but it is less clear to what extent it affected their formation. For communal reading to significantly affect the formation of the Gospels, extensive note-taking must be presumed to have already existed. Although this was touched upon in an excursus (pp. 119-20), it was simply beyond the scope of this book.

Overall a well-written book on the widespread nature of communal reading in the first century.

David Graieg
Murdoch University

www.ingramcontent.com/pod-product-compliance
Lightning Source LLC
Chambersburg PA
CBHW042038100526
44587CB00030B/4476